TRAFFICKING

Modern Slavery in

Sylvia Walby and Karen A. Shire

B BRISTOL
UNIVERSITY
PRESS

First published in Great Britain in 2024 by

Bristol University Press
University of Bristol
1-9 Old Park Hill
Bristol
BS2 8BB
UK
t: +44 (0)117 374 6645
e: bup-info@bristol.ac.uk

Details of international sales and distribution partners are available at bristoluniversitypress.co.uk

British Library Cataloguing in Publication Data
A catalogue record for this book is available from the British Library

ISBN 978-1-5292-3235-6 paperback
ISBN 978-1-5292-3237-0 ePub
ISBN 978-1-5292-3236-3 OA PDF

Cover design: Qube Design
Front cover image: iStock/Georgeclerk
Bristol University Press use environmentally responsible print partners.
Printed and bound in Great Britain by CPI Group (UK) Ltd, Croydon, CR0 4YY

FSC
www.fsc.org
MIX
Paper | Supporting
responsible forestry
FSC® C013604

Due to its subject matter, this book deals with sensitive issues, including: coercion and violence, historic and current racialized violence, enslavement and forced labour, forced marriage, organ selling, and trafficking for purposes of sexual and labour exploitation, including of women and children.

Contents

List of Figures and Tables

Figures

Tables

List of Abbreviations

BBC	British Broadcasting Corporation
BGB	Bundesgesetzbuch (German Law Book, generally civil law)
BKA	Bundeskriminalamt (German Crime Office, federal government)
BMFSFJ	Bundesministerium für Familie, Senioren, Frauen und Jugend (German Federal Ministry for Family, Seniors, Women and Youth)
BufaS	Bündnis der Fachberatungsstellen für Sexarbeiterinnen und Sexarbeiter (Coalition of Expert Consultancies for Sex Workers, Germany)
CSR	corporate social responsibility
CTDC	Counter Trafficking Data Collaborative (led by the International Organization for Migration)
EU	European Union
Europol	European Union agency for law enforcement cooperation
FCSE	forced commercial sexual exploitation
GDP	gross domestic product
GRETA	Group of Experts on Action against Trafficking in Human Beings (Council of Europe)
ICAT	Inter-Agency Coordination Group against Trafficking in Persons
ILO	International Labour Organization
IOM	International Organization for Migration
ISIL	Islamic State of Iraq and the Levant
ITUC	International Trade Union Confederation
KOK	Koordinierungskreis gegen Menschenhandel e.V. (Coordination Organization against Human Trafficking, Germany)
MDGs	Millennium Development Goals (of the United Nations)
MiMOSA	Migrant Management Operational System Application (of the IOM)

NATO	North Atlantic Treaty Organization
NGO	non-governmental organization
NRM	National Referral Mechanism
NRW	North-Rhine Westphalia (the most populated of the 16 German federal states)
OECD	Organisation for Economic Co-operation and Development
ONS	Office for National Statistics (UK)
OSCE	Organization for Security and Co-operation in Europe
SDGs	Sustainable Development Goals (of the United Nations)
SoFFi.K	Sozialwissenschaftliches Frauenforschungsinstitut Freiburg (Social Scientific Women's Research Institute Freiburg, Germany)
StGB	German Criminal Law Book
TiP	Trafficking in Persons (Report of the US Department of State)
TVPA	Victims of Trafficking and Violence Protection Act (US)
UN	United Nations
UNCTAD	United Nations Conference on Trade and Development
UNODC	United Nations Office on Drugs and Crime
UN OHCHR	United Nations Office of the High Commissioner for Human Rights

Acknowledgements

This book, linking theory and practice, draws on a series of reports commissioned by the European Commission between 2016 and 2020 under the direction of Sylvia Walby. We would like to thank Myria Vassiliadou who, as the former Anti-Trafficking Coordinator (2011–20), strongly supported research through numerous discussions over many years. Myria pioneered the European Union anti-trafficking strategy and the implementation of the 2011 Anti-Trafficking Directive, established an impressive network of non-governmental organizations active in eradicating trafficking, and established an evidence-based body of knowledge about trafficking of human beings, to which we were honoured to contribute.

Numerous colleagues contributed to and co-authored the series of European Commission reports. Without their knowledge, inquisitiveness, and research competence we would not have achieved the state of knowledge necessary for launching off in the more theoretical analysis of trafficking/ modern slavery that has resulted in this book. We thank: Birgit Apitzsch, Jo Armstrong, Susie Balderston, Patricia Bell, Janet Bowstead, Amy Elliott, Gene Feder, Karolina Follis, Adam Fish, Brian Francis, Abigail Fraser, Claire Hardaker, Annie Herbert, Valmira Hoti-Llabjani, Liz Kelly, Stuart Kirby, Corinee May-Chahal, David Mansley, Sally McManus, Stephan Morris, Sian Oram, Becky Pattinson, Moira Peelo, Jessica Phoenix, Merili Pullerits, Awais Rashid, Emma Palmer, Jude Towers, Markus Tünte, and Rachel Verrall.

We especially wish to thank Birgit Apitzsch, Brian Francis, Jude Towers, and Markus Tünte for their contributions to our thinking. We have been supported by several institutions and associations while writing this book from our presentations. We thank the International Sociological Association's Thematic Group 11 Violence and Society and Research Committee 02 Economy and Society, and the Society for the Advancement of Socio-Economics Network G Labour Markets. An early version of the concept of 'trafficking chains' was presented at a workshop of the research group In Search of Global Labour Markets at the Centre for Interdisciplinary Research (ZIF) at Bielefeld University. Sylvia Walby thanks the policy makers and practitioners in the European Commission, European Parliament, EU Network of National Rapporteurs, EU Anti-Trafficking Civil Society

Platform, UN Women, and policy makers and practitioners in the UK for their time and feedback during the research process that helped to advance our thinking. Karen Shire thanks the ZIF, the Ochanomizu Women's University Centre for Global Leadership, and the Max Planck Institute for the Study of Societies Scholar-in-Residence programme for fellowship support and the chance to present preliminary analyses of exploitation in modern economies.

We would like to thank friends and colleagues who read drafts and engaged us in fruitful conversations: Brian Francis, Aisha Gill, Celia Lury, Sue Penna, Mieke Verloo, and Ines Wagner.

We acknowledge the support of the Alexander von Humboldt Foundation Anneliese Maier Research Award to Sylvia Walby in enabling frequent and intensive collaborations in Essen and London in the last year of writing this book. The kind support of the Essen College for Gender Research, especially the managing director Maren Jochimsen and staff member Linn Hendricks, relieved us of many organizational and administrative tasks. We also wish to thank Maria Frolova for her accurate editorial assistance.

We thank our mutual friend Heidi Gottfried who has provided intellectual support, read drafts, and discussed many of the over-arching ideas in this book on complex inequalities, the economy and violence over many years.

Although we draw on the results of research for the European Commission, the views are ours alone and should not be considered to represent the contracting authority's official position. Our thanks to people does not imply their endorsement. And, of course, all errors are our own.

1

Introduction

The use of coercion to extract profit did not end with modernity. Trafficking/ modern slavery is driven by a search for profits, for value, for material benefit, that uses coercion to exploit the vulnerability of others. While the specific forms are varied, it forms a single field of enquiry. The most frequent victims are migrants and women. Trafficking/modern slavery is not an outcome of capitalism alone but depends on situations of vulnerability that are systematically structured by colonial and gendered inequalities. It is systemic, not merely a result of a few bad individuals. While trafficking/ modern slavery is a crime under international law, the regulation of the economy is critically important and draws on bodies of law other than the criminal. Society as a whole – economy, violence, polity, and civil society – creates the situations of vulnerability that are exploited, so interventions need to be wide-ranging and comprehensive. The most important of these sites of intervention into trafficking/modern slavery is that of third-party profit-taking. The alternative forms of modernity – social democratic, neoliberal, authoritarian – provide different contexts and opportunities for exploitation, situations of vulnerability, and interventions. The change to thinking about development as sustainable development rather than simple growth in gross domestic product (GDP) creates new opportunities for policy development. These include an appreciation of the significance of reducing violence/coercion for sustainable development, security, and human rights.

Theories of society are advanced when attention is paid to the coercion used to exploit situations of vulnerability in trafficking/modern slavery. This book offers a theory of trafficking/modern slavery as a contribution to the debates on the laws, data, and policies required to reduce and end this coercion.

What is trafficking/modern slavery?

The question 'what is trafficking/modern slavery?' is answered through discussions of the definition, the centrality of coercion, the distinctions between chattel and modern slavery, the concepts of harm and consent, the multiple types of trafficking/modern slavery, whether mobility is always present, the multiple epistemologies involved, profit-taking from the exploitation of the vulnerability of others, and the development of the concept of multi-sided transactions in trafficking chains.

Coercion is core to the definition of trafficking/modern slavery (UN 1956; Bales 1999; UN 2000a; Kelly 2003; Brass 2011; Cockayne 2021). Trafficking/modern slavery is the use of coercion to extract profits from activities. It is the exploitation of the vulnerability of others. The use of coercion means that this is not free wage labour. Trafficking/modern slavery will often involve violence, a physical form of coercion, but physicality is not necessary since coercion is sufficient. Coercion may involve the mobilization of debt, or threats against the individual or against their loved ones. It occurs when one party is in a situation of vulnerability. This situation of vulnerability is exploited, using coercion. Coercion and violence are a distinctive form of power not reducible to other forms of power, constituting a specific institutional domain of interrelated practices. Coercion is a form of power in which one person makes another person do their bidding even when they do not want to and are harmed by this, or they are in a situation where they have no reasonable alternative. Consent does not exclude a person from being considered a victim of trafficking/modern slavery. Violence is a form of power in which physical actions are intended to cause physical harms, so all violence is coercive. Coercion is a wider concept than violence since it does not require a physical element.

Trafficking in persons is defined by a UN Convention, known as the Palermo Protocol (UN 2000a), as:

(a) 'Trafficking in persons' shall mean the recruitment, transportation, transfer, harbouring or receipt of persons, by means of the threat or use of force or other forms of coercion, of abduction, of fraud, of deception, of the abuse of power or of a position of vulnerability or of the giving or receiving of payments or benefits to achieve the consent of a person having control over another person, for the purpose of exploitation. Exploitation shall include, at a minimum, the exploitation of the prostitution of others or other forms of sexual exploitation, forced labour or services, slavery or practices similar to slavery, servitude or the removal of organs.

(b) The consent of a victim of trafficking in persons to the intended exploitation set forth in subparagraph (a) of this article shall be irrelevant where any of the means set forth in subparagraph (a) have been used.

(c) The recruitment, transportation, transfer, harbouring or receipt of a child for the purpose of exploitation shall be considered "trafficking in persons" even if this does not involve any of the means set forth in subparagraph (a) of this article.

Modern slavery is different from chattel slavery. In chattel slavery, the control of another person is both legal and real, while in modern slavery there is not legal ownership, even though the power to control is real (Allain and Bales 2012). The absence of legal ownership in trafficking/modern slavery makes a significant difference, although some reject the concept of modern slavery (O'Connell Davidson 2015). Du Bois describes the difference between chattel slavery and other forms of coerced labour in his account of the failure to fully emancipate slaves in the 19th-century US, which led to highly coercive labour relations despite the removal of the legal entitlement to own another human after the American Civil War (Du Bois 1998 [1935]). Chattel slavery was transformed into a system of coerced labour marked by debt bondage, in an environment hostile to racial equality. There is a continuum of degrees of control in contemporary labour relations (Skrivankova 2010; Hyman 2022; Shahadat and Uddin 2022). International legal instruments created a category of 'practices similar to slavery' in 1956 that included debt bondage, serfdom, child exploitation, and forced marriage (UN 1956). There are further related terms in use, including 'forced labour' (ILO 1930), and 'unfree labour' (Brass 2011).

Consent is not relevant to the legal definition of trafficking/modern slavery. The issue is coercion, not consent. Some consider the two concepts to be close, for example, Cockayne (2021), following Sen (1999), focuses on lack of consent as if it were indicative of harm, while the concept of unfree labour (Brass 2011) similarly assumes such an alignment. O'Connell Davidson (2015) argues that consent is important, and that prioritizing harm over consent leads to an over-extension of the concept of trafficking/modern slavery. Barry (1979, 1995) argues that 'harm' should trump 'consent' in the justification of public interest intervention into trafficking/modern slavery. Gupta (2008, 2016) objects to O'Connell Davidson's narrowing of the concept of trafficking/modern slavery which would exclude many cases. In international legal instruments following the Palermo Protocol (UN 2000a), the key concept is coercion in the exploitation of the vulnerabilities of others, rather than harm or lack of consent.

Trafficking/modern slavery is best understood as a single field with multiple sub-types (Gallagher 2010; Allain 2013; Cockayne 2021; ILO, Walk Free, and IOM 2022). The unity concerns the use of coercion to exploit the vulnerability of others for material benefit. The different sub-types concern the area of activity, and the social relations of the exploiter and exploited. The major types concern forced labour, sexual exploitation, state forced labour, and forced marriage. The different types are articulated in slightly different ways during the development of international legal instruments

(Gallagher 2010; Allain 2013). In the Palermo Protocol, the main types are trafficking in human beings for purposes of labour exploitation, for purposes of sexual exploitation, and for other purposes including sale of organs and forced criminality (UN 2000a). Earlier legal instruments concerned forced labour, both state and commercially based (ILO 1930); and practices similar to slavery that includes forced marriage (UN 1956). The step-by-step development of the legal field with its multiple instruments should not be treated as an obstacle to the identification of trafficking/modern slavery as a single field for social science and policy.

Trafficking/modern slavery does not require mobility, nor the migration of people over state frontiers, though this is a feature in around one third of the cases of registered victims (UNODC 2021). The core aspect is control over the person: coercion is sufficient. The Palermo Protocol does not require movement of people, of corporeal bodies, despite the term trafficking seeming to imply movement (UN 2000a). However, flows of people and value are entangled with situations of vulnerability and the exploitative extraction of profits (Boris et al 2023). In practice, contemporary trafficking/modern slavery often intersects with movement over borders, especially of those without legal entitlements to citizenship, since this generates situations of vulnerability that can be exploited (Anderson and O'Connell Davidson 2003). There are flows of value and of people from the periphery to the core, understood in both spatial and social terms (Wallerstein 2011 [1974]; LeBaron 2021).

Epistemologically, three types of entities are active in defining trafficking/modern slavery: victims/survivors, authorities, and scientists. The victims or survivors, who report their experiences to friends and family, non-governmental organizations (NGOs) and authorities, or social science investigators, define their own lived experience. Legislatures, political projects, legal, and judicial authorities identify, generate, and adjudicate boundaries as to what is or is not trafficking/modern slavery at both national and transnational levels, as well as in specific individual instances in judicial processes. Scientists (including sociologists, criminologists, political scientists, and other social scientists) generate their own concepts, definitions, measurement practices, and theoretical frameworks within which coercion, trafficking, and modern slavery are analysed. These three epistemologies are distinct and co-exist. However, they are linked via the object with which they are concerned. In this context of multiple alternative concepts and understandings linked to different epistemological stances, this book prioritizes social science. It recognizes and takes account of the lived experience of victims but does not give this epistemological privilege. It recognizes the definitions of international legal instruments, and their significance in structuring trafficking/modern slavery but does not restrict its remit to the legal or democratic domain. This book positions itself as a work of science, evidence, theory, and analysis. It adjudicates disagreements over the concept and consequences of coercion in the economy, over trafficking and modern slavery, drawing on a range of academic disciplines.

Trafficking/modern slavery does not only concern commercial activities in neoliberal contexts. While this is important (LeBaron 2020a), the coercion of labour, activities, and bodies can also be done by states (LeBaron and Roberts 2010; LeBaron 2012; LeBaron and Phillips 2019; Cockayne 2021) and by kin (Anitha and Gill 2017). While trafficking/modern slavery by commercial entities is more often a feature of neoliberal contexts, state forced labour is more likely to be a feature of authoritarian regimes. The people whose labour is forced by the state are likely to be of a different ethnic, religious, national group or political persuasion from those that control the state in authoritarian societies, for example, Nazi Germany (Tooze 2007), Russia in the context of the invasion of Ukraine (Lewis and Blitz 2023), and the short-lived Islamic State (Al-Dayel et al 2022). Forced marriage (Anitha and Gill 2017) is one of the practices similar to slavery identified in the 1956 UN Convention (UN 1956); the proximate beneficiaries may be the parents or wider kin group, structured by regimes of gender inequality. While neoliberal regimes are significant forms of social system that generate trafficking/modern slavery, so too are authoritarian ones, and both are in contrast to more social democratic regimes.

So, is it a market (Hayek 1948; Smith 1986 [1776]; Friedman 2002 [1962])? Trafficking/modern slavery is not a market in the sense of voluntary exchanges, since the exploited person is coerced rather than freely contracting. There are, however, more than two sides to the processes in trafficking/modern slavery, usually including third parties selling the services of others. Trafficking/modern slavery is a multi-sided set of transactions rather than a simple exchange of ownership of a commodity between sellers and buyers, of supply meeting demand (Vogel and Cyrus 2017; Wismer et al 2017). In addition to the person whose work, body, or activities are being sold and the person buying these services, there is a third party that extracts profits from this encounter. It is the profit-seeking third party that drives these illegal activities. In some cases, the multi-sided transactions may be considered a form of platform (Gillespie 2010; Poell et al 2019), which distances the profit-taker from the routine transactions between those seeking livelihoods and customers buying services. Figure 1.1 illustrates the multi-sided nature of the transactions, where the points of the triangle represent: the entities taking profits from the exploitation of the vulnerabilities of others; the vulnerable persons seeking livelihoods; and the entities exploiting the vulnerabilities of others.

Without this third-party profit-seeking to drive the repetition of this activity, the activities would likely be small scale and not grow. Illegal markets are often interwoven with legal markets to disguise and hide their illegality (Beckert and Dewey 2017; Mayntz 2017). In trafficking/modern slavery, criminal activities

Figure 1.1: Multi-sided transactions in trafficking/modern slavery

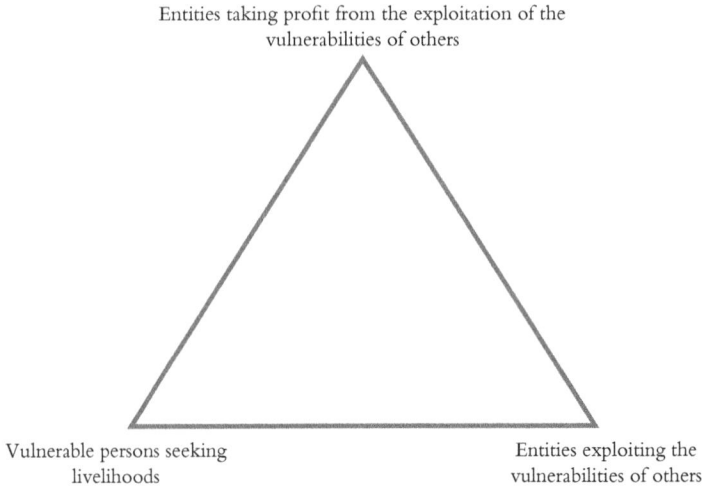

Entities taking profit from the exploitation of the
vulnerabilities of others

Vulnerable persons seeking
livelihoods

Entities exploiting the
vulnerabilities of others

become entangled with legal and legitimate business and market exchanges (Hulme et al 2021). The economy is a larger concept than that of market. Only part of the economy is monetized or commodified (Waring 1988; Walby 2009). Some forms of livelihood are not monetized (for example, domestic servitude, forced marriage) or contain elements where the freedom of the market is restricted (for example, tied visas). The driving force, however, in trafficking/modern slavery is the profit-taker, rather than the buyer of the end services or the victim of trafficking/modern slavery who is treated as the object of this exchange. Figure 1.2 outlines the main sources of profits and sides of the relations where they are taken. It illustrates the sets of relations through which this value is extracted. Profits are derived from profit takers in relation to vulnerable persons through charging fees for migration or job placement, by collecting interest on credits extended to vulnerable persons for paying fees and other expenses, thereby also creating debt dependencies, and from collecting rents for services like housing or transport above the costs of these services. Profits are also derived when profit-takers collect fees and rents for selling the services and labour of vulnerable others to buyers; and these buyers themselves profit not only from exploiting labour and services of vulnerable others through low labour costs, but also from rents collected for services like housing and transport above their cost, and through illegal practices like unpaid wages and unpaid social insurance contributions.

The concept of 'chain' is used to illustrate the processes of extraction and flow of value over space and time. Value extracted at one location or triangle of exploitation flows to another, in spatial terms away from the periphery towards the core of the economic system (Hopkins and Wallerstein 1977,

Figure 1.2: Relations of exploitation in multi-sided transactions of trafficking/modern slavery

Entities taking profit from the exploitation of the vulnerabilities of others

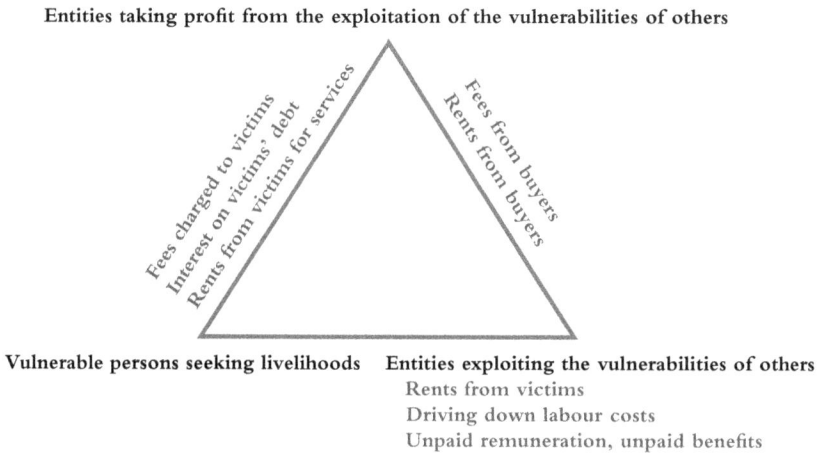

Vulnerable persons seeking livelihoods

Fees charged to victims
Interest on victims' debt
Rents from victims for services

Fees from buyers
Rents from buyers

Entities exploiting the vulnerabilities of others
Rents from victims
Driving down labour costs
Unpaid remuneration, unpaid benefits

1994; Gereffi and Korzeniewicz 1994), and in social terms, as vulnerable persons seeking livelihoods are recruited for profit and sold into exploitative situations. Each specific site and relation of value generation and extraction is linked with others in a chain over space and time, with value sometimes moving across frontiers between states. The concept of a trafficking chain is developed from the literature about commodity, supply, production, and care chains (Hopkins and Wallerstein 1977, 1994; Gereffi and Korzeniewicz 1994; Ehrenreich and Hochschild 2003; Crane et al 2019; LeBaron 2020a, 2021) to denote those forms where there is coercion, and covered in more detail in the next chapter. We illustrate how the sets of relations of exploiting the vulnerably of others are linked over space and time in Figure 1.3. There may be many profit-taking entities involved in a trafficking chain, each deriving profits in the forms of fees, interest, and rents for a specific part of the process, linked together over time and space. The practices of exploitation include charging excessive fees to those seeking jobs elsewhere (Jaegers and Rijken 2014), extending credits to finance migration and use of social media to control migrants in destination countries (ITUC 2014), and may involve the mobilization of kin networks (Ollus et al 2013; Lawthorn et al 2015). The distinctive nature of the trafficking chain is that it includes coercion at some point along the chain and that profit-taking relies on coercion.

Emerging multi-disciplinary field

This critical review and development of social theory of trafficking/modern slavery is multi-disciplinary, from political economy to criminology, from

Figure 1.3: Trafficking chains

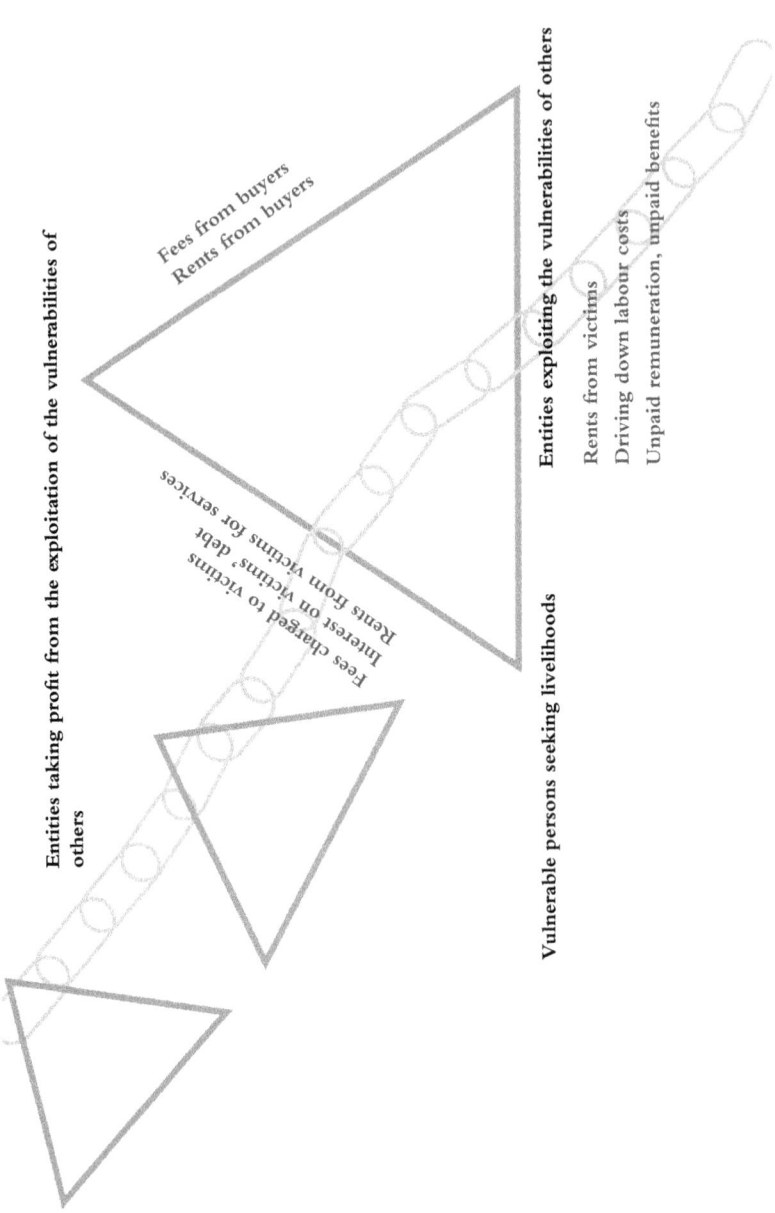

Entities taking profit from the exploitation of the vulnerabilities of others

Entities exploiting the vulnerabilities of others

Rents from victims
Driving down labour costs
Unpaid remuneration, unpaid benefits

Fees from buyers
Rents from buyers

Fees charged to victims
Interest on victims' debt
Rents from victims for services

Vulnerable persons seeking livelihoods

sociology to economics, from public policy to business studies, from post-colonial to gender studies. Contributions are to the disciplines of business/management studies, criminology, data science/social statistics, economics, gender studies, geography, law, political economy, political science, post-colonial studies, social work, and sociology. Trafficking/modern slavery is a multidisciplinary and interdisciplinary field. This book is a contribution to the component disciplines of this multidisciplinary field as well as to building an interdisciplinary field.

This emerging field of trafficking/modern slavery, that theorizes coercion in the economy, builds on several key classic and contemporary writers: Du Bois (1998 [1935]), Barry (1995), Bales (1999), Gallagher (2010), Brass (2011), O'Connell Davidson (2015), LeBaron (2020a), and Cockayne (2021). Bales (1999) demonstrates the existence of trafficking/modern slavery as a form of coercion, violence, and exploitation in the contemporary world, not consigned to history. Brass (2011) argues that unfree labour is an endemic feature of contemporary capitalism, rather than a form of primitive accumulation that will disappear with economic growth. LeBaron (2020a) develops the analysis of the extraction of profits in global labour supply chains. Du Bois (1998 [1935]) analyses the reasons that the attempts to free slaves in the 19th century resulted in only partial success. Cockayne (2021) argues that the international regulation of capital to reduce trafficking/modern slavery is possible. Barry (1995) shows the importance of gendered sexual exploitation as a distinct form of coercion and trafficking/modern slavery. O'Connell Davidson (2015) discusses potential limits to the concept of modern slavery mobilizing concepts of agency and choice. Gallagher (2010) documents over a century of gradual development of this field in international law and the contributions of global civil society to this long process of making coercion illegal in the economy. The chapters in this book return to these key insights in developing theory, and understandings of legal developments and policy pathways.

Root causes

This book develops four contributions to the investigation of the root causes of trafficking/modern slavery. The first concerns whether the root causes of trafficking/modern slavery lie in the individual agency of a few bad individuals or organized criminals, or in social systems. The analysis sets the focus on social systems, while not denying the agency of individual actors. The second concerns whether the root causes are part of universal processes or diverge across varieties of modernity. Building on prior research on theories of society (Walby 2009, 2020, 2021a, 2023), human trafficking/modern slavery is found differently in three varieties of modernities: social democratic, neoliberal, and authoritarian. The third concerns whether trafficking/modern slavery is located in one or more institutional domain, for example, just the economy. Here the contribution demonstrates that trafficking/modern slavery involves all institutional domains: economy, violence, polity, and civil society. The fourth concerns whether the root causes lie in class inequalities and (neoliberal) capitalism or if other regimes of inequality need to be addressed. This book expands the analysis to include regimes of coloniality and gender. An analysis of capital and capitalism is insufficient to understand the root causes, which lie in the intersection of capitalism with coloniality (both legacies and current) and gender regimes.

Agency or systems?

Is trafficking/modern slavery the individual agency of a few bad individuals or the outcome of intersecting social systems? Approaches differ in the extent of their focus on individual traffickers and their victims or on situations, institutions, and systems (Bales 1999; O'Connell Davidson 2015; LeBaron 2020a). This is linked to different priorities for prevention: the former focuses on improving the prosecution of traffickers and special services for registered victims; the latter on regulating institutions to reduce exploitative situations. O'Connell Davidson (2015: 135) is critical when the 'primary focus is on the morality of individual employers, creditors or labour-brokers who violently abuse workers, not the structures and systems within which they operate, which are only very selectively questioned'; yet focuses on the agency and choices of individuals when discussing what constitutes the boundaries of what is trafficking for sexual exploitation. There is a balance to be found between 'prosecution and assistance' (Gallagher 2017) and a focus on institutional and systemic change; both are needed. While the greed of the individual traffickers and the lack of power of victims are part of the problem, trafficking/modern slavery is more than individual traffickers and victims of trafficking. Experiences and practices of trafficking/modern slavery are rooted in larger institutions and systems. Trafficking/modern slavery is a chain of linked practices in institutions and systems. While the prosecution of traffickers and welfare support to victims of trafficking/modern slavery are important, the most important, and challenging, issues concern prevention, for which the identification of the root causes of trafficking/modern slavery in institutions and social systems is needed.

Not the dustbin of history: varieties of modernity

(Modern) slavery is not over. The existence of trafficking/modern slavery challenges traditional linear notions of modernity and progress. Modern slavery is part of the contemporary as well as classical world, in high-income as well as low-income countries. The existence of trafficking/modern slavery in all countries in the contemporary world challenges the notion that economic development inevitably generates progress. An alternative position is that there are multiple varieties of modernity, with varying levels of inequality, democracy, and violence, generating varying levels of trafficking/modern slavery.

Traditional modernization theory suggested that economic development would lead to progress in all other areas of society (Lipset 1959; Giddens 1990; Ingelhart 1997), including violence (Elias 1939; Pinker 2011, 2018). Pinker argues that violence is declining as civilization advances, with a growth in enlightenment and self-control. This is contested by analyses of multiple modernities (Eisenstadt 2000), the Holocaust (Bauman 1989; Tooze 2007), war (Braumoeller 2019), the post-colonial (Bhambra 2007; Boatcă 2015; Go 2016), and gender (Shire and Walby 2020; Walby 2020, 2023a; Gottfried et al 2023; Shire 2023).

There are multiple modernities rather than a universal form, of which three major varieties are social democratic, neoliberal, and authoritarian (Walby 2009, 2023a). Discussed in more detail in Chapter 2, these vary by levels of inequality in the economy, the depth of democracy in the polity and civil society, corruption and the rule of law, and the extent of violence. These varieties of modernity are shaped by intersecting regimes of inequality of capitalism, coloniality, and gender. The level and form of trafficking/modern slavery varies with these varieties of social system.

Institutional domains: economy, violence, polity, civil society

Trafficking/modern slavery is generated in each of the institutional domains of economy, violence, polity, and civil society. The tendency to focus on just one of these institutional domains rather than including all of them can be the result of disciplinary practices in the academy that limit the understanding of the field.

Trafficking/modern slavery is generated in the economy in that it concerns the extraction of value from material activities. Extraction is organized along multi-sided sets of transactions in which third parties take profits and material advantage from the activities of others. Trafficking chains are often transnational in structure, in which case value flows from periphery to core. Trafficking/modern slavery is not only an activity associated with illegal markets, but also encompasses forced labour organized by states, and forced marriages organized by kin or other groups.

Trafficking/modern slavery is generated in the domain of violence and coercion in that value is extracted by means of coercion through private and state actors. Coercion is understood as wider than violence, though all violence is coercive. Further, war generates trafficking/modern slavery through the vulnerabilities of those fleeing war zones, which are themselves opportunities for crime and exploitation.

Trafficking/modern slavery is structured by the polity in that it can be reduced, or increased, by state policies, laws, and institutions. The depth of democracy shapes these practices. Polities can reduce trafficking/modern slavery by the provision of welfare that can reduce vulnerabilities and by regulating the economy to remove opportunities for exploitation. In contrast, states can also be responsible for organizing forced labour, and corrupt states can be captured by trafficking/modern slavery interests.

Trafficking/modern slavery is structured by civil society through the negotiation of the meaning of the concepts of exploitation and vulnerability. Actions of civil societal projects aim to reduce situations of vulnerability and encompass the advocacy and services of groups from trade unions and feminist NGOs to faith groups supporting diaspora.

Capital, coloniality, and gender regimes

Trafficking/modern slavery concerns exploitation: the extraction of profits and material benefits from those in situations of vulnerability using coercion. It is generated by capital, intersecting with coloniality and gender regimes. While the drive for profits that is core to the dynamics of capital is central (Brass 2011; LeBaron 2020a), the situations of vulnerability that are exploited are shaped by coloniality (both legacy and contemporary) (Du Bois 1998 [1935]) and by gender regimes (Barry 1995). These global and national structures of power are contested by political projects to reduce this exploitation and can be significant in shaping the outcome (Du Bois 1998 [1935]; Gallagher 2010; Brass 2011, 2016).

The inequalities driving trafficking/modern slavery are articulated in value chains structured by world systems of capital (Wallerstein 2011 [1974]; Brass 2011; LeBaron 2020a), the ethnic constructions of empires (Du Bois 1998 [1935]; Boatcă 2015; Go 2016), contemporary authoritarian regimes (Al-Dayel et al 2022; Lewis and Blitz 2023) and by gender regimes (Barry 1995; Walby 2009, 2020, 2023a; Shire and Walby 2020; Shire and Nemoto 2020; Gottfried et al 2023). While states can be important in implementing laws, they can also be captured by trafficking/modern slavery interests, and significant aspects of the political shaping of the environment for trafficking/modern slavery takes place at a global level. Processes of neoliberal globalization have removed some of the regulations developed in earlier times, creating situations of vulnerability (Harvey 2005). The situations of vulnerability are structured by the intersection with further regimes of inequality, including the ethnicized legacies and contemporary practices of coloniality and gender regimes.

Migrants are more than three times more likely than non-migrants to be victims of trafficking/modern slavery (ILO, Walk Free, and IOM 2022) and are more likely to be of a minority ethnicity within the country within which the exploitation takes place. The mobility of migrants from lower income to higher income countries in part arises out of economic inequalities rooted in legacies of coloniality (Du Bois 1998 [1935]; Boatcă 2015; Go 2016). Migrants have fewer entitlements than citizens to the protections of welfare and justice systems (van der Leun 2011), and visas tied to a particular employer or household remove the free movement that offers opportunities to escape exploitation (Demetriou 2015). New forms of exploited ethnicities and nationalities emerge as authoritarian regimes both directly coerce labour (Al-Dayel et al 2022; Lewis and Blitz 2023) and expand their power beyond their borders through war, threats, and coercion, generating forced movement of people who are vulnerable to exploitation along their migration pathways.

Women and girls are more likely to be victims of trafficking/modern slavery than men and boys, especially for forced marriage and for trafficking for purposes of sexual exploitation (UNODC 2021; ILO, Walk Free, and IOM 2022). Forced marriage disproportionately affects girls and is conducted in the context of family and kin relations in highly unequal gender regimes (Anitha and Gill 2017). The sex trade creates situations of vulnerability that especially concern women and girls (Barry 1979; O'Connell Davidson 2015). The nature and consequences of attempts to regulate the sex trade depend on the context of the gender regime in which this occurs. Situations of gendered vulnerability are generated in different ways in varieties of gender regime, with consequences for the specific kinds of exploitation and opportunities for resistance (Gupta 2008, 2016; Walby 2023a).

Law

Legal definitions matter. Trafficking and practices similar to slavery are defined in international legal instruments, most recently those of the United Nations in 1956 and 2000. Core to its definition is the concept of control over another person. This builds on earlier international law on slavery, which made illegal actual ownership of another person, culminating in the 1926 *Convention to Suppress the Slave Trade and Slavery* (League of Nations 1926). Thereafter there was the extension of law to forms of control that were not actual ownership:

1930 *Convention Concerning Forced and Compulsory Labour*, developed by the International Labour Organization (1930).
1956 *Supplementary Convention on the Abolition of Slavery, the Slave Trade and Institutions and Practices Similar to Slavery* (UN 1956).
1998 Rome Statute of the International Criminal Court (UN 1998).

2000 United Nations *Protocol to Prevent, Suppress and Punish Trafficking in Persons, Especially Women and Children, supplementing the United Nations Convention against Transnational Organized Crime* (UN 2000a).

There are multiple areas of law relevant to trafficking/modern slavery. This is not only criminal law. There are several relevant international legal instruments. This is best understood as the development of a single field of trafficking/modern slavery, even though there are multiple bodies of relevant law, leading up to the most recent legal instrument, the 2000 UN Palermo Protocol (UN 2000a).

This international law treats trafficking/modern slavery as a crime. But it does more than that. It mobilizes several bodies of law, some of which are not usually thought of as criminal law. The 2000 UN Palermo Protocol (UN 2000a) mandates the use of these wider bodies of law and of policy to implement them effectively. The new laws reach out beyond criminal individuals to groups, practices, organizations, and institutions, thus, potentially reaching into root causes not only individuals. These laws are applied to the economy, to the regulation of supply chains in which trafficking/modern slavery might be located, to the regulation of welfare to support the mitigation of harms to victims of trafficking, to the activities needed to prevent trafficking/modern slavery, and to the regulation of conduct during war. The interpretation of the limits and boundaries to the concepts are subject to negotiation in civil society, so the practical definition of what counts as sufficient exploitation and vulnerability is settled according to their meaning in different national contexts.

There are, however, simultaneous legal developments that run counter to these developments and are conducive to trafficking, perhaps by reducing regulations in the name of economic development. The outcome is a balance, that changes over time.

There is a history of development of laws over more than two centuries to prevent the slave trade, slavery, practices similar to slavery, forced labour, and trafficking in human beings. Each has a slightly different emphasis and consequences. There are divergences, even fractures. One of these concerns the significance and legal strategy to address trafficking/modern slavery in relation to gender and sexuality. The complex debates on this are addressed further in Chapter 6 on sexual exploitation. The nuanced analysis of these polarized issues as developed in this book offers a way forward to overcoming some of the divisions in research on trafficking/modern slavery.

Trafficking/modern slavery laws are global, ranging historically from before the foundation of the League of Nations to the current United Nations. However, the interpretation of key concepts and the implementation by courts are the tasks of national and regional states and polities. The varied interpretation and implementation can have diverse outcomes.

The significance of the global in issues of 'law and order' challenges some understandings of sovereignty.

Changes in these laws are embedded in the struggles of global civil society, including transnational feminism (Barry 1995; Gallagher 2010); in contexts of war, civil war, empire and coloniality (Tooze 2007; Al-Dayel et al 2022; Lewis and Blitz 2023); and in which states supported or resisted these changes (Du Bois 1998 [1935]).

All aspects of society are involved in the developments and implementation of these laws. They concern coercion and violence, polities (both global and national), the economy (since this is about economic exploitation and the regulation of processes that are understood to be in the economy), and by civil society. They are structured by multiple regimes of inequality: capitalism; empire and coloniality, in which (modern) slavery originated and has been reproduced; and the specificity of gender and sexuality in varieties of gender regimes. Law is a key point of condensation in society of all these matters.

Data

Data on trafficking/modern slavery is used to test theories and to evaluate policies. A range of data has been collected in different ways using administrative methods and population surveys, at local, national, regional (EU), and international levels. There are debates over the priorities over data collection and over the selection of the indicators that summarize the data. This is a new and important field under rapid development.

There are quantitative estimates of the extent and nature of trafficking/ modern slavery using data gathered in several ways.

One statistic concerns the number of victims identified by the authorities with whom they have registered for assistance. Another concerns the number of traffickers (investigated/suspected or arrested; prosecuted; and convicted). These are data on people in contact with the authorities in specific countries.

Estimates of the number of victims in the population (including those not in contact with the authorities) have been generated by population surveys. There are gaps in data which are filled in various ways, including statistical modelling and expert judgements. Data on trafficking/modern slavery is often disaggregated by the type of exploitation (whether labour, sexual, forced marriage, other), and by the sex and age (adult/child) of the victim. There can be data on other characteristics, including migration status and country of origin.

The process of setting the priorities for indicators, which summarize complex data, and data collection is important, since indicators can crystalize a field of enquiry. The UN Sustainable Development Goals (UN 2015) comprise a measurement framework that is supported by the authority of the UN, which might be considered a data 'platform'. The UN SDG Goals,

Targets, and Indicators help to set the framework for priorities of other UN organs and agencies, and other actors.

The collection of data is challenging, as the phenomenon is illegal. There are debates as to the reliability of the data. The quality of the estimates require improvement through further research.

Policy

The way to address trafficking/modern slavery is contested. Is the prosecution and conviction of traffickers the best way to stop trafficking? Or are such 'traditional penalization and rescue approaches' Chuang (2015a: 1519) 'carceral', merely leading to further forms of inequalities (Bernstein 2010)? Or does this underestimate the range of forms of regulation, including multiple bodies of law beyond criminal justice used in multiple sites of intervention (Ayers and Braithwaite 1992; Gallagher 2010)? Do critiques of anti-trafficking/modern slavery underestimate the range of support for victims that is provided, wider welfare supports, and strategic interventions into the institutions and systems that are the root causes of trafficking? What would a comprehensive approach to policy interventions look like? Reducing inequalities and poverty and ensuring access to a way to obtain a livelihood is an important part of policy to reduce situations of vulnerability to trafficking, including of women and migrants. Could trafficking/modern slavery be prevented if political capacities to regulate and govern were deployed more appropriately and the depth of democracy increased? The following are areas of policy under investigation and development.

There has been a call for better coordination at the UN level (Cockayne 2021). Trafficking/modern slavery policy and law is shaped in global arenas (Gallagher 2010), including the UN, transnational civil society including global feminism, and multiple entities linked to the UN that have trafficking/modern slavery in their remit, including the International Labour Organization (ILO), UNODC, International Organization for Migration (IOM), UN Women, UN Special Rapporteur on Contemporary Slavery, Special Rapporteur on Trafficking in Persons, World Bank Group, and the UN Statistics Commission.

Global financial investment is subject to some forms of global governance. The UN has developed as a platform for setting standards, including the Sustainable Development Goals (Cockayne 2021). The World Bank Group adopted the Sustainable Development Goals in 2016 (World Bank Group 2016), with implications for their policies relevant to trafficking/modern slavery as part of their conditions for financial investment. However, not all financial investment is governed in this way, with China a particular exception (Cockayne 2021).

All polities have strategies to encourage economic growth and have preferred forms of development. In many countries, this strategy includes prioritizing some industries over others in 'industrial policy'. Some activities and parts of the economy are more prone to trafficking/modern slavery than others. The sex trade is prone to trafficking/modern slavery (Europol 2015a), as are domestic labour, seasonal agricultural work, and seafaring. Hence industrial policy, to ban or constrain industries that are conducive to trafficking, is a relevant, if controversial, policy tool.

Businesses are increasingly being made responsible for trafficking/modern slavery in their supply chains. In some jurisdictions, companies are required to report on their due diligence (UK Modern Slavery Act 2015). The use of voluntary codes has been growing but is relatively weak in effect (LeBaron 2020a, 2020b). There is emerging development of laws and policies with sanctions.

Businesses are subject to local and national regulations. This may include licensing, for example, to regulate the recruitment industry that supplies labour, and for health and safety matters.

Regulations standardizing and protecting labour and regulating employment relations can reduce opportunities for exploitation. The loosening of restrictions on temporary and contract labour, the expansion of outsourcing, the rise of non-standard employment, and the legitimation of private recruitment and brokering in the 'management' of temporary labour migration (Barrientos 2013; Fudge and Strauss 2014; Theodore and Peck 2014) open a 'low road' to economic growth that increases opportunities for exploitation and trafficking/modern slavery. The use of restrictions on migrants, such as temporary and tied visas, further increases opportunities for exploitation. Preventing trafficking/modern slavery by improving regulation is a significant strategic development, but it depends upon state capacity and democratic activity to mobilize this capacity appropriately. In the context of trafficking/modern slavery concerning labour exploitation, the cooperation of trade unions can be important; in the context of trafficking/modern slavery concerning sexual exploitation, the cooperation of NGOs can be important. In both contexts, organizations supporting migrants, ethnic minorities, women, and diaspora can be important.

Ensuring the rule of law and the elimination of corruption are important in preventing trafficking/modern slavery. Criminal justice is a necessary part of combatting trafficking; of using the authority and capacity of the state to stop the powerful exploiting the weak (Gallagher 2010). Potentially the criminal justice system is a social justice project on the side of the weak; but it can be punitive and exacerbate inequalities if poorly targeted. This is especially the case in relation to migrants. This rearticulates some of the classic debates in criminology between punitive and welfare-oriented criminal justice systems (Garland 2000; Braithwaite 2023) in the context of trafficking/modern slavery. Further, the successful prosecution of traffickers has proved challenging. This is partly the case when it is cross-border, as criminal justice systems remain largely national in jurisdiction; and partly because it is intrinsically difficult to prosecute the powerful in a crime that is often divided into relatively modularized sections of a chain over space and time (Kirby and Penna 2010). Moving forward with criminal prosecution requires the identification of appropriate points of prosecution along the trafficking chain and transnational action on enforcement (European Commission 2022a).

The depth of democracy (Walby 2009; V-Dem 2022) is significant for the policy and legal developments to reduce both impunity of the exploiters and to reduce situations of vulnerability to trafficking/modern slavery (Global Initiative against Organized Crime 2021). Deeper democracy supports the rule of law, the reduction of corruption, greater welfare support, and the more effective involvement of civil society.

Developing welfare provision helps to prevent the development of vulnerable situations. This includes provision of income support, housing, health care, and other services. But this wider welfare provision depends on state funding, which is only varyingly available (see Chapter 5, on policy). Further, the exclusion of those without full citizenship because of migration status leaves those excluded in situations of vulnerability. Migration policies attempting to restrict these migration flows generate forms of vulnerability that can be exploited by traffickers (Anderson 2010, 2014a).

Assistance is needed by victims of trafficking/modern slavery; it is legally required for victims who are registered with the authorities. The services mandated under the UN Palermo Protocol (UN 2000a) can include residence for non–citizen victims, though sometimes this is only for the duration of the prosecution after which survivors are returned to the vulnerable situations from which they came (Lindquist 2013a). Programmes to more fully support victims to rebuild their lives, for example, through training and integration in viable economic activities, have been recommended, but not always funded.

Sexual exploitation

The sex trade contains elements of trafficking/modern slavery. The effectiveness of different interventions to stop the elements of the sex trade that are trafficking/modern slavery is debated. The debate is polarized along several dimensions: whether the sex trade is inherently oppressive to women regardless of trafficking/modern slavery or not; and, whether the intervention of the criminal justice system is appropriate or carceral, especially because of entanglements with migration policy. The questions that have arisen concern evaluation of both theory and policy. They include philosophical as well as social scientific questions as to the nature of freedom, agency, choice, consent, and intention. They concern the nature of social systems of contemporary forms of capitalism, varieties of gender regime, the legacies of empire and coloniality in borders, migration and ethnicity, and global processes. They concern practical policy issues as to what works at the intersections of the multiple inequalities and illegalities of trafficking/ modern slavery for purposes of sexual exploitation, forced commercial sexual exploitation of adults, commercial sexual exploitation of children, and sexual slavery.

There is a tendency in the existing debates to polarize between calls for decriminalization or for more criminalization of the sex trade. Two distinctions contribute to more nuance in resolving or at least broadening the parameters of the debate. The first is to distinguish between different bodies of law, between criminal and non-criminal law, and different forms of non-criminal law including the regulation of profit-taking through licensing and company law, due diligence, labour rights, enforcing labour standards, and welfare. Second is the distinction between three sides of the relations constituting trafficking/modern slavery, each of which can be the object of regulation: the seller; the end user; the profit-taker. The argument is to shift the focus of regulatory activity from seller and end user to the profit-taker, the person or entity, that is benefitting from the vulnerability of others at the peak and across the links of trafficking chains.

Empirically, the different regulatory approaches are investigated with a focus on Germany, in comparative context with the UK, Sweden and the US. Like all EU Member States and signatories to the UN Palermo Protocol (UN 2000a), Germany has criminalized coercion, but at the same time it has legalized all sides of the sex trade. The intent to implement the UN Palermo Protocol and to transpose the EU Directive on Preventing and Combatting Trafficking in Human Beings (European Commission 2011) led Germany to enact a major reform of prostitution law in 2016, in an attempt to regulate the legal sex trade to eliminate coerced sexual exploitation. The evaluation of this attempt is informative for building theory as well as for policies to eradicate trafficking/modern slavery both specially in the sex trade, and more broadly.

Approach of this book

This book contributes to the development of the theory of change needed to inform the development of the policies, law, and data required to prevent trafficking/modern slavery. Next, Chapter 2 on theory engages with theories and research on trafficking/modern slavery across multiple disciplines. Theory is necessary to provide the connection between the pieces of empirical data to support an understanding of what works to prevent and eradicate trafficking. Theory is constructed at multiple levels and has a range of key concepts that specify the objects used in the theory and the potential relations between them. This is followed by Chapter 3 on law. The legal instruments for ending trafficking/modern slavery begin with the laws to end the slave trade and span the last two centuries. International law has played an important role in efforts to end trafficking/modern slavery. The United Nations is an important agent in this endeavour, including through the 2000 Palermo Protocol. Chapter 4 on data provides information on the extent and nature of trafficking/modern slavery and addresses the ways in which data collection is being, and can be, improved. Chapter 5 on policy develops a comprehensive analysis of policies to reduce trafficking/modern slavery. At the most abstract level, this concerns sustainable development, democracy, and war. The detailed policy fields include finance, industrial policy, business regulation, employment regulation, welfare, building democratic institutions, international security, criminal justice, human rights, specialized services, and research. Chapter 6 offers an empirical study of changes in the regulation of the sex trade, the context for sexual exploitation mainly of women, and a contested policy field among feminist scholars. The chapter moves beyond the polarized debates about abolition or empowerment in the sex trade, by mobilizing the analyses of all sides of selling, buying, and profit-taking in the sex trade, and examining the different bodies of law, civil and criminal, that attempt to regulate coercion out of the sex trade.

The contribution of this book, summarized in Chapter 7 (Conclusion), lies in the analysis of the root causes across different institutional domains, regimes of inequality, and varieties of modernities. The conclusion returns to the multidisciplinary and interdisciplinary approach developed in this book, to argue for more research and debate, including between development, criminal justice, human rights, gender, migration, and labour research.

2

Theory

Introduction

This book builds a theory of trafficking/modern slavery in society at the intersection of coercion and the economy and of multiple regimes of inequality. It develops the concept of trafficking/modern slavery as a single field and identifies its 'root causes'. Trafficking/modern slavery is generated by the whole society; hence root causes are located within a theory of society. The chapter builds the theory across three dimensions of social systems: institutional domains; regimes of inequality; and varieties of modernity. Trafficking/modern slavery is generated within all the institutional domains of economy, violence, polity, and civil society. It is shaped by the intersection of multiple regimes of inequality: capitalism, coloniality, and gender. It exists in different levels and forms across different varieties of modernity: social democratic, neoliberal, and authoritarian.

The book makes the following contributions to social theory. First, it develops the concept of trafficking/modern slavery as a single field. Second, it identifies the significance of third-party profit-taking in trafficking/modern slavery, in multi-sided transactions, entwining legal and illegal activities. Third, it develops the concept of 'trafficking chain' as flows of value that involve coercion, building on and adapting the concepts of commodity and supply chain. Fourth, it includes coercion alongside economy, polity, and civil society, transcending the traditional disciplinary separation of these fields/domains, especially between criminology and political economy. Fifth, it applies the lens of intersectionality to the social relations of trafficking/modern slavery, in which capitalism is shaped by colonial and gender relations, and identifies the pathways that link coloniality and gender regimes to trafficking/modern slavery. Sixth, it links variations in trafficking/modern slavery to varieties of modernity, including social democratic, neoliberal, and authoritarian, rather than to a unilinear modernization.

Trafficking/modern slavery as a single field

Trafficking/modern slavery is the exploitation of the vulnerability of others that uses coercion to extract profit and other material benefits. It is best treated as a single field, though there are distinct forms and processes. These include: labour exploitation (commercial forced labour); sexual exploitation; state forced labour; forced marriage; as well as other forms. As discussed in Chapter 1, modern slavery is different from chattel slavery, in that a person is controlled but not legally owned. Lack of consent is not part of the definition; control over the person is key. Mobility is not needed, but is common.

Third–party profit-taking from multi–sided trafficking/modern slavery transactions

Is trafficking/modern slavery: a market; an illegal market, since some things are not legally sold; not a market at all, because of the presence of coercion; the interweaving of legal and illegal markets; or an illicit economy (but not a market)?

Trafficking/modern slavery is challenging to traditional understandings of markets as two-sided locations of free exchange, of supply and demand. In commercial forms of trafficking/modern slavery, the extraction of value takes place in multi-sided transactions, in which third-party profit-takers extract profit from transactions involving a coerced person. In state-based forced labour, market mechanisms are not central. In forced marriage, the exchange does not usually take place under market conditions, although it can.

The neoclassical idea of free markets and their contribution to economic growth is articulated in the work of Hayek (1948) and Friedman (2002) [1962], who understand markets as naturally fair and efficient mechanisms to organize economic activity, and hence best kept free from (state) interference. This framework has traditionally underpinned the Washington Consensus and the workings of international financial institutions (Reich 2016). The neoclassical concept of market is problematic, since there is a tendency to naturalize it as a self-correcting self-balancing entity in which supply and demand are in equilibrium because of the 'magic' of the 'price mechanism' (Hayek 1948). Even Adam Smith (1986) [1776] (see also Friedman 2002 [1962]) knew this not to be the case, because of issues of fraud and power that distort markets. It is also problematic because of the assumption that markets operate best without state 'interference'. Markets are not self-balancing but social institutions that are regulated by states to prevent corruption, instability, and excessive exploitation and profit-taking (Keynes 1936; Fligstein 2002; Minsky 2008 [1986]; Beckert 2009; Callon 2021). The drive to expand the proportion of human activity to be treated as if it operates as a market is central to the neoliberal project (Harvey 2005; Davies and Gane 2021).

The neoliberal project usually contrasts itself with authoritarianism (Hayek 1948; Friedman 2002 [1962]), but it also diverges from social democracy (Giddens 1998; Walby 2009, 2021b).

In relation to trafficking/modern slavery, the simple use of the term 'market' is inappropriate, since the person being sold does not have agency in any market. Nonetheless, there have been attempts to develop the concept of demand in relation to some aspects of trafficking, despite it having a more complex ecology of elements than individual sellers and buyers (Vogel and Cyrus 2017). The notion of reducing demand to prevent trafficking is included in the Palermo Protocol (UN 2000a). Vogel and Cyrus (2017) discuss the concept of demand in the context of reducing the demand that leads to trafficking. They argue for the importance of conceptual clarity: demand requires that it is possible to identify who wants to buy what. If this is not possible then the concept of market is not helpful. They start from simple models of demand in markets and progress to more complicated models of markets that include brokers or intermediaries. They conclude that 'a market contract implies the absence of coercion through other people' and that 'coercive relations may be embedded in market contexts, but they are not market relations' (Vogel and Cyrus 2017: 389). Thus, the coercion that is central to trafficking/modern slavery precludes it being conceptualized as a simple market.

In illicit economies, illegal markets can be interwoven with legal markets (Beckert and Dewey 2017; Mayntz 2017) and with forms of transactions that are not markets. Rents and fees are taken, and money is laundered. Trafficking/modern slavery is organized in various ways, as: a governance type of organized criminal groups who wield security governance in a community by fear and violence; business-like organized crime; opportunistic associations of traffickers; and individual traffickers (UNODC 2023: 48). Some forms of trafficking/modern slavery corrupt otherwise legitimate activities as it seeks to hide from authorities and justice (UNODC 2011). The attempts to suppress trafficking/modern slavery involve interventions to regulate and intervene in the 'non-market' criminal activities covering financial flows (Broad et al 2022), money laundering, tax havens (secrecy jurisdictions), and corruption (UNODC 2011; Global Initiative against Transnational Organized Crime 2021; Hulme et al 2021).

The analysis of trafficking/modern slavery requires the development of concepts of economies that go beyond conventional notions of markets. It is an illicit economy, but not a simple market. The person who is being exploited is not acting freely, but is coerced. Their work and services are being exchanged by others, rather than themselves engaging in free exchange. Profit-taking in trafficking/modern slavery is usually by third parties from transactions between others (Chapter 1, Figure 1.3). Persons prosecuted for trafficking are usually much further downstream from these peak profit-takers (Chapter 4, on data). These profits can take the form of fees, rents, and interest (Chapter 1, Figure 1.2). The illegal activities are interwoven with legal markets. The multi-sided nature of trafficking/modern slavery transactions may also be understood through the concept of platform (Gillespie 2010; Plantin et al 2018; Poell et al 2019), in which the controller of the platform on which others conduct exchanges is the entity that derives the profits. 'Platforms as profit-takers' becomes increasingly important with the digitalization of market operations and financial transactions.

Third-party profit-takers are the driving factor behind trafficking/modern slavery. Trafficking chains link together illegal activities with legal markets, voluntary and coerced transactions, market exchanges and non-market relations.

Trafficking chains

As introduced in Chapter 1, trafficking chains are flows of value that involve coercion. The concept of 'trafficking chain' builds on the earlier uses of the concept of chain in commodity chains, supply chains, labour supply chains, production chains, value chains, and care chains. It adds the dimension of coercion to identify a specific kind of chain. There are many points along the chain at which value is added and extracted; some, but not all, points involve coercion and cross the criminal threshold of the exploitation of the vulnerability of others; both objects and services are involved.

The concept of chain has developed in several ways. The early concept of commodity chain (Hopkins and Wallerstein 1977, 1994; Gereffi and Korzeniewicz 1994) captures the links needed to create goods and services out of parts sourced from around the world, in which value extracted at each stage flows towards the core of the world system. In this way, Wallerstein combined both the global and the local levels of analysis, showing how both were needed to fully grasp the inequalities that both generated and were generated by these processes. The value that is extracted flows upwards towards the 'core' and away from the 'periphery'. The concept of core/periphery, while often referring to processes that are spatial, is primarily concerned with the social relations involved.

The concept of commodity chain developed at a macro level and the concept of global value chain at a more meso level (Bair 2005). Further developments include the concepts of production chains, and labour supply chains (Crane et al 2019; Voss et al 2019; LeBaron 2020a). For LeBaron (2021: 35): 'A labor supply chain is comprised of the employment relationships that a worker passes through in order to arrive on a work-site. They can involve multiple layers of contracting and intermediaries, where agencies, recruiters, labor providers, or other intermediaries are involved in the supply of workers to producers.' The development of the concepts of global value chain and global production network put the state back into the analysis (Gereffi 2014; Neilson et al 2014). The increasing mobilization of the concept of 'global value chain' is consolidating a move beyond the old Washington Consensus, midway between state-minimalist and state-coordinated approaches (Werner et al 2014). The concept of chain has been mobilized to address issues of gender and care. Transnational production is gendered at a macro as well as micro level (Bair 2010). The global value chain is gendered (Barrientos 2019, 2023; Barrientos et al 2019). The concept of 'care chain' has been developed (Ehrenreich and Hochschild 2003; Yeates 2009; Gottfried 2013) to focus on the mobility of those (usually women) from the Global South (periphery) to supply care work to the Global North (core). Dunaway (2001, 2014) notes that the inputs into commodity chains could include the unpaid household labour of women, thereby including non-monetized, non-market sources of value in the chain. LeBaron notes that some labour supply chains include forced labour (LeBaron et al 2017; LeBaron 2021). Her analysis includes 'debt bondage' (LeBaron 2014) and the role of penal labour in social and labour discipline (LeBaron 2012).

All these concepts of 'chain' capture the sourcing of materials and labour from around the world needed to make a final product or service in one place, noting that this may involve the movement of value over frontiers (LeBaron 2015, 2021; Crane et al 2019). The connections are not a simple hierarchy but may involve subcontracting and informal connections. The processes of subcontracting act to prevent a simple and direct connection between the links of the chain. This process is important in diminishing responsibility and accountability for an activity even while value and profits are accrued (Barrientos 2013; Phillips 2015; LeBaron 2020a). The concept of chain recognizes that there may be many sites or links in the chain at which value is added and extracted, which may have a different set of people from the other sites, which are connected.

The concept of trafficking chain builds on this intellectual infrastructure. A trafficking chain is when the flow of value includes coercion. The flow may include crossing borders, but this is not essential.

Institutional domains, including violence/coercion

Trafficking/modern slavery chains are constituted within economy, violence and coercion, polity, and civil society. They are economic, with the extraction of value. There is coercion, since this is how control over the person is obtained. Polities reduce, support, or even carry trafficking/ modern slavery out. Within civil society the meaning of trafficking/modern slavery is contested. All are structured by capitalist, colonial, and gender relations. Their forms vary by the variety of modernity (Walby 2023a). The theoretical framework draws on Walby (2009, 2021a).

Trafficking/modern slavery is driven by the hunt for profits and material advantage, so the economic dimension is central (Bales 1999). The economy includes sectors that are monetized and marketized as well as ones that are not, the household, and the state (Walby 2009). Each sector has associated forms of trafficking/modern slavery. Trafficking for purposes of labour and sexual exploitation are in the monetized/marketized sector, forced marriage in the household, and state forced labour in the state sector. There are different strategies for economic development: inclusive sustainable development (SDG); economic growth (GDP); or subordinate to the priorities of the state. The intersection of the economy and coercion/violence makes trafficking/modern slavery a distinctive object for social theory, since these two domains have often been addressed as if they were separate matters.

The use of coercion to extract profits and material benefits marks the distinctiveness of trafficking/modern slavery. Although the use of coercion as a means of control is sufficient to define trafficking in the Palermo Protocol (UN 2000a; Kelly 2003), violence is common (UNODC 2021, 2023; Chapter 4). Violence is an institutional domain that includes multiple forms of practices and social relations of violence, including interstate, intergroup, state–individual, and interpersonal (Walby 2009, 2013). There are variations in levels of violence, in policies towards violence, and in the use of violence by the state (Garland 2000; Loader and Walker 2007; Lacey 2009; Wacquant 2009; Walby 2009). Violence shapes the environment, including the political economy (McIlwaine and Moser 2003; Moser and McIlwaine 2014). These variations of violence in the environment have implications for the amount and form of trafficking/modern slavery in a society and against specific groups (Hynes 2004; UNODC 2023).

Violence and coercion are part of the causes of trafficking/modern slavery in several ways. War can cause trafficking, both directly, and indirectly through migration. War can lead to state forced labour; indeed, this is sometimes intended. The conquered people are subjected to forced labour, sometimes in camps, to the benefit of the victors; sometimes, during war, a minority population will be subjected to forced labour, sometimes intended, sometimes an indirect feature of imprisonment, sometimes in camps (Tooze 2007; Cockayne 2021; Al–Dayel et al 2022; Lewis and Blitz 2023). War, conflict, and disaster increase situations of vulnerability to trafficking/modern slavery. The concept of security can be used more broadly to encompass not only war, but also various forms of disaster resulting from climate, floods, famine, earthquakes, tsunami, and terrorism. These may cause state collapse, deterioration in the rule of law and thus the impunity of offenders, forced displacement, social fragmentation and family breakdown (UNODC 2018a, 2018b; 2022a, 2022b). They increase situations of vulnerability to several forms of trafficking and modern slavery (Peyroux 2015). War, conflict, and disaster cause migration which increases vulnerability to trafficking/modern slavery. People flee war zones in fear for their lives: they are refugees, displaced persons, and asylum seekers. Without the full range of normal social practices and organizations, they are vulnerable. They have left behind economic resources and their justice institutions/state that protect against predators, violence, and coercion. They lose civil societal capacity and organizations in the disruption. Migration generates trafficking/modern slavery for labour and sexual exploitation as a result of these increased vulnerabilities. It may increase forced marriage, with the coercion of children into marriages in times of crisis.

The polities that regulate and govern the conditions under which trafficking/modern slavery is generated operate at multiple levels: global, regional, national, and local (Cockayne 2021). This global dimension challenges the notion that states have effective sovereign control over matters of law and order. All aspects of the state apparatus are relevant. While economic inequality is often considered as governed by regulation of economic institutions and violence/coercion is usually considered as governed by criminal justice and the security apparatus, in the case of trafficking/modern slavery not only are both relevant, but so also is the provision of welfare for potential and actual victims. Criminal justice is relevant to the governance of the economy, since trafficking/modern slavery is a crime as well as part of the economy. While trafficking/modern slavery is a crime, it is significantly affected by the regulation of the economy and the state provision of welfare (see Chapter 5, on policy). The depth of democracy is key to the nature of the responses of polities and civil societies.

Walby (2009: 179) proposes a specific conceptualization of the depth of democracy in ten principles and procedures: no hereditary or unelected positions, including a monarch, and members in either chamber of parliament; no colonies (that is, no governance of territories that do not also meet these criteria); no powers of governance held by an additional non-democratic polity (for example, organized religion); universal suffrage, de facto as well as de jure; elections, especially those that are free, fair, and competitive, in a context of free speech and free association and developed civil society associations; a low cost for electioneering, either by law or by custom; an electoral system with proportional representation; an electoral system with quotas for underrepresented groups such as women; a proportionate presence in parliament of women and minorities; a range of institutions (for example, welfare services) that are governed by the democratic polity. The depth of democracy is one of the most important differences between varieties of modernities, as discussed later in this chapter. The depth of democracy also matters for regimes of inequalities, since it affects the representation of women and other disadvantaged groups in political institutions.

Civil society is the domain where there is negotiation over what counts as trafficking/modern slavery. Civil society generates multiple projects and associations, from anti-slavery projects to feminism and trade unions, at multiple scales from global to local. The meaning of exploitation and vulnerability are debated and negotiated. If someone consents to exploitation, can they be a victim of a crime, or is the harm or their situation of vulnerability more important? Is effective agency the norm and vulnerability an exceptional state, or should this characterization of agency and vulnerability be reversed (Fineman 2008)? In anti-trafficking law, any apparent consent of the victim is irrelevant; by contrast, in popular understanding, consent to an action is often understood to mean that the action cannot be a crime. Does criminality require that a person knows the consequences of their actions and not merely be a beneficiary? Are impressions of greater choice in modern society real (Giddens 1984, 1990; Beck 2002), or a myth in which false perceptions of freedom enfold people into agreeing to the legitimacy of an increasingly unequal society (Foucault 1991; Rose 1999; Bauman 2000)? Is the extension of the market into more areas of life to be interpreted as greater choice and individual freedom, including sexual freedom (Amnesty International 2016), or is this destructive of human well-being (Polanyi 2001 [1944]; Statz 2010), especially of women (Banyard 2016)? In some contexts, the social norms are very different, with expectations that women and girls will defer to male kin, including over the selection of marriage partners (Anitha and Gill 2017). Hegemony is constituted by the negotiation of common-sense understandings of the world (Gramsci 1971). The struggles over the meaning of trafficking/ modern slavery are numerous and complex (Gallagher 2010; Kotiswaran 2021). Different understandings are supported by different projects and political forces, sometimes aligned in historic blocs. These understandings can change gradually but also more rapidly in times of crisis, depending on the conjunctural balance of forces.

The generation of trafficking/modern slavery takes place in the institutional domains of economy, violence, polity, and civil society. Each institutional domain is structured by capitalist, colonial, and gender relations.

Regimes of inequality

Trafficking/modern slavery concerns exploitation: the extraction of profits from those in situations of vulnerability using coercion. The profits are extracted in multi-sided transactions linked in trafficking chains though which profits flow from periphery to core. These social relations of inequality are constituted at the intersection of capitalism, coloniality, and gender regimes, where capitalism is shaped by intersecting colonial and gender regimes. This section discusses the relationship of trafficking/modern slavery to capitalism, whether it benefits the whole system or only the rogues, and how it is contested, regulated, and governed. It identifies the pathways that link coloniality (historic and contemporary) to trafficking/modern slavery. It provides a framework for making sense of the complexities of gendered trafficking for purposes of sexual exploitation. The drive for profits that is core to the dynamics of capital is central to trafficking/modern slavery (Brass 2011; LeBaron 2020a); the situations of vulnerability that are exploited are shaped by coloniality (both legacies and contemporary) (Du Bois 1998 [1935]) and by gender inequality (Barry 1995; Cameron et al 2023). The inequalities driving trafficking/modern slavery are articulated in value chains structured by world systems of capital (Brass 2011; Wallerstein 2011 [1974]; LeBaron 2020a;), the ethnic and national legacies of empires (Du Bois 1998 [1935]; Boatcă 2015; Go 2016) and contemporary authoritarian regimes (Al-Dayel et al 2022; Lewis and Blitz 2023); and by gender regimes (Barry 1995; Shire and Walby 2020; Walby 2009, 2023a; Gottfried et al 2023). These global and national structures of power are contested by intersectional political projects that can be significant in shaping the outcome (Du Bois 1998 [1935]; Gallagher 2010; Brass 2016; Kotiswaran 2021). The regimes are understood to be mutually shaping (Walby 2007; Walby et al 2012).

Capitalism

The drive for profit that is central to capitalism is also central to trafficking/modern slavery. Capitalism and trafficking/modern slavery are linked in multiple connections. Issues concern: inequalities and their contestation; the identification of the beneficiaries of trafficking/modern slavery; the spatial distribution of economic inequalities and the flow of value and people from periphery to core; the structuring of these systems by interventions; the intersection of capitalism with coloniality and gender regimes; and varieties of modernity.

Inequalities drive trafficking. The drive for profit can lead to pressure to employ people in situations vulnerable to exploitation through coercion. This search for profit is intrinsic to the capitalist system, though it is resisted, and the outcomes can be moderated. While in Western societies many take free wage labour without coercion for granted, Brass (2011, 2016) argues that this is contingent and the outcome of struggle. Unfree labour matters for capitalism (Rioux et al 2020). Global economic inequalities drive migration from lower-income to higher-income countries, which can generate situations of vulnerability along the migration pathway and in the destination country, especially if the migrant does not have access to the benefits of citizenship there (LeBaron 2015). These inequalities are contested in multiple ways. These include: changing regulations of financial investment via polities at international and national levels (Gallagher 2010; Cockayne 2021); governance of supply chains (Crane et al 2019; LeBaron 2020a); war, civil war, and rebellion to resist conquest and to free those enslaved (Du Bois 1998 [1935]); Simic and Blitz 2019) and civil societal justice projects (Barry 1995; Gallagher 2010; O'Connell Davidson 2015).

Who are the main beneficiaries of trafficking/modern slavery and how does this vary with the form of social organization? Do benefits flow to the whole capitalist system or only the rogues? Does trafficking/modern slavery only exist because of the lack of effective governance of the economic system, so the rogues freeride on a poorly regulated social system? Does the whole society lose since trafficking/modern slavery produces distortions and profits/incentives in the wrong places (Cockayne 2021), illuminated in studies on the cost of trafficking/modern slavery to the whole economy and society (Reed et al 2018; Walby et al 2020). Are slavery and similar practices a form of primitive accumulation that speeds capitalist development (Harvey 2003)? Or does the extraction of such profits benefit only a criminally corrupt elite? However, despite such questions, it is clear that the possibility of trafficking/modern slavery existing is shaped by the nature of the capitalist system, with significant variations between social democratic, neoliberal, and authoritarian forms.

Trafficking/modern slavery has a relationship with the spatial, since trafficking chains often involve flows of value from the periphery to the core. The spatial and temporal reach of social systems varies (Walby 2009). The economic system is worldwide, even though there are multiple nationally based polities (Wallerstein 2011 [1974]) and competing hegemons (Arrighi 2007). Value flows from the periphery to the core, these terms signifying both spatial and social dimensions (Wallerstein 2011 [1974]). The periphery (in terms of social categories) can be located in the core (in terms of spatial categories) (Castells 1996). There are flows and mobilities of value, of labour, of capital (Urry 2007), and of civil societal projects (Moghadam 2005; Walby 2011; Weldon et al 2023). Movement across borders can be understood in different ways: as part of mobility in general (Urry 2007); as a migration infrastructure (Xiang and Lindquist 2014); and within analyses of specific cross-border labour markets constructed by multiple players (Shire 2020). Law enforcement, often nationally based, is challenged to follow transnational traffickers across national frontiers (Penna and Kirby 2012). The development of trafficking/modern slavery takes place during processes of globalization that restructure social relations (Bales 1999). Globalization involves the restructuring of space and of governance (Brenner 1999; Harvey 2005; Brenner et al 2010; Gottfried 2023). These spatial complexities have implications for the analysis of root causes and for sites of policy intervention into trafficking/modern slavery, requiring multiple spatial levels to be addressed.

Capitalism is structured by political processes and varied forms of state formation. While states can be important in implementing laws to reduce coercion in the economy, they can also be captured by trafficking/modern slavery interests to promote deregulation and facilitate forced labour. The regulation of global financial investment can be achieved at the global level, in a context where national level states have limited effectivity on capital that flows across national borders (Cockayne 2021, see Chapter 5, on policy). Changes in the global regulation of capital have implications for vulnerabilities to trafficking/modern slavery and for opportunities for exploitation. The institutions of global financial governance of the World Bank Group are relevant to the regulation of new capital investments to prevent trafficking/modern slavery (Cockayne 2021), despite their changing organizational ecology (Hannan and Freeman 1989), meaning that these institutions – established in the Bretton Woods settlement inspired by Keynes (1936) to stabilize unstable finance capital (Minsky 2008 [1986]) and to prevent a repeat of the financial crash of 1929 (Galbraith 2009 [1954]) – have been shifting since the neoliberal wave (Reich 2016; Fioretos and Heldt 2019).

However, not all financial investment is governed in this way, with China a particular exception (Cockayne 2021). The regulation of employment relations is shaped by international entities as well as national ones. The ILO (the tripartite body of employers, governments, and trade unions, established in 1919 in the Treaty of Versailles) continues to engage on the quality of employment relations, including forced labour and decent work. International legal instruments have developed over two hundred years to reduce slavery, practices similar to slavery, and trafficking, under pressure from global civil society (Gallagher 2010). State regulation led by organized civil society may be more effective than the self-regulation of companies. LeBaron is critical of the effectiveness of private corporate self-governance through corporate social responsibility (CSR) (LeBaron 2020a) and 'ethical audits' (LeBaron 2015; LeBaron et al 2017) in reducing severe exploitation. Indeed, she argues further that this is not only ineffective but also a distraction from the real causes of exploitation in profit maximization (LeBaron and Lister 2022), by a focus on a few extreme cases of modern slavery rather than exploitation more widely (LeBaron 2020a: 8), enabling corporate leaders to secure weak rather than strong regulations: 'CSR was used as a strategy to deflect more stringent legislation' (LeBaron and Rühmkorf 2019: 729), and to falsely claim the moral high ground (LeBaron 2020a). LeBaron (2020a) documents the failure of private governance, including the 'audit industry', while underlining the importance of public (state) and international regulatory initiatives in anti-trafficking policies. The provision of welfare, which is important in reducing situations of vulnerability, including specialized welfare for victims, depends on the development of state welfare, which is an uneven and important outcome of long historical struggles.

The use of coercion to extract value has not ended with economic development. Nevertheless, some of the terminology still used in social theory could be understood to imply its reduction. For example, the use of the concept of 'primitive accumulation' to refer to the use of violence and coercion to extract value might suggest declines over time because of the strong temporal connotations of the term 'primitive'. Harvey (2005) appears ambiguous as to such temporal connotations, though it is unlikely that he intended to consign coercion in the economy to the past. Brass (2011, 2016) argues that free wage labour – labour without coercion – is rare, and only contingently produced as a result of political struggle. The use of coercion in the economy varies with the variety of capitalism and modernity. It declines with social democracy; likely increases with the advance of neoliberalism; and is the more likely, the more authoritarian the context. Processes of neoliberal globalization (Harvey 2005) have removed some of the regulations developed in more social democratic times, creating situations of vulnerability. In authoritarian contexts, there is more likely to be state forced labour and forced marriage.

Analysis of capitalism is necessary but not sufficient for an analysis of trafficking/modern slavery, which is also structured by coloniality and gender inequality. The situations of vulnerability are structured by the intersection of capitalism with the ethnicized legacies and emergent practices of coloniality and with gender regimes.

Coloniality

Coloniality shapes trafficking/modern slavery both as legacies from past forms and from current forms (Lazzarino 2019). These legacies structure global inequalities, borders, ethnicity and nationality (Bhambra 2007; Virdee 2014, 2019; Boatcă 2015; Go 2016; Williamson 2017), relations of core/periphery, and pathways of migration. Legacies of coloniality (Du Bois 1998 [1935]; Boatcă 2015; Go 2016) still structure situations of vulnerability, including those along migration pathways between lower- and higher-income world regions. Current forms of coloniality, disproportionately associated with war and conflict zones, can generate forced labour (Al-Dayel et al 2022; Lewis and Blitz 2023). Migrants are much more likely to be victims of trafficking/modern slavery than non-migrants (ILO, Walk Free, and IOM 2022) and to be of a minority ethnicity within the country within which the exploitation takes place.

Coloniality is a distinctive configuration of power, which is not reducible to capitalism though shaped by it and by gender regimes. It is distinctive in: the lack of democracy for those subjugated; its rule of the periphery (colonized) by the core (colonizers); prioritization of the goals of the state over economy; in the extent of violence/coercion (war, conquest, forced migration, slavery, practices similar to slavery); and in its civil societal projects of colonial ethnic, racialized, and religious supremacy. It is shaped by its intersection with capitalism (Virdee 2019) and gender regimes (Mies 1986). Resistance to coloniality takes many forms from rebellion and war (Du Bois 1998 [1935]; 2019 [1903]) to the development of international law (Gallagher 2010). The outcome of the history of these conflicting forces continues to shape trafficking/modern slavery (Barry 1995; Cockayne 2021).

Du Bois (1998 [1935]) analysed the transition from chattel slavery to modern slavery in his sociological history of reconstruction in the US after the Civil War, explaining why there was a transition from one form of coerced labour to another rather than to real emancipation. Slavery, which was marked by state-legitimated ownership and the use of physical force, was transformed into a system of coerced labour marked by debt bondage. Du Bois shows that there was a brief moment when there was a possibility of transition to freedom for the former slaves. It did not happen because of the power of capital seeking profits, the White supremacist identity of the White working class, the denial of suffrage, the criminal justice powers of the polity, the violence of lynching, and the refusal to hand over land, in a complex set of interactions. The use of violence by White people and the failure to establish democratic participation for those former enslaved were key to the maintenance of Black labour as subject to excessive exploitation. In his analysis, Du Bois mobilizes an account of the full spectrum of institutions in society and theorizes their systemic interaction. Political economy is not enough to explain the failure of the legal emancipation of enslaved people to 'free' waged labour. The violence of the White Southerners, both landowners and White labour, was key to this blocked modernization of labour relations. Du Bois argues that scholars who attributed the failure of the reconstruction to ideology and culture are wrong; he critiques this as the 'propaganda of history'. Rather the failure is rooted in racism and multiple forms of power within and across all societal domains, including economic, political, and violence, as well as civil society. For Du Bois, violence and the denial of political citizenship were critical to his theory of change in the form of slavery rather than to its ending, despite the victory of the North in the Civil War. Without land, or other means of livelihood, full emancipation would not be possible. Du Bois provides a theory of slavery and changes in its form that is a classic sociological theory of society.

Coloniality is linked to trafficking/modern slavery in several ways. Colonial and authoritarian states directly use forced labour. Coloniality generates global inequalities with uneven access to the entitlements of citizenship including access to justice, welfare, and livelihood. Global inequalities drive migration, which generates situations of vulnerability to trafficking/

modern slavery. Migrants are several times more likely than non-migrants to be victims of trafficking/modern slavery (ILO, Walk Free, and IOM 2022) and to be of a minority ethnicity within the country within which the exploitation takes place, globally. Around half the people identified as victims of trafficking/modern slavery are not citizens in the country where they are being exploited, the proportion varying by global region (ILO, Walk Free, and IOM 2022).

Colonial and authoritarian states force labour. Those minoritized by colonial and authoritarian states on grounds of ethnicity, religion, political beliefs, or other status, are vulnerable to be put to forced labour by the state. This is both historic, as in Nazi Germany (Tooze 2007) and the short-lived Islamic State (Al-Dayel et al 2022); and contemporary, in the Russian war on Ukraine (Lewis and Blitz 2023); and some minorities in China (Zenz 2023).

Colonial legacies in authoritarian and neoliberal regimes can be associated with very high rates of imprisonment, especially of racialized minorities, and the coercive use of labour in prisons (Garland 2000; Davis 2003; Wacquant 2009; Davis et al 2022).

War (often an outcome of contesting or would-be colonial powers) drives migration. War generates displacement and migration, as people flee, with varying degrees of choice and coercion. Fleeing war creates situations of vulnerability for refugees, asylum seekers, and migrants. Authoritarian regimes seeking to expand their power through war, threats, and coercion generate movement of people, leading to situations of vulnerability to exploitation along those migration pathways.

Coloniality created and creates global inequalities. Global inequalities lead to flows of value and of people from peripheries to cores. Migration generates situations of vulnerability. These situations of vulnerability during migration can be exploited. When the cause of the mobility is a disaster (war, famine), migration is less likely to include access to citizenship entitlements. The vulnerable situation of migrants moving from lower-income to higher-income countries is partly a legacy of coloniality which structured these global inequalities (Du Bois 1998 [1935]; Boatcă 2015; Go 2016). The fees and costs of travel some migrants pay to intermediaries to obtain employment in another country create forms of debt that are hard to pay back, leading to their being effectively controlled. Low-wage and labour-intensive economic sectors have high proportions of both legal migrant labour and those who have been trafficked (Rijken 2011; Wagner and Shire 2019). Temporary agency (Strauss 2014) and labour subcontracting (Wagner and Shire 2019) practices create situations of vulnerability.

The lack of rights held by migrants is partly a legacy of coloniality. This is a situation of vulnerability. It contributes to trafficking for labour and sexual exploitation through exclusions for migrants: sometimes all migrants have reduced rights, sometimes it is those migrants who are without legal citizenship, sometimes as a result of the threat of deportation, sometimes while on a migrant journey/pathway. This can entail less or no access to justice (criminal, employment law), welfare (income support, health care, emergency housing), and to free wage labour (tied visas). There is differential access to the entitlements and rights of citizenship (welfare, justice, mobility, democratic participation). Migrants who do not have citizenship of the country in which they are living have reduced entitlements which increases vulnerability. This is exacerbated if they have irregular migration status. Migrants have fewer entitlements than citizens to the protections of welfare and justice systems (van der Leun 2011), while visas tied to a particular employer or household removes the free movement that offers opportunities to escape exploitation (Demetriou 2015). Immigration controls reduce the entitlements of non-citizens to the protections of welfare and justice systems and so make migrants easier to exploit (van der Leun 2011). Visas that are tied to a particular employer or household reduce the capacity for escape by seeking a new employer or home if there is abuse (Anderson 2015; Demetriou 2015).

Borders can create situations of vulnerability to trafficking in human beings by the limits they place on migration (Anderson and Davidson 2003). The increased securitization of borders to reduce in-migration can subordinate justice concerns about trafficking/modern slavery to security concerns about migration (Aradau 2008). Borders and migration are entwined with issues of perceived threats to security, which generates complex contexts in which people can be identified as trafficked or smuggled (Aradau 2008). Policies on migration/security can be in tension with policies to provide human rights, to the detriment of the victims of trafficking/modern slavery.

Coloniality generates several pathways to trafficking/modern slavery, in both legacy and contemporary forms. Coloniality is linked to authoritarian varieties of modernity, though legacies can be found in societies that have become more social democratic or neoliberal. Coloniality is shaped by its intersection with capitalism and gender. The situations of vulnerability faced by many migrants from lower-income countries are embedded in legacies of coloniality.

Gender regimes

Women and girls are more likely to be victims of trafficking/modern slavery than men and boys (UNODC 2021). Gender regimes generate situations of vulnerability to trafficking/modern slavery, especially sexual exploitation and forced marriage, among women and girls to a greater extent than among men and boys. These vulnerabilities are exacerbated at the intersection with capitalism and coloniality.

A gender regime is a system of gender inequality, constituted in economy, violence, polity, and civil society. Gender regimes can take multiple forms (Walby 2009, 2020, 2023a; Shire and Walby 2020; Gottfried et al 2023; Shire 2023). These varieties include, at least, domestic and public, in which the public can take social democratic, neoliberal, or authoritarian forms (Walby 2023a). Situations of gendered vulnerability are generated in different ways in varieties of gender regime, with consequences for the specific kinds of exploitation, situations of vulnerability, and opportunities for resistance.

Gender regimes variously generate situations of vulnerability for women and girls in their lesser access to independent livelihoods, lesser economic reward for their labour, greater vulnerability to gender-based violence, lesser access to political and policy decision-making, and lesser access to civil societal organizations that shape meaning (Walby 2009, 2020; Shire and Walby 2020). The situations of greatest vulnerability lie at the point of intersection with capitalist and colonial relations, generating situations of extreme vulnerability for migrant women and girls without formal employment and citizenship entitlements.

Forced marriage is marriage without consent, although a previous threshold was set at the higher level of 'with menace' (Gallagher 2010; Cockayne 2021). It is not the same as arranged marriage, which is with consent. Forced marriage disproportionately affects girls rather than boys (ILO, Walk Free, and IOM 2022) and is conducted in the context of family and kin relations in highly unequal gender regimes (Anitha and Gill 2017). Forced marriage is more likely to be found in domestic gender regimes and in authoritarian societies.

Women and girls are more likely than men and boys to be victims of trafficking for purposes of sexual exploitation (UNODC 2021; ILO, Walk Free, and IOM 2022). The sex trade creates situations of vulnerability that especially concern women and girls (Barry 1979, 1985; Sanders 2004; MacKinnon 2011; Cho et al 2013; O'Connell Davidson 2015). The regulation and legitimacy of the sex trade are shaped by the variety of gender regime and modernity. In neoliberal regimes sexuality is more likely to be commodified, and in more social democratic regimes more likely to be assumed to be a matter of non-commercialized mutuality. Authoritarian regimes tend to publicly attempt to suppress the sex trade using coercive means.

Discussions as to the contemporary regulation of the sex trade engage with debates on agency, consent, and harm. There are significant differences in how Barry (1995) and O'Connell Davidson (2015) address the shaping of experience, with implications for the legitimacy of regulation and governance of the sex trade. The difference is linked to differences in epistemology and social theory. Barry (1995) argues that consent can obscure harms. People make their lives in conditions not of their choosing and which shape what people choose to do. Barry argues that it is inappropriate to move from recognizing the significance of agency to apparently endorsing the systems which structure people's lives. Consent to activities that are harmful does not mean that those activities are not harmful. Consent does not trump harm. O'Connell Davidson (2015) argues that the agency and choice of individuals take priority. If a person does not experience an activity as more harmful than another activity, then it is not more harmful. People should not be prevented from engaging in activity that others think is harmful if they themselves do not think it is. Consent trumps harm. Gupta (2016) argues that O'Connell Davidson is inappropriately 'defining modern slavery out of existence', by hollowing out the meaning of slavery by excessive focus on loose usage of the term, and by excessive focus on agency and choice.

The different epistemologies and social theories deployed by Barry (1995) and O'Connell Davidson (2015) underpin these differences in approach to regulation and governance. Barry's epistemology is centred on structural knowledge, and she treats the knowledge of her respondents as true for them but not necessarily for others or a structural analysis. O'Connell Davidson takes a standpoint epistemology approach, that prioritizes the subjective experiences of victims and has less room for systemic analysis. Barry and O'Connell Davidson differ in the extent to which their social theory is structured by systems or by agency. The approach taken in this book is systems led, while recognizing the importance of listening to and learning from survivors. In international trafficking law, consent is not relevant. There is a complex ecology of epistemic systems generating the knowledge on trafficking/modern slavery.

The nature and consequences of attempts to regulate the sex trade depend on the context of the gender regime in which this occurs. Attempts to resist and oppose the trafficking/modern slavery of women and girls are shaped by the intersection of the gender regime, capitalism, and coloniality (Crenshaw 1991; Aradau 2008; Gupta 2008, 2016; Walby 2009; Withers and Piper 2023).

Globalization: space and the social

The spatial and social levels of the legal instruments on trafficking/modern slavery are entwined, including the global/international/world, regional powers, (national) states, and varieties of modernity (social democratic, neoliberal, authoritarian). These processes are both spatial and social, partly due to the physical aspect of the spatial/mobility component of some (but not all) of its forms, and partly due to differences in social relations – and thus in power – that are contingently geographically and historically distributed (shaped by regimes of inequality of capitalism, coloniality, and gender). The concept of core/periphery is an example of a concept that entwines both spatial and social components.

The globalization thesis – of the increasing pertinence of the global level relative to (national) states – has focused on political economy: on the emergence of a single world economic system that is more powerful than (national) states. In world systems theory, the development of a world economic system occurred centuries ago (Wallerstein (2011) [1974]; Chase-Dunn 1997), while for others it was in more recent decades (Held et al 1999; Robinson 2004). This process reterritorializes and rescales governance (Brenner 1999). It restructures the hierarchical relations between the core and periphery, linked by commodity chains in which value flows from periphery to core (Hopkins and Wallerstein 1994). There is a restructuring of the relationship between social and spatial dimensions of core and periphery in which some of the social periphery moves to the spatial core, and some of the global poor live and work in the global north (Castells 1996). These processes are gendered (Gottfried 2023).

The globalization of the regulation of coercion, as in the case of the international legal instruments on trafficking/modern slavery, significantly extends the implications of the globalization thesis because of its concern for violence/coercion in addition to political economy. Globalization is taking place in the domain of violence/coercion/security in relation to trafficking/modern slavery, with law and powers traditionally assigned to states/polities concerning violence/coercion/security/law and order moving from the national to the global level. The development of the legal capacity of the UN over trafficking/modern slavery is a challenge to simple notions of full national state sovereignty on violence/coercion/security/law and order. The UN (and its associated agencies) is an emerging polity at the global level. All Member States participating in the UN de facto pool some of their sovereignty, even though the legal and political rhetoric still describes this as inter-national, that is, relations between states. The UN is further shaped by its environment, including regional hegemons, the global economy, and global civil society. The traditional notion has been that (national) states have sovereignty. Even when it is accepted that sovereignty in the economic sphere is compromised by global processes, it is often assumed that states still have sovereignty over violence/security/law and order. This is challenged by the development of UN/transnational governance of crime/violence/law and order in relation to trafficking/modern slavery.

There are spatialized systems of regulation and governance linking the UN, regional hegemons, and almost 200 Member States of the UN; this system is shaped by further systems, including global capital, violence, and civil society. This global system of violence/coercion is not homogenized, with significant variations in the form of modernity (social democratic, neoliberal, authoritarian). The regional powers (including the US, EU, and China) are important for these variations. They are significant in mediating and shaping the processes and outcome of the implementation of the international legal regulations of the UN.

The mechanisms through which the regional powers produce variations in the implementation of the international legal instruments on trafficking/modern slavery are several. They include: the interpretation of the legal meaning of the concepts of exploitation and vulnerability (as discussed earlier in this chapter); the processes through which international regulations are incorporated or transposed into domestic (national) legal systems; the implementation of the legal regulations in judicial systems; and, the context of different regimes of inequality of capitalism, coloniality, and gender.

The actions and structure of polities matter for the level of trafficking/modern slavery (Cho 2015), including whether there is deregulation (Peksen et al 2017), the rule of law (Cho 2015; ILO, Walk Free, and IOM 2022), corruption (Bales 2007b; Global Initiative against Transnational Organized Crime 2021) and the degree of democracy (Global Organized Crime Index 2021). Since the response of the polity varies with deregulation, the rule of law, the level of corruption, and the depth of democracy, it is likely to vary with the variety of modernity, including its social democratic, neoliberal, and authoritarian forms. The varieties of modernity align with regional powers and their spheres of influence. The different practices of the EU, US, and China impact on the governance of trafficking/modern slavery in their respective territories and regions of influence.

Varieties of modernity

Trafficking/modern slavery has not ended with modernity. This challenges simple theories of modernization. Its extent and nature vary over time and space. Multiple reasons have been identified that might explain these variations. Here, these varieties of modernity are clustered into social democratic, neoliberal, and authoritarian.

Traditional modernization theory suggested that economic development would lead to progress in all other areas of society (Lipset 1959; Ingelhart 1997) including violence (Elias 1939; Pinker 2011). Pinker (2011, 2018) argues that violence is declining as civilization advances, with a growth in enlightenment and self-control. While recognizing continuing exploitation, Harvey (2003) ambiguously uses the concept of 'primitive' accumulation to capture forms of exploitation that involve violence, as if this might disappear in later times. Modernization theory has been nuanced and challenged in multiple ways. A detailed reading of Pinker (2011) finds that he recognizes fluctuations and, in later work, Elias (1997) did acknowledge the reversals associated with fascism. Pinker's thesis on a decline in war is challenged by Braumoeller's (2019) analysis of both the relevant statistics and the underlying arguments. The best conclusion is that there are uneven fluctuations in the rate of violence over time.

Variations in the form of society can be better understood as multiple varieties of modernity (Eisenstadt 2000) resulting from different trajectories through modernity (Moore 1966; Therborn 1995), rather than a single universal pattern of development. These varieties of modernity are shaped by capital (Brenner et al 2010), post-colonial (Bhambra 2007; Boatcă 2015; Go 2016) and current colonial (Al-Dayel et al 2022; Lewis and Blitz 2023) relations, and by gender regimes (Shire and Walby 2020; Shire 2023; Walby 2023b; Gottfried et al 2023). There are extensive debates as to how varieties might be distinguished (Esping-Andersen 1990; Hall and Soskice 2001; Bruff 2014; Shire and Walby 2020; Gottfried et al 2023; Moghadam 2023). While the location of the boundary between social democratic and neoliberal forms has been a key site of debate (Giddens 1998), there is increasing interest in authoritarianism in the context of de-democratization (Verloo 2018; Lombardo et al 2021; V-Dem 2022). Within these debates, there is a cluster of work that focuses on political economy (Esping-Andersen 1990; Brenner et al 1999; Hall and Soskice 2001; Bruff 2014) and another relatively separate cluster focused on the regulation of violence (Garland 2000; Lacey 2009; Wacquant 2009; Bernstein 2010; Hörnqvist 2020; McGlynn 2022; Ballesteros Pena et al 2023).

The debates on the regulation of violence focus on whether the response of the state is carceral, poorly targeted, and disproportionate (Davis 2003; Wacquant 2009; Bernstein 2010; Davis et al 2022) or is potentially providing justice to those who suffered violence and reducing the impunity of offenders (Taylor 2018; McGlynn 2022). The former is associated with neoliberal and authoritarian forms where democracy is thin or non-existent, while the latter is associated with social democracy and greater depth of democracy. The response of the polity may vary with the depth of democracy, the rule of law, and level of corruption, which may vary with the variety of modernity, social democratic, neoliberal, and authoritarian.

Democracy comes in degrees in which some forms are deeper than others. The most basic is the holding of elections; but also significant is whether there is proportionality of representation; and, further, whether the democratic principle is extended to a narrow or wider range of institutions. The depth of democracy matters (Walby 2009).

At least three major varieties of modernity can be identified, including social democratic, neoliberal, and authoritarian, which vary by levels of inequality in the economy, the extent and nature of violence, the depth of democracy, and the extent of free association in civil society (Walby 2009, 2020, 2023a). These are ideal types so, while there are examples, they do not fit exactly. The EU is an example of the social democratic variety, the US of the neoliberal variety, and Russia and China of the authoritarian variety.

There are significant variations in the extent and nature of trafficking/modern slavery between different social groups and different regions of the world (UNODC 2021; ILO, Walk Free, and IOM 2022). There is a range of evidence that links variations in the level and form of trafficking/modern slavery with variations in the form of modernity. Multiple factors correlated with trafficking/modern slavery can be clustered in ways relevant to theory. While economic inequality, the extent of violence, the depth of democracy, and free association in civil society are all relevant, probably the most important is the depth of democracy, which drives many of the other factors.

There are multiple sources of evidence, although its quality is still undergoing improvement. Chapter 5 on policy and Chapter 6 on sexual exploitation address the qualitative data sources in more detail. Findings from comparative quantitative studies (Bales 2007b; Rao and Presenti 2012; Cho et al 2013; Cho 2015; Peksen et al 2017; Cameron et al 2023) are presented in the following paragraphs, while the quality of the underlying quantitative data (UNODC 2021; ILO, Walk Free, and IOM 2022) is discussed in Chapter 4.

Economic inequality is associated with trafficking/modern slavery, both interpersonal (Rao and Presenti 2012; Cho 2015; Williamson 2022) and interstate (Cho 2015). The actions and structure of the polity matter (Cho 2015), including deregulation (Peksen et al 2017), rule of law (Cho 2015; ILO, Walk Free, and IOM 2022), corruption (Bales 2007b; Global Initiative against Transnational Organized Crime 2021) and the depth of democracy (Walby 2009; Global Organized Crime Index 2021). Trafficking/modern slavery is associated with migration (Rao and Presenti 2012; Cho 2015; ILO, Walk Free, and IOM 2022) and with gender inequality (Williamson 2022; Cameron et al 2023).

When considering the varieties of modernity previously identified alongside the range of evidence, it is reasonable to suggest the following ideal types.

In the social democratic variety, there are relatively low rates of trafficking/modern slavery. This is concentrated in the less well-regulated areas of the economy and where there are exemptions to full citizenship due to migration status. There is very little state forced labour or forced marriage. The strategy for economic growth is more inclusive and sustainable, the economy is less unequal, with less poverty, livelihoods are available to all in the market economy, capital is regulated, industrial policy restricts damaging sectors, supply chains are regulated, and employment relations are regulated. There are relatively low levels of violence, interpersonal and group violence/coercion is criminalized, using targeted and proportionate state interventions, with low militarization, and low rates of violence from the state to the individual. In the polity there is the greatest depth of democracy, relatively proportionate representation in elected assemblies, significant general welfare and specialized welfare, and few exclusions to state services (including welfare) based on citizenship/migration and gender status, the rule of law is respected and there is relatively low corruption. In civil society, there is equal participation, free speech, free association, and civil liberties.

In the neoliberal variety there are moderate rates of trafficking/modern slavery, especially where there are exemptions to full citizenship due to migration status. Trafficking/modern slavery for labour exploitation is enabled by the overall less well-regulated areas of the economy. Trafficking for sexual exploitation is found in the sex trade, which can be criminalized in some instances. There is some state forced labour in prisons, which have typically increased in scale as a securitized response to crime. There is little forced marriage. The strategy for economic growth is focused narrowly on GDP and removing state regulations, resulting in more inequality, more poverty, livelihoods dependent on the market economy, less regulated capital, little industrial policy, less regulated business, and less regulated employment relations. There are high rates of violence linked to high levels of inequality; while interpersonal and group violence/coercion (including trafficking/modern slavery) are criminalized, state interventions tend to be disproportionate and poorly targeted. There are higher levels of militarization with consequences for situations of vulnerability as a consequence of war. In the polity, there is a moderate depth of democracy, with full electoral processes leading to: forms of representation that are not consistently proportionate; low levels of state provision of general welfare and moderate levels of specialized welfare, with exclusions to state-provided services (including welfare) based on citizenship/migration status; the rule of law is varied, with middle levels of corruption. In civil society, there is democracy, free speech, free association, and civil liberties; however, capacities are uneven because of the levels of inequality.

In the authoritarian variety, there is the highest rate of trafficking/modern slavery. This is found in several locations: among those who are minoritized and lack full citizenship entitlements. There is state forced labour, especially of minorities, especially in war and conflict zones. There are some forced marriages, depending on the nature of the gender regime. Restrictions on property ownership for women make them more dependent on marriage overall. The economic strategy subordinates growth to state priorities, resulting in more inequality, more poverty, fewer livelihoods in the market economy, capital regulated by state interests, industrial policy to promote state interests, business regulation to promote state interests, and employment relations regulated to promote state interests. There are high rates of violence, uneven criminalization of interpersonal violence, state interventions are disproportionate and targeted to support state interests, high militarization, high state–individual violence, some state coerced labour; and some forced marriage. In the polity, there is thin if any democracy (though there may be some elections), low levels of general and specialized welfare, exclusions to state services (including welfare) on grounds of citizenship/migration status, the rule of law is varied, and there are high levels of corruption. In civil society, there is state interference to restrict associations and free speech, and low levels of civil liberties.

The existence of trafficking/modern slavery is a challenge to notions of unilinear universal progress driven by economic development and enlightenment. Trafficking/modern slavery is part of the contemporary as well as classical world, in high-income as well as low-income countries. It is not in the dustbin of history. It requires the theorization of multiple modernities. There is variation in the core, not only a division between core and periphery.

Theorizing trafficking/modern slavery at a macro level requires contemporary forms of systems analysis. This theorizing requires adding violence/coercion to the typology of institutional domains of economy, polity, and civil society, and requires addressing the intersection of regimes of inequality of capitalism, coloniality, and gender. This theorization requires the application of systems thinking (Castellani and Hafferty 2009; Byrne and Callaghan 2023). This enables the analysis to keep the capacity for explanation while addressing multiple social systems (Walby 2007, 2009, 2021a) that intersect and mutually shape each other (Walby et al 2012). Theorizing trafficking/modern slavery requires the use of systems theory to analyse the multiple regimes of inequality and the multiple varieties of modernity.

Conclusion

Key to the specificity of trafficking/modern slavery is that it is the use of coercion to extract profits and material benefits. The profit is often taken by third parties in multi-sided transactions. The concept of 'trafficking chain' builds on the concepts of commodity and supply chains, to capture the specificity of coercion in the flow of value along chains from peripheries to cores, both spatially and socially understood.

The locating of trafficking/modern slavery in a theory of society requires addressing the institutional domains of economy, violence, polity, and civil society, the intersecting regimes of inequality of capitalism, coloniality, and gender, and the main varieties of modernity, of social democracy, neoliberalism, and authoritarianism.

These processes develop at the point of intersection of three regimes of inequality – capitalism, coloniality, and gender – to generate exploitative practices and situations of vulnerability. The use of coercion in extracting value has not ended with economic development and modernization. The extent and nature of trafficking/modern slavery vary across time and place with the variety of modernity, including social democratic, neoliberal, and authoritarian.

This theoretical framework is applied and further developed in the following chapters on law, data, policy, and sexual exploitation.

3

Law

Introduction

This book situates law on trafficking/modern slavery in a theory of society. Trafficking/modern slavery is illegal and a crime, yet the legal field is not a simple carceral development of criminal law. Multiple bodies of law address the multiple sides of the links in trafficking chains, and the extraction of profit or other material benefit through coercion and control of a person. The laws span over two centuries of gradual and cumulative development internationally, regionally, and with transpositions, implementation measures, and further law-making by national states. The legal field as a whole includes, but goes well beyond, criminal law to cover employment, business regulations, and equal opportunity. The associated policy fields are addressed in Chapter 5 on policy.

This chapter engages with the interpretation of the concepts of exploitation, vulnerability and consent that are contained in the Palermo Protocol (UN 2000a), the most far-reaching of the UN legal instruments. This supports the development of the concept of 'trafficking chain', and its focus on prevention, rather than just a reactive focus on prosecuting offenders and assisting victims. The Protocol allows for different national implementation of ostensibly universal concepts, which can extend and shrink the boundaries of trafficking/modern slavery in different contexts.

The chapter discusses the global, national, and regional levels in the development and implementation of these laws for their implications for theories of globalization, the challenges to notions of state sovereignty, and the significance of differences between varieties of modernity.

The chapter also considers the implications of legal developments for trafficking/modern slavery in society, noting their effects across the institutional domains of economy, violence, polity, and civil society, and the intersecting regimes of capitalism, coloniality, and gender.

The development of trafficking/modern slavery as a single field

Trafficking/modern slavery is best treated as a single field, though there are differences between sub-types. It is a single field because of the shared core meaning around coercion and control for the purposes of exploitation, as discussed in Chapters 1 and 2. The cumulative historical development in international legal instruments to oppose slavery, forced labour, practices similar to slavery, and trafficking in human beings – in which each development builds on previous instruments – further demonstrates, it is argued, the underlying unity of the field.

There are, however, discussions about some aspects of its treatment as a unified field in relation to: the significance of the difference between chattel slavery and modern slavery (Chuang 2015a; O'Connell Davidson 2015); whether the summary term should derive from legal, social science, or advocacy contexts (Bales 1999; LeBaron 2020a; Cockayne 2021); and, the preferred hierarchical organization of the sub-types, especially for the presentation of data and the treatment of overlapping crime categories (ILO, Walk Free, and IOM 2022; UNODC 2023).

The legal instruments

This section provides a summary and chronological account of each of the major international legal instruments on trafficking/modern slavery, and the context of their implementation.

International legal instruments have been developed over more than two centuries to stop trafficking and slavery (Gallagher 2010: xxiii–lvi; Allain 2013). The most recent law concerns trafficking in human beings: the 2000 United Nations *Protocol to Prevent, Suppress and Punish Trafficking in Persons, Especially Women and Children, supplementing the United Nations Convention against Transnational Organized Crime* (UN 2000a). Of major historical importance are the international laws to stop the slave trade, slavery, and practices similar to slavery. The most important definitions are in the 1926 *Convention to Suppress the Slave Trade and Slavery* (League of Nations 1926). An extension of legal prohibition concerns forced labour in the 1930 *Convention Concerning Forced and Compulsory Labour* developed by the International Labour Organization (ILO) (ILO 1930). A further extension concerns practices similar to slavery, which include forced marriage, in the 1956 *Supplementary Convention on the Abolition of Slavery, the Slave Trade and Institutions and Practices Similar to Slavery* (UN 1956). A further extension which includes sexual slavery is in the 1998 *Rome Statute of the International Criminal Court* (UN 1998). These are the most important instruments:

1926 *Convention to Suppress the Slave Trade and Slavery* (League of Nations).

1930 *Convention Concerning Forced and Compulsory Labour* (International Labour Organization).

1956 *Supplementary Convention on the Abolition of Slavery, the Slave Trade and Institutions and Practices Similar to Slavery* (UN).

1998 *Rome Statute of the International Criminal Court* (UN).

2000 *Protocol to Prevent, Suppress and Punish Trafficking in Persons, Especially Women and Children, supplementing the United Nations Convention against Transnational Organized Crime* (UN).

Slavery

An earlier line of legal development concerned the slave trade, slavery itself, and practices similar to slavery. International legal instruments – including the 1814 Treaty of Paris, 1815 Congress of Vienna, 1841 *Treaty of London for the Suppression of the African Slave Trade*, 1862 *Treaty between the United States of America and the United Kingdom of Great Britain for the Suppression of the African Slave Trade*, 1885 *General Act of the Berlin Conference Regarding Africa*, and 1890 *General Act of the Brussels Conference* – prohibited first the slave trade, then slavery (Gallagher 2010; Allain 2013).

The 1926 *Convention to Suppress the Slave Trade and Slavery* Article 1 (League of Nations 1926) introduced a definition of slavery that is still an international benchmark:

> Slavery is the status or condition of a person over whom any or all of the powers attaching to the right of ownership are exercised.

This definition was an attempt to capture the conditions of slavery, not only when there were the legal conditions of ownership of another person.

There have been multiple attempts to extend the international legal prohibition of practices that meet this definition of slavery, which does not require actual ownership, only the use of the powers attached to ownership. The boundaries between slavery, practices similar to slavery, and not-slavery have been extensively debated. The most authoritative statement of these boundaries is in the Bellagio-Harvard *Guidelines on the Legal Parameters of Slavery* (Research Network on the Legal Parameters of Slavery 2012).

Forced labour

Forced labour was introduced into international law in 1930 in the *Convention Concerning Forced and Compulsory Labour* (ILO 1930). 'Forced or compulsory labour' is defined in the 1930 ILO Forced Labour Convention at Article 2 (ILO 1930) as:

> [A]ll work or service which is exacted from any person under the menace of any penalty and for which the said person has not offered himself voluntarily.

There are some exemptions, including 'military service', 'civil obligations', 'a consequence of a conviction in a court of law', 'cases of emergency', and 'minor communal service'. These exemptions exclude many of the ways in which states compel labour.

The 'guardian' of the law is the ILO, founded in 1919, which was an agency of the League of Nations and is now an agency of the UN. The ILO is made up of representatives of three constituencies – governments, employers, and workers – and has Conventions that are legally binding on those of its members that sign and ratify them (ILO 2002).

The ILO today treats sexual exploitation as a sub-category of forced labour. The ILO makes interventions on trafficking for purposes of sexual exploitation, for example, producing a list of indicators by which this might be identified (ILO 2022b); in producing this list, the ILO is treating trafficking for purposes of sexual exploitation as within its remit. The joint work of the ILO with the Walk Free Foundation and the International Organization on Migration on data includes 'forced commercial sexual exploitation of adults and commercial sexual exploitation of children' as a sub-category of forced labour (ILO, Walk Free, and IOM 2022).

Practices similar to slavery

There have been several steps in the extension of the international legal prohibition of practices that are similar to slavery. The key instrument is the 1956 *Supplementary Convention on the Abolition of Slavery, the Slave Trade and Institutions and Practices* (UN 1956). This identified several practices similar to slavery, including forced labour and forced marriage. However, the definition of the concept of 'servitude' was not included in the Convention, despite the discussions of this matter during the development of the Convention (Gallagher 2010; Allain 2013).

Practices that are often understood as servitude are recognized as practices similar to slavery. Debt bondage, serfdom, child exploitation, and servile marriage are identified thus in Article 1 of the 1956 *Supplementary Convention on the Abolition of Slavery, the Slave Trade and Institutions and Practices Similar to Slavery* (UN 1956).

Debt bondage is defined thus:

(a) Debt bondage, that is to say, the status or condition arising from a pledge by a debtor of his personal services or of those of a person under his control as security for a debt, if the value of those services as reasonably assessed is not applied towards the liquidation of the debt or the length and nature of those services are not respectively limited and defined.

Serfdom is defined thus:

(b) Serfdom, that is to say, the condition or status of a tenant who is by law, custom or agreement bound to live and labour on land belonging to another person and to render some determinate service to such other person, whether for reward or not, and is not free to change his status.

Child exploitation is defined thus:

(d) Any institution or practice whereby a child or young person under the age of 18 years, is delivered by either or both of his natural parents or by his guardian to another person, whether for reward or not, with a view to the exploitation of the child or young person or of his labour.

Forced marriage

Three forms of forced or servile marriage – bride purchase, wife transfer, and widow inheritance – are identified but not named using these terms as similar to slavery in the 1956 *Supplementary Convention on the Abolition of Slavery, the Slave Trade and Institutions and Practices Similar to Slavery* (UN 1956) at Article 1(c):

  (i) A woman, without the right to refuse, is promised or given in marriage on payment of a consideration in money or in kind to her parents, guardian, family or any other person or group; or
 (ii) The husband of a woman, his family, or his clan, has the right to transfer her to another person for value received or otherwise; or
(iii) A woman on the death of her husband is liable to be inherited by another person.

In Article 2, the Convention extends the issue to young age of marriage and further processes to ensure free consent to marriage:

With a view to bringing to an end the institutions and practices mentioned in article 1 (c) of this Convention, the States Parties undertake to prescribe, where appropriate, suitable minimum ages of marriage, to encourage the use of facilities whereby the consent of both parties to a marriage may be freely expressed in the presence of a competent civil or religious authority, and to encourage the registration of marriages. (UN 1956)

Resolutions of the UN General Assembly and Recommendations of the Economic and Social Council have further addressed the issue of forced marriage, including marriage at early ages before a person could be considered capable of consent (Allain 2013). There has been development of the operationalization of the concept of consent, so that the threshold has moved from 'use of menace' to 'lack of consent' (ILO, Walk Free, and IOM 2022). These are developed in the 1979 *Convention on the Elimination of all Forms of Discrimination against Women* (UN 1979).

The ILO, Walk Free, and IOM (2022) include forced marriage as a form of modern slavery alongside forced labour, not as a sub-type of forced labour, in their global estimates of modern slavery.

The Rome Statute

The UN set up a special court to deal with cases of serious violence in times of war and conflict that the usual national courts were felt to be unable to address sufficiently. This was precipitated by wars in the former Yugoslavia and on the African continent. A statute to govern its practices was adopted, the 1998 Rome Statute of the International Criminal Court (UN 1998).

The Rome Statute included enslavement, sexual slavery, and forced marriage in Article 7:

(c) 'Enslavement' means the exercise of any or all of the powers attaching to the right of ownership over a person and includes the exercise of such power in the course of trafficking in persons, in particular women and children.

(g) Rape, sexual slavery, enforced prostitution, forced pregnancy, enforced sterilization, or any other form of sexual violence of comparable gravity.

The 2000 UN Protocol on trafficking in human beings

Trafficking in human beings is a category constructed in international law, as well as in popular culture and social science. The leading legal instruments are those of the UN (UN Office of the High Commissioner for Human Rights (UN OHCHR 2014). The concept, 'the exploitation of the vulnerability of others', is central to the acts, means and purpose of trafficking in UN, US, EU, and UK law. The concepts of 'exploitation' and 'vulnerability' are noted in UN legal instruments and yet open to different interpretation and thus implementation in varied national legal and social contexts (UNODC 2013, 2015).

The key international legal instrument is the UN (2000b) *Convention against Transnational Organized Crime* and the associated *Protocol to Prevent, Suppress and Punish Trafficking in Persons, especially Women and Children* (sometimes known as the Palermo Protocol) (UN 2000a). These instruments can be understood as a hybrid of the human rights and crime schools of law (Gallagher 2010).

This Convention built on the earlier UN 1949 *Convention for the Suppression of the Traffic in Persons and of the Exploitation of the Prostitution of Others* which built on two Conventions of the League of Nations (the precursor to the UN), the 1921 *International Convention for the Suppression of Traffic in Women and Children* and the 1933 *International Convention for the Suppression of Traffic in Women of Full Age*.

All states that are members of the UN participated in the decision to create the Convention and are expected to sign and ratify it, committing themselves to criminalize trafficking, to assist victims, and to develop policy to prevent it.

Trafficking is defined in the UN 2000 Palermo Protocol Article 3 thus:

(a) 'Trafficking in persons' shall mean the recruitment, transportation, transfer, harbouring or receipt of persons, by means of the threat or use of force or other forms of coercion, of abduction, of fraud, of deception, of the abuse of power or of a position of vulnerability or of the giving or receiving of payments or benefits to achieve the consent of a person having control over another person, for the purpose of exploitation. Exploitation shall include, at a minimum, the exploitation of the prostitution of others or of other forms of sexual exploitation, forced labour or services, slavery or practices similar to slavery, servitude or the removal of organs;

(b) The consent of a victim of trafficking in persons to the intended exploitation set forth in subparagraph (a) of this article shall be irrelevant where any of the means set forth in paragraph (a) have been used;

(c) The recruitment, transportation, transfer, harbouring or receipt of a child for the purpose of exploitation shall be considered 'trafficking in persons' even if this does not involve any of the means set forth in subparagraph (a) of this article;

(d) 'Child' shall mean any person under eighteen years of age.

In this definition, movement across borders is noted as a part of the crime of trafficking but it is not a necessary part of the crime. The definition includes a range of terms drawn from earlier Conventions of the UN and League of Nations, including forced labour, and practices similar to slavery, while adding to them further concepts, including servitude and removal of organs. The explicit exclusion of the relevance of the consent of the victim is noteworthy (UNODC 2014b).

The United Nations Office on Drugs and Crime (UNODC), established in 1997, is an agency of the UN that assists UN Member States to interpret and implement the Convention on trafficking in human beings (UNODC 2023).

Implications

The conclusion drawn is that there is a single field of trafficking/modern slavery because there is a core common concern with the coercive control of another person to exploit them and extract profit or other material benefit. There are different sub-types, but these are not sufficiently great to divide the field.

There is significant difference between chattel slavery and modern slavery (Chuang 2015a; O'Connell Davidson 2015). Chattel slavery means the legal ownership of a person, while modern slavery, which is the main form of contemporary slavery (UN Special Rapporteur on Contemporary Forms of Slavery 2023), means the powers of ownership but not the legal ownership of the person. Chuang (2015a) argues against treating trafficking and modern slavery as a single field because of the importance of the distinction between chattel slavery and modern slavery, suggesting that this 'is not only legally inaccurate, but it also risks undermining effective application of the relevant legal regimes' and further, 'strategic use of slavery imagery by defense counsel in trafficking prosecutions can raise jurors' expectations of more extreme harms than anti-trafficking norms actually require' and 'depoliticises and absolves – behind a humanitarian agenda' (Chuang 2015a: 146–7). However, while it is important that the distinction between chattel slavery and modern slavery is maintained, this is not a reason to reject treating trafficking and modern slavery as a single field.

The term used here, trafficking/modern slavery, is long. The reason for the use of this term is to merge the term 'trafficking' that is defined in international legal instruments, most recently in 2000, and the term 'modern slavery' that, while not defined in international legal instruments, is widely used in social science and advocacy (Bales 1999; Cockayne 2021) and in some national legislation including that of the UK (UK Modern Slavery Act 2015). The hybrid term is the best way to communicate the concept as a single field.

There are practical decisions as to how to treat sub-categories, which have different legal histories, and which have consequences for the collection and presentation of data. The incremental history of the legal developments is associated with the development of multiple UN agencies to assist their implementation, especially by the ILO and the UNODC (but also by UN Special Rapporteurs on Contemporary Forms of Slavery and on Trafficking in Persons, the IOM, UN Women, and the UN Statistics Commission). This means that more than one categorization and hierarchical organization of the sub-types have developed. This is especially relevant to the gendered categories of trafficking for sexual exploitation/forced prostitution and forced marriage/other form of trafficking/modern slavery (ILO, Walk Free, and IOM 2022; UNODC 2023). The practice here is to use the trafficking terminology for sexual exploitation and not to subsume it to forced prostitution (since the trafficking legal instrument in 2000 is more recent than the forced labour instrument in 1930), while keeping forced marriage as a separate category, rather than part of 'other', given its scale and significance. There are further nuances concerning the treatment of overlapping crime categories, where the same event could be categorized in more than one way, such as homicide (where the victim of trafficking is killed) and rape (where the sex is without consent and known to be without consent). These sub-types are discussed further in Chapter 4 on data. They do not detract from the use of the term trafficking/modern slavery to encompass the whole field.

Multiple legal areas

There is a discussion as to whether recent legal developments including for trafficking/modern slavery are carceral (Bernstein 2010). This is situated in wider debates as to whether the actions of the criminal justice system are targeted and proportionate or unfairly sanction poor Black men (Davis 2003; Wacquant 2009; Davis et al 2022), whether there is an over-use of criminal law over other forms of engagement (Lacey 2009; Ashworth and Zedner 2012; Walklate et al 2018), a turn to a culture of control (Garland 2000), and to governing through crime (Simon 2007). The development of the use of criminal justice to protect women from violent and coercive predators has been defended in the context of the previously incomplete criminalization of violence when it is against women (Taylor 2018; Terwiel 2020; McGlynn 2022), which is a consequence and cause of gender inequality. These are situated in wider debates as to the balance of different forms of regulation and governance beyond the criminal (Ayers and Braithwaite 1992; Black 2002, 2008).

The issue as to whether trafficking/modern slavery law is carceral can be addressed empirically along two dimensions: whether the legal instrument concerns solely criminal law or is more widely drawn; whether, in the context of multiple available interventions, criminal law is used disproportionately. This is addressed in relation to the most recent of the international legal instruments on trafficking/modern slavery, the Palermo Protocol (UN 2000a). It is argued that this legal instrument contained multiple areas of law in addition to criminal law; and that the sources of variation in the use of criminal sanctions as compared with other interventions are to be found in national and regional contexts, not the legal instrument itself: hence, that the Palermo Protocol is not carceral in itself.

The Palermo Protocol

The legal instruments not only define trafficking in persons, but also outline approaches to the actions required of states to prevent trafficking. The UN

Palermo Protocol requires that states: criminalize trafficking (Article 5); provide certain services to victims of trafficking to assist them (Articles 6, 7, and 8); and establish policies to prevent trafficking, including discouraging the demand that fosters the exploitation that leads to trafficking (Article 9) (UN 2000a). The wording of Articles 6 and 9 show the range of practices that State Parties (the state in which the victim has been identified) are legally mandated to perform:

Article 6 spells out assistance to and protection of victims of trafficking in persons:

1. In appropriate cases and to the extent possible under its domestic law, each State Party shall protect the privacy and identity of victims of trafficking in persons, including, inter alia, by making legal proceedings relating to such trafficking confidential.
2. Each State Party shall ensure that its domestic legal or administrative system contains measures that provide to victims of trafficking in persons, in appropriate cases:
   (a) Information on relevant court and administrative proceedings;
   (b) Assistance to enable their views and concerns to be presented and considered at appropriate stages of criminal proceedings against offenders, in a manner not prejudicial to the rights of the defence.
3. Each State Party shall consider implementing measures to provide for the physical, psychological and social recovery of victims of trafficking in persons, including, in appropriate cases, in cooperation with non-governmental organizations, other relevant organizations and other elements of civil society, and, in particular, the provision of:
   (a) Appropriate housing;
   (b) Counselling and information, in particular as regards their legal rights, in a language that the victims of trafficking in persons can understand;
   (c) Medical, psychological and material assistance; and
   (d) Employment, educational and training opportunities.
4. Each State Party shall take into account, in applying the provisions of this article, the age, gender and special needs of victims of trafficking in persons, in particular the special needs of children, including appropriate housing, education and care.
5. Each State Party shall endeavour to provide for the physical safety of victims of trafficking in persons while they are within its territory.
6. Each State Party shall ensure that its domestic legal system contains measures that offer victims of trafficking in persons the possibility of obtaining compensation for damage suffered.

Article 9 of the UN Protocol (2000a) addresses the 'prevention of trafficking in persons':

1. States Parties shall establish comprehensive policies, programmes and other measures:
   (a) To prevent and combat trafficking in persons; and
   (b) To protect victims of trafficking in persons, especially women and children, from revictimization.
2. States Parties shall endeavour to undertake measures such as research, information and mass media campaigns and social and economic initiatives to prevent and combat trafficking in persons.
3. Policies, programmes and other measures established in accordance with this article shall, as appropriate, include cooperation with non-governmental organizations, other relevant organizations and other elements of civil society.
4. States Parties shall take or strengthen measures, including through bilateral or multilateral cooperation, to alleviate the factors that make persons, especially women and children, vulnerable to trafficking, such as poverty, underdevelopment and lack of equal opportunity.
5. States Parties shall adopt or strengthen legislative or other measures, such as educational, social or cultural measures, including through bilateral and multilateral cooperation, to discourage the demand that fosters all forms of exploitation of persons, especially women and children, that leads to trafficking.

A wide range of bodies of law and policy are identifiable in the concepts used in the Protocol. While Article 5 is focused on criminalization, Articles 6, 7 and 8 are focused on mitigating the harms to the victims, by providing counselling and welfare, and Article 9 is focused on prevention, including research and information. The UN Protocol on trafficking identifies the organization and regulation of the economy, with reference to employment, poverty, underdevelopment, lack of equal opportunity, and the demand that fosters exploitation, polity actions relevant to criminalization and to the provision of welfare in counselling, medical assistance, material assistance, education, training, housing, and care, and to civil society in relation to research, to information and mass media campaigns, and the need for cooperation between the state and non-governmental bodies.

This wide-ranging set of legal and policy issues is variably implemented. This variation is allowed for in the Protocol since, while some immediate issues of criminalization and protection of victims are considered essential, as in the phrase, 'Each State Party shall ensure', in many of the other issues States Parties are mandated only to 'consider' them. The outcome is varied.

Each legal instrument has an associated UN entity to assist its implementation. There are several UN entities relevant to trafficking/ modern slavery, including the ILO, IOM, UNODC, Special Rapporteurs on Trafficking in Persons and on Contemporary Forms of Slavery, UN

Women, UN Security Council, and the UN Statistics Commission. They are relevant to several legal and policy fields (crime, employment, migration, human rights, gender equality, security, data) as discussed in Chapter 5 on policy. At national and regional levels of governance a range of governmental entities and other organizations interpret and implement the legal concepts in slightly different ways, according to their remits and contexts.

The Palermo Protocol calls for 'comprehensive policies, programmes and other measures' to 'prevent and combat trafficking in persons' (Article 9) to engage with several sites of potential intervention. It is not only focused on criminal law. It engages with a wide range of legal fields. Anti-trafficking law is not in itself carceral. The interpretation and implementation of the law does allow for variation between countries, as discussed in the next section and in Chapter 5 on policy.

Interpreting the law in context: what are 'exploitation' and 'vulnerability'?

There is varied interpretation of the key concepts in the international legal instruments, including those of 'exploitation' and 'vulnerability'. Although the law is international, it is applied in courts and judicial systems at national (UN Member State) level; and this implementation is shaped by interpretation of its terms and concepts within the national context. This extends or shrinks the extent to which an individual is found by the courts to be a trafficker or a victim of trafficking. Concepts that have been subject to discussion include those of 'exploitation' and 'vulnerability'. This varied interpretation of concepts establishes the boundaries of the trafficking chain.

The UNODC assists Member States of the UN with the implementation of the Palermo Protocol. It offers practical guidance, for example in interpretation of the Convention. It is a conduit for funding to states to support their building the institutional practices needed for implementation. For example, the European Commission has funded joint actions with the UNODC to assist low- and middle-income countries to revise their regulation and welfare systems to meet the requirements of the UN 2000 Convention (Walby et al 2016a).

The 'exploitation of the vulnerability of others' is core to the legal definition of trafficking in human beings. However, even though definitions are included in the UN Convention and Protocol, the exact meanings of the concepts of 'exploitation' and 'vulnerability' are debated. The UNODC (2013, 2015) states that the loose definitions of the concepts in international law were intentional, in order that the same legal instrument could be considered relevant to the varied circumstances in different countries, thereby diplomatically allowing agreement by national politicians negotiating the UN Convention. This means that different 'thresholds' of exploitation and vulnerability could be applied in different national legal systems, depending on local circumstances. The consequence is that social context, political struggle, and negotiation are important in the interpretation of the concepts of exploitation and vulnerability.

Exploitation

The law on trafficking includes the concept of exploitation. There are alternative interpretations of this term.

Exploitation – the purpose of trafficking – is defined in the UN Protocol (2000a), Article 3:

> Exploitation shall include, at a minimum, the exploitation of the prostitution of others or other forms of sexual exploitation, forced labour or services, slavery or practices similar to slavery, servitude, or the removal of organs.

The EU 2011 Directive is similar, adding to the list of purposes of exploitation 'begging' and 'the exploitation of criminal activities'. According to the UN (and EU), the definition includes the 'means' of securing 'control over another person', referring to 'the threat or use of force or other forms of coercion, of abduction, of fraud, of deception, of the abuse of power or of a position of vulnerability'. Thus, the means to achieve exploitation defined in law are wider than the use of force, including threat of force, coercion, fraud, deception, and abuse of power or of vulnerability.

The interpretation of these definitions is debated. The approach to the inclusion of forms of coercion and abuse other than physical force in the definition of trafficking/modern slavery is sometimes contested, even though these means are explicitly encoded in law (Kelly 2003).

The definition of exploitation in the UN Protocol, and the domestic legislation that it informs, focuses on the control over a person, which is distinguished from mere direction of their labour or actions. Trafficking/ modern slavery thus includes some aspect of non-market processes, where the forms of control of the person are outside of or additional to market mechanisms. While market-based forms of inequality are often considered legitimate, since they entail some degree of choice and freedom simultaneous with the inequality, the use of coercion prevents this form of legitimation of inequality.

The differing interpretations of the term 'exploitation' are raised in several ways. The UN definition of trafficking includes 'the exploitation of the prostitution of others'. This means that it is illegal for third parties to exploit commercialized sex. Hence, the exploitation of the prostitution of others is illegal under UN law. In some locations, including the UK, this is interpreted to mean any taking of profits by any person other than the person selling sex is illegal, indeed a crime. This means that it is illegal in the UK for anyone to live off earnings from the sale of sex, other than the person selling sex, and illegal to set up brothels as businesses. Under this interpretation, if sex is commercialized, then the only legitimate beneficiary is the person themself – no one else can legitimately profit. By contrast, in other locations, including recently in the Netherlands and Germany, the term 'exploitation' is used to refer to taking 'excessive' profits, not reasonable profits. This interpretation means that profit-taking from the sale and purchase of sex, under regulated conditions, is legal in the Netherlands and Germany. This interpretation of exploitation to mean excessive rather than reasonable profit-taking is disputed: sometimes in principle, sometimes in its practical application. It is disputed in principle, on the argument that the intention of the UN law was to rule out any profit-taking by third parties. It is disputed in its practical application in relation to where the line is to be drawn between excessive and reasonable profit-taking, and how and by which agency this line is to be adjudicated.

The location of the boundary between 'reasonable' and 'excessive' profits is central to the adjudication of what is and what is not trafficking. The concept of 'reasonable' concerns what constitutes the 'normative'. This discussion of the concept of exploitation is not specific to the context of the sex trade but applies also to the exploitation of labour. The 'normative' is dependent on specific social location, as interpreted by the courts.

There is a position that any individual should be entitled to do as they please with their bodies. Hence selling organs, selling sex, abortion, taking one's own life are legitimately the concern only of a person themself. This is represented in the position that selling sex should be legal (Outshoorn 2001; O'Connell Davidson 2015). This should be kept separate from the position that profit-taking from the sale of sex should be illegal. EU Member States have decriminalized the sale of sex (Kelly et al 2014). There has recently been a tendency to conflate these two positions, merging the decriminalization of the sale of sex with the decriminalization of profit-taking from the sale of sex (Amnesty International 2016). It is important to distinguish between these two positions.

There is debate as to whether some forms of human activity can ever be legitimately commercialized at all; and whether any commercialization of such activities constitutes exploitation (Satz 2010). The focus of this debate is usually the selling of sex and of organs, which concerns the use and abuse of bodies, and which has wider consequences for social inequality. In the example of buying and selling sex, from one perspective any commercialization of buying or selling sex is considered exploitation (Barry 1979, 1995; Jeffreys 2008). However, in the UN Protocol, the decision as to how to address this matter is assumed to be a matter for the national/Member State level rather than international law. This allows for national specificities in the legal regulation of the buying and selling of sex, which are discussed in detail in Chapter 6 on sexual exploitation. In some countries, such as Sweden, the purchase of sex is illegal while the sale of sex has been decriminalized. The European Parliament has called for the purchase of sex to be made illegal across the whole of the EU (European Parliament 2014). This debate deploys a wide analysis and theorization of the relationships between: intimacy, sexuality and society; sexuality and gender regimes; and, sexuality and the economy.

The meaning of the term 'exploitation' is debated. This means that what constitutes trafficking in human beings is contested. The different interpretations, including those mobilized in national legal systems, are embedded in different theoretical frameworks and in different varieties of modernity.

From traffickers to trafficking chains

'Who is a trafficker'? This question is more complex than usually assumed. A trafficker may be defined as a person who directly trafficks another person, or the focus may be widened to include actions linked together in a chain of activities, or still wider to the social institutions and regimes that are conducive to trafficking. The focus may be narrow, on individuals, or widened to include institutions and regimes. These ontological questions are relevant to determining the sites and types of legally supported interventions to prevent trafficking.

Is a trafficker a person? Is it a group (as in organized crime)? Does a trafficker include those who benefit from trafficking, for example, 'aiding and abetting' (does it matter if they know and intend this, or not)? Can a trafficker be a business (a legal person)? The UNODC (2023) distinguishes between organized crime (both governance and business) and other traffickers (both a group and individuals). Trafficking/modern slavery may be one part of a wider set of business transactions, in a supply chain, which may be referred to as a trafficking chain. Trafficking/modern slavery may be assisted by facilities to corruptly launder funds (Levi 2002; Shaxson 2012; Penna and O'Brien 2018). A still wider focus includes the social relations (regimes of inequality of capitalism, colonialism, gender), and institutions in which trafficking/modern slavery is generated – the trafficking-conducive environment. Some industries appear to be either inherently or contingently conducive to trafficking. Some forms and levels of economic regulation may also be inherently or contingently conducive to trafficking. Regimes of high inequality are conducive to trafficking. Indeed, some varieties of modernity may be considered trafficking-conducive environments.

Reducing exploitation by traffickers is assisted by more effective prosecution. This depends on defining who exactly is a trafficker. There are variations as to whether the category of 'trafficker' is drawn broadly or narrowly in law and analysis. In law, criminal liability extends to those that aid and abet a crime, so might include a range of financial beneficiaries in the industries that directly and indirectly profit from trafficking. These include those who launder illegal profits through legal enterprises and banks (Levi 2002) and hide them away from legal scrutiny (Shaxson 2012). While criminal law usually requires the concept of 'intention' for liability, other forms of law, such as those of employment law, company law, and concerning planning regulations, do not require this. Thus, if 'a trafficker' is not a natural person (who can have 'intention'); then non-criminal forms of law (that do not require intention for prosecution) are relevant. This includes placing responsibility on firms to check that their own supply chains are free from trafficking/modern slavery (as in the UK Modern Slavery Act 2015 and the EU External Action Service (2022) guidance on due diligence in their supply chains) (see also EU Parliament 2020).

Traffickers are embedded in trafficking chains. The concept of 'chain' (developed in Chapters 1 and 2) is used to indicate the multiple social components that are linked together in a way that produces trafficking/modern slavery. Each link in the chain is part of a trafficking chain, but only some links may be illegal under the law on trafficking/modern slavery. Some actors and businesses may be unaware that they are connected to trafficking/modern slavery. But together they form the chain that constitutes trafficking/modern slavery. Trafficking/modern slavery is a process spanning space and time, that includes profit-takers. A trafficking chain is a set of linked social entities and processes that produce trafficking, whose gains are rooted in the illegal exploitation of the vulnerabilities of others.

End consumers of the services produced by a victim of trafficking/modern slavery are part of the trafficking chain. Some know that they are part of it; others do not. The development of criminal law concerning trafficking/modern slavery is increasingly criminalizing those that use the services of those that are trafficked, either knowingly or unknowingly, as indicated in Articles 18 and 23 of the EU 2011 Anti-Trafficking Directive (European Commission 2011), which is proposed to be reinforced in the European Commission (2022b) proposal for a revised Directive, following reporting on actual practice (European Commission 2022c). Criminal law usually but not always requires the 'intention' to commit the act for that act to be identified as a crime. The issue of knowing or not-knowing is not a simple dichotomy, since the law recognizes several positions along a continuum, for example, 'reckless disregard'. 'Knowing' is thus both a conceptual and practical issue.

Trafficking chains are embedded in wider social systems. The extension of legal regulation to the industries and institutions that generate the incentives for trafficking/modern slavery is important. The form and density of regulation of institutions and industries vary significantly between the EU, US, China, and other global regions. In the EU, there is often a dense layering of multiple forms of legal regulation, which can be nuanced and specific, the monitoring of which engages civil society as well as the state. For example, most of the EU, unlike elsewhere in the world, has decriminalized the sale of sex but not profit-taking from the sale of sex (with exceptions), which significantly shapes the industry into which people might be trafficked for purposes of sexual exploitation. The regulation of the industries into which people might be trafficked to reduce the exploitation of vulnerability is relevant to issues of prevention. The extent to which economic sectors are regulated can be linked to the wider regimes of inequality and varieties of modernity in which they are located.

Analysing the reduction of exploitation by traffickers through law requires the concept of 'trafficking chain' and a framework that includes organizations, institutions, regimes of inequality, and varieties of modernity.

What is vulnerability?

The law on trafficking/modern slavery includes the concept of vulnerability. There are several interpretations of the meaning of this concept. Victims are addressed most visibly but narrowly when the focus is on identifying, protecting and assisting victims of trafficking. When the focus is widened to include the social relations and systems in which vulnerability is generated, then a wider range of processes becomes relevant. There are issues concerning agency and consent.

Vulnerability is defined in EU 2011 Anti-Trafficking Directive Article 2.2 thus: 'A position of vulnerability means a situation in which the person concerned has no real or acceptable alternative but to submit to the abuse involved.' When any of the specified means (the threat or use of force or other forms of coercion, of abduction, of fraud, of deception, of the abuse of power or of a position of vulnerability) are used then: 'The consent of a victim of trafficking in human beings to the exploitation, whether intended or actual, shall be irrelevant.' (UN 2000a: Article 3.b; EU 2011: Article 2.3). A child (someone under 18 years) is treated as if they are vulnerable, so that if there is exploitation (as discussed in the section on exploitation) the additional requirement of these 'means' is not needed for the exploitation to count as trafficking (UN 2000a: Articles 3.c, 3.d; EU 2011: Articles 2.5, 2.6).

There are ambiguities in the definition of vulnerability over which there are debates. If a person consents to exploitation, does this mean that they are not being trafficked or subjected to modern slavery? Or can trafficking/modern slavery exist even when people have consented to their own exploitation?

The legal definition of trafficking does not allow the consent of the victim to negate trafficking. Trafficking is defined in law as the exploitation of the vulnerability of others, even if the victim consents. The intent of the law is directed at individuals acting under duress, for whom apparent 'consent' does not negate the illegality of the excessive exploitation. These circumstances are tightly defined, and the pressures that make this illegal are specified.

This irrelevance of 'consent' to the determination of victimhood is relatively unusual in criminal law. Some consider that if there is consent, then there is not a crime and the actions under consideration are not wrong (O'Connell Davidson 2015). Then people are not victims of trafficking/ modern slavery but rather exercising their choice in difficult circumstances.

There is an issue as to the point at which economic duress (for example, debt) constitutes 'no real or acceptable alternative but to submit to the abuse involved' (European Commission 2011). For example, the point at which economic duress deriving from structural economic inequalities becomes so great that there is 'no real or acceptable alternative' but to submit to activities that would otherwise be unacceptable. This might include: sex in exchange for food and shelter ('survival sex') under duress that is the consequence of citizenship and migration regimes in the context of war and flight from war zones.

Another issue concerns the irrelevance of 'consent' if any of the 'means' are used. Although the irrelevance of consent in these circumstances is encoded in the UN Protocol, this irrelevance has been disputed if a person is considered to have agency (O'Connell Davidson 2015). This concerns whether, if a person has capacity for 'agency', despite the use of the 'means', it is reasonable to treat consent as irrelevant. Specifically, the argument is whether an adult woman selling sex can ever be considered sufficiently 'vulnerable' to need the protection offered by anti-trafficking legislation. This is a challenge to the legitimacy of the UN Protocol. Arguments over the interpretation of the location of the practical boundary as to what counts as 'a situation of vulnerability' are shaped by the position taken on 'agency'. Gupta (2008, 2016) argues that O'Connell Davidson inappropriately narrows the definition of trafficking. Barry (1979, 1995) argues that harm trumps consent.

There are three main positions: that some things should never be sold (Satz 2010); that some things should not be the subject of third-party profit-taking but individuals can sell them; and that this is always a matter of individual choice. The use of bodies (including organs and sex) lies at moral, social, and legal fault lines. Organs may be donated but not sold, in most countries. Sex may be mutually given; but what sexual services may be sold or subject to profit-taking varies between countries and over time. The law is unequivocal: consent is irrelevant to the definition of trafficking if any of the means is used.

Reducing the situations of vulnerability requires more than provision of services to victims after they have been trafficked, although these are important in mitigating harms and have the potential to make wider contributions. Reducing vulnerability requires reducing the situations that generate vulnerability; this means the practices, institutions, and regimes that generate these situations.

Strategies of institutions relevant to reducing vulnerability include: increasing sustainable development; reducing violence; and reducing inequalities. The regulation of the practices, institutions, and regimes that generate vulnerability requires an understanding of wider forms of governance.

The international legal instruments allow for this wider interpretation of the causes of situations of vulnerability but do not mandate this, thus leaving scope for variation. These are addressed in Chapter 5 on policy.

Global, national, and regional law

The international level, especially the UN, is key for the legal instruments on trafficking/modern slavery. By 2023, 181 out of 193 UN Member States had signed the Convention on Trafficking (UN Treaty Collection 2023). National states, which participated in the creation of the legal instruments at the international level, have incorporated UN Conventions and Protocols into their domestic law. Yet, the implementation of the law is varied, with different interpretations of legal concepts, the nature of the judicial/justice system, the role of regional polities, and wider societal contexts, giving rise to different patterns of legal practice and policy in different countries and varieties of modernity (social democratic, neoliberal, and authoritarian).

The EU governs its Member States on trafficking/modern slavery through the process of transposition of Directives, including the one on Trafficking in Human Beings, into domestic law. In Member States of the EU, the EU Directive has direct legal force in their national law courts. The EU has Strategy to implement the Directive (European Commission 2012, 2021a). The EU has significant influence over countries that would like to join the EU, which must eventually adopt the acquis (the total body of EU law), some influence over countries in its neighbourhood, and influence via funding of projects to assist countries to implement the UN Protocol. The EU economic model is influential (Bradford 2021).

The US Trafficking in Persons programme (TiP) has trade sanctions against countries that the US considers are insufficiently addressing trafficking in persons. In 2000, the US adopted the Victims of Trafficking and Violence Prevention Act (TVPA), using a definition of trafficking close to that of the UN (United States 2000), though with the addition of a sub-type of 'severe' forms. The purpose of the Act is defined in Section 102: 'The purposes of this division are to combat trafficking in persons, a contemporary manifestation of slavery whose victims are predominantly women and children, to ensure just and effective punishment of traffickers, and to protect their victims.' (United

States 2000: 4). The US Act instituted an annual review of countries around the world to see if there were severe forms of trafficking and if they met their legal and policy standards and, if not, applied trade and aid sanctions to them (US Department of State 2022a).

China has influence via its financial investment for development, which does not go through UN and World Bank Group processes (Cockayne 2021). China is identified in the US TiP as engaging in state-led trafficking in persons. China is currently the target of a new US law, the Uyghur Forced Labor Prevention Act (United States Department of Homeland Security 2022) that strives to stop trade from the Uyghur region (US Department of State 2022b).

The law on trafficking/modern slavery is a global system, with multiple scales at which the regulation and governance are constituted. The multiple co-existing legal instruments, legal and implementation systems interact with each other and change each other, generating a global legal system (Teubner 1997). The cascading transposition of the crime of trafficking in human beings from the UN legal instruments to regional powers and to Member States of the UN is a challenge to simple notions of the sovereignty of (national) states on issues of law and order. Nevertheless, there are significant variations in the implementation of the law, which tend to align with varieties of modernity. These variations are discussed further in Chapter 5 on policy and Chapter 6 on sexual exploitation.

Conclusion

The development of international legal instruments has been important in developing trafficking/modern slavery as a single field. These instruments have developed over two hundred years, incrementally and cumulatively building the range of issues that are subject to law. This legal field does not only include criminal law, though that is an important part, but multiple bodies of law, including employment, welfare, company regulation, and equal opportunities, across several institutional domains. This means that there is no necessary carceral impulse associated with the legal developments. There is support for victims and a wide repertoire of legal initiatives that are focused on prevention by engagement with a wide range of relevant institutions. There is varied interpretation and implementation of these legal instruments between countries, showing patterns aligned with varieties of modernity. The legal concepts, including exploitation and vulnerability, are open to interpretation; and, while some aspects of the laws are mandatory, others only ask countries to consider implementation. Despite the variation in implementation, this is a legal development that is global in scale, thereby challenging the simple notion that states alone determine law and policy on matters of law and order.

4

Data

Introduction

How much trafficking/modern slavery is there worldwide? How is it distributed between social groups and how does it vary across time and place? The various estimates are contested from multiple directions with many calls for the improvement of data (Weitzer 2013, 2015; Guth et al 2014; David 2017; Fedina and DeForge 2017; Raphael 2017; Yea 2017; Barrick and Pfeffer 2021; Cameron et al 2023).

Data crystalizes definitions and understandings of phenomena. Indicators summarize complex data using measurement frameworks. These include the number of victims who are registered by relevant authorities, and the estimated number of victims in the population. Different organizations use measurement systems rooted in different legal remits and histories, which has generated more than one typology for trafficking/modern slavery, including one for trafficking in human beings (UNODC) and one for modern slavery (ILO, Walk Free, and IOM). The UN Sustainable Development Goals (SDGs) locate policies, targets, and indicators in the same framework, potentially aiding the integration of the field of trafficking/modern slavery. We offer a way to integrate diverse contributions in alignment with the UN SDGs.

What is the nature of trafficking/modern slavery? Data is available on the extent and nature of exploitation of victims, when they are registered with authorities and agencies, and on the organization of (alleged) traffickers in contact with the criminal justice authorities. Data is available on the policies in place to counter trafficking/modern slavery in different countries around the world. There is some information about correlations between trafficking/modern slavery and potential causes and drivers. There are estimates of the cost of trafficking/modern slavery for economy and society. The data is contested. We discuss the strengths and weaknesses of existing data, and plans and possibilities for its improvement. We reflect on the measurement frameworks and epistemic systems involved in generating this data.

Indicators, data, and epistemic indicators

Indicators are key numbers. From a multitude of possible numbers, key numbers are selected from a mass of data to summarize it in an indicator in a meaningful way. Data on trafficking/modern slavery has been produced by several international organizations, including the UNODC, ILO, IOM, and Walk Free. The criteria for selecting which numbers to use includes that they are meaningful for the policy remit of the organization and are technically feasible. There is debate over the criteria, process of selection, and scientific and technical merit.

Data is collected and structured in measurement systems which are embedded in epistemic systems that generate knowledge according to a set of rules, or methodology (Walby et al 2017). This involves coordination to select, collect, curate, and present a lot of data within a system of knowledge in which the indicator, the key number, has meaning in relation to a concept, which is itself related to the intellectual and organizational framework within which it is located. Definitions of indicators matter. Indicators are based on concepts and on the technical practicalities of collecting and organizing data in a field. Some of these key concepts are defined in international legal instruments. Trafficking is so defined. Modern slavery is not, although its meaning is very close. Collecting and organizing data to exactly match the intended concept behind the indicator is challenging. The match is not exact, with debate as to how to achieve greater alignment, and what trade-offs might be made in the process.

Indicators consolidate a field of knowledge and influence around a presentation of that knowledge preferred by the organization platforming that indicator. Indicators and data contribute to the epistemological infrastructure that supports scientific development in specific fields (Star and Griesmer 1989; Star 1999). Classification matters (Bowker and Star 1999). Data is collected and structured in systems which are collections of institutions that generate knowledge (Kitchin 2021). The datafication of society increases the importance of these processes and of institutions concerned with data (Kitchin 2021). Social relations are embedded in these epistemic systems, in the measurement frameworks, indicators, datasets, and the structuring of the data (Harvey et al 2017; Nakazora 2017). Numbers exist in ecologies of social relations (Day et al 2014). These social relations include multiple relations of inequality, including gender (Walby 2023b).

Not everyone thinks that quantification aids the evidence base for theory and policy development. Merry (2016), for example, considers that reliance should not be placed on indicators to guide policy in trafficking since they are not well done. While Gallagher (2017) does not object to metrics in themselves, she criticizes any turn to metrics without sufficient quality, arguing that current data, especially from Walk Free, over-state their reliability and that the data practices are too speculative to generate robust estimates. However, the current pace of development of indicators and data in the field of trafficking/modern slavery is rapid.

Data is power in contemporary society (Porter 1996). Indicators are assets (Birch and Muniesa 2020) in systems of power and influence. Problem spaces are shaped by critical numbers (Lury 2021) which contain the social relations that they represent in summary form (Day et al 2014). Indicators are both shaped by the field in which they are generated and have the capacity to further shape this field and adjacent fields. An indicator is a distillation of a lot of data into a single number. Influence over its definition is sought after.

Rather than direct control, an indicator has influence because of its location on a platform. A platform is a multi-sided configuration of social relationships that has the capacity to elevate some things (here, indicators) into powerful forces (Gillespie 2010; Plantin et al 2018; Poell et al 2019). The concept of platform embeds multiple dimensions, drawing on spatial and architectural metaphors as well as social ones (Gillespie 2010; Lury 2021). The UN can be understood to be a kind of platform in its role as global standard setter. The UN Sustainable Development Goals are an example of a platform that elevates a set of indicators to a position of influence (Walby 2023b). The UN SDG indicators include an indicator for trafficking in human beings.

There are alternative indicators, measurement frameworks, and priorities for data in the field of trafficking/modern slavery, including from the UNODC, ILO, Walk Free, and the IOM. Each of these organizations is embedded in an epistemic system. This includes a measurement framework and the organizational context in which that indicator is located, is produced, and is meaningful. This conceptualization draws on and goes beyond the notion of 'boundary object' and 'epistemological infrastructure' (Starr and Griesemer 1989; Star 1999) by adopting the notion of complex systems to better capture the fluidity in this situation (Walby 2023b).

There is competition and cooperation between epistemic systems over the best indicator and data for use in evaluating theory and policy on trafficking/ modern slavery. Each epistemic system has slightly different definitions of its key concepts and indicators that draw variously on international legal instruments, and slightly different criteria as to what is likely to constitute good policy. This is a consequence of the path-dependent development of the various organizations, their legal remit, and their positioning in relation to other organizations and systems of influence.

UN Sustainable Development Goals

Trafficking is included in the UN instruments for the Sustainable Development Goals (SDGs) as an Indicator and in the Targets. The UN has developed a set of key measurements of progress in its 17 Sustainable

Development Goals and their associated policy Targets and quantitative Indicators (UN 2015). This is part of the UN's role as a standard setter.

The SDGs are important in influencing the agenda for global governance institutions linked to the UN and have further resonance beyond. The SDGs build on the history of the earlier Millennium Development Goals (MDGs) (UN 2000c). The MDGs and SDGs have been important mechanisms in the process of establishing an agenda for economic growth that builds in sustainability and inclusion by design, rather than being focused solely on growth in GDP. The UN rarely has direct power over the activities of other organizations: it orchestrates more than it directs or delegates (Abbott and Snidal 2010). It may be described as a 'platform' (Gillespie 2010; Plantin et al 2018; Poell et al 2019) in relation to the development of the key indicators of the SDGs (Walby 2023b).

In the UN SDGs, trafficking in human beings is named in three Targets (5.2, 8.7 and 16.2) and one Indicator (16.2.2) within three of the Goals (5, 8, 16), while modern slavery and forced labour are named adjacent to human trafficking in Target 8.7, and forced marriage is named in Target 5.3. Target 5.2, 'Eliminate all forms of violence against all women and girls in the public and private spheres, including trafficking and sexual and other types of exploitation', and Target 5.3, 'Eliminate all harmful practices, such as child, early and forced marriage and female genital mutilation', are linked to Goal 5, 'Achieve gender equality and empower all women and girls'. Target 8.7, 'Take immediate and effective measures to eradicate forced labour, end modern slavery and human trafficking and secure the prohibition and elimination of the worst forms of child labour, including recruitment and use of child soldiers, and by 2025 end child labour in all its forms', is linked to Goal 8, 'Promote sustained, inclusive and sustainable economic growth, full and productive employment and decent work for all'. Target 16.2, 'End abuse, exploitation, trafficking and all forms of violence against and torture of children', and Indicator 16.2.2, the 'Number of victims of human trafficking per 100,000 population, by sex, age and form of exploitation', are linked to Goal 16, 'Promote peaceful and inclusive societies for sustainable development, provide access to justice for all and build effective, accountable and inclusive institutions at all levels'.

Indicator 16.2.2, the 'Number of victims of human trafficking per 100,000 population, by sex, age and form of exploitation', is the sole part of the SDG framework that refers to the numbers that underpin the Targets and Goals. The Targets are largely aspirations for policy outcomes concerning trafficking, using the key words of 'eliminate', 'eradicate', and 'end', together with references to policy actions to 'take immediate and effective measures', and 'secure the prohibition'. The 17 high level Goals do not separately identify trafficking.

There is rapid development of data that could meet the requirements of Indicator 16.2.2. But there are challenges. Generating this data requires a measurement framework which includes definitions that align with international legal instruments and data collection that includes all countries and extends over time and is consistent and comparative.

Registered victims

Data is collected on victims of trafficking/modern slavery who register with authorities and agencies in most countries of the world. This is a sub-set of victims, since most do not register with authorities (as discussed towards the end of this section). Several international organizations collect and collate this data, as do national states. There is information on numbers, sex, age (adult/child), type of exploitation, citizenship and nationality, and some details about the exploitation. Data on the traffickers is reported in the next section.

The UNODC (2009, 2012, 2014a, 2016, 2018c, 2021, 2023) collects data from UN Member States and aggregates this for the world every two years. The International Organization for Migration (IOM) (2007, 2012, 2017, 2022) collects data on those to whom they provide services, and leads a coalition on data with Polaris (2021) and Liberty (CTDC 2023) in the Counter Trafficking Data Collaborative (CTDC) (CTDC 2022). The EU collates data for its Member States (European Commission 2018a, 2020).

UNODC data concerns victims of trafficking in each country who are registered by competent authorities, including the police, non-governmental organizations (NGOs), doctors, and other service providers. This is provided to central national authorities who process the data and give it to relevant entities, including the UNODC.

The UNODC (2009, 2012, 2014a, 2016, 2018c, 2021, 2023) has collected data during the period 2003–22 on over 450,000 victims and 300,000 suspected offenders around the world (UNODC 2023: 10). The detailed analysis of data on victims reported here is centred on the year 2018 and includes information from 148 countries that encompass more than 95% of the world's population and 49,032 detected victims (UNODC 2021: 25). Data is missing on some countries. The 'UNODC elaboration on national data' (2021) shows that gaps where countries have provided no data are filled by extrapolation from the other countries in that world region. Most of their reporting of characteristics is presented as percentages rather than as raw numbers. The base number for these percentages of characteristics is the number of victims for whom information about that characteristic is available. So, for example, the form of exploitation was reported in 39,805 cases out of 49,032 reported. Women were 46%, girls 19%, men 20%, and boys 15% of detected victims (UNODC 2021: 31), amounting to 65% female and 35% male, as shown in Table 4.1.

The most frequent form of exploitation was sexual exploitation (50%), followed by forced labour (38%), with 12% for other forms (6% criminal

Table 4.1: Trafficking/modern slavery estimates: percentage of detected victims by sex and age – UNODC

	Men	Boys	*Male*	Women	Girls	*Female*	Total
All victims of trafficking	20	15	35	46	19	65	**100**

Note: Year is 2018; boys and girls defined as those under 18 years of age. N= 48,478

Source: Derived from data in UNODC 2021: 31

Table 4.2: Trafficking/modern slavery estimates: percentage of detected victims by form of exploitation, sex, and age – UNODC

Form of trafficking	Men	Boys	Women	Girls	Total
Sexual exploitation	17	23	77	72	50
Labour	67	66	14	21	38
Other	15	11	9	7	12
Total	**100**	**100**	**100**	**100**	**100**

Note: Year is 2018; boys and girls defined as those under 18 years of age; N=48,478

Source: Derived from data in UNODC 2021: 33, 34

activity; 1.5% begging; 1% forced marriages; 1% mixed forms, including baby selling and removal of organs) (UNODC 2021: 34). The sex and age distribution varies between forms of exploitation. Trafficking for sexual exploitation was most frequent for women (77% of victims) and girls (72%), trafficking for forced labour was most frequent for men (67% of victims) and boys (66%) (UNODC 2021: 33, see Table 4.2). Among victims of sexual exploitation, 67% were women, 25%, girls, 5% men, and 3% boys, so females made up 92% of such victims (UNODC: 2021: 36). The distribution of victims across sex, age, and form of trafficking varies between world regions (UNODC 2021: 31, 35).

Migrants make up 35% of registered victims (15% from another region, 8% within the same region, and 12% within the same sub-region), while 65% are trafficked domestically (UNODC 2021: 55). These proportions vary by global region. Migrants are 65% of victims in Western and Southern Europe, 60% in the Middle East, 55% in East Asia and the Pacific, 50% in Central and South-Eastern Europe, and 25% in North America (UNODC 2021: 10).

In the European Union (EU-27) in 2018, victims were trafficked for sexual exploitation in 60% of the cases, for labour exploitation in 15%, and 25% for other forms; 72% of registered victims were female (European Commission 2020). Within the EU-27, around half (49%) of registered victims of trafficking are EU citizens, and around half (51%) are migrants (European Commission 2020).

The IOM collects data on the registered victims who it assists (DiRienzo 2022) through the IOM Migrant Management Operational System Application (MiMOSA) Counter Trafficking Module (IOM 2012, 2017). The IOM leads the Counter Trafficking Data Collaborative (CTDC) which also includes data from Polaris and Liberty in its reports (CTDC 2023).

Victims who come to the attention of the authorities are only one sub-set of the victims of trafficking/modern slavery, since others will not have had such contact. So, these data do not provide reliable information on the extent of trafficking/modern slavery. Nonetheless, they are important since they are a measure of something real, that is, the number of victims recognized and supported by the national authorities. It is generally assumed that the distribution of registered victims across forms of trafficking/modern slavery, sex, and age (adult/child) reflects their distribution in the population.

An increase over time in the recorded numbers of victims cannot be relied upon to indicate an increase in the 'real' population of victims, since it may be a result of an improvement in the actions of these services that leads to a higher proportion of the 'real' population coming to the attention of the authorities.

There are new developments in statistical methods to address the gap between the number of victims who are registered with the authorities and the number of victims in the population. The 'capture-recapture' or multiple systems technique potentially offers an important contribution to the estimation of the scale of trafficking/modern slavery by providing a method of estimating the number of victims in the population using data from the victims who have contact with several different authorities (Bales et al 2015; Bales et al 2020; Chan et al 2021). However, the method depends on assumptions that not all accept (Whitehead et al 2021, 2022), especially over how to address victims who do not report to any authority. It may be best regarded as an experimental technique (ONS 2020).

The Indicators and data on registered victims have strengths and weaknesses. They use a definition based in international legal instruments, the UN 2000 Protocol. The data concern victims registered with the authorities. They are not the numbers of victims in society; they are a sub-set of the victims in the population in a country. It is probably a significant under-count of the number of victims in a country. The data is not useful comparatively either over time or between countries, since it is a measure of two things combined: the activity of the authorities in identifying victims to help; and the number of victims in a society. It is not known if an increase is due to an improved response by the authorities or due to an actual increase in numbers. It is not known if more registered victims in one country than another indicates a better response by the authorities in that country or more actual victims in that country. However, despite these limitations, the number of registered victims and their distribution are important. They are an absolute minimum number of victims, who cannot be denied. They are an indication of the need and use of resources to support victims.

Registered traffickers and trafficking cases

The UNODC collects data from states on traffickers apprehended by their criminal justice systems and on trafficking cases that have resulted in convictions in the courts. One dataset concerns people who are investigated, prosecuted, or convicted. The other is drawn from records of court cases. Data on those in contact with the criminal justice system concerning trafficking is relevant to the SDG Targets concerning policy actions to 'take immediate and effective measures' and 'secure ... prohibition' to 'eliminate', 'eradicate', and 'end' trafficking. Data is available on people who are apprehended by the criminal justice system, as persons investigated/suspected or arrested, those prosecuted, and those convicted, and from the narratives of court cases of those convicted.

The UNODC (2009, 2012, 2014a, 2016, 2018c, 2021, 2023) collates data on persons investigated/suspected or arrested, prosecuted, and convicted from data collected by national states. In 2018, there were 9,429 persons reported as investigated/suspected or arrested; 7,368 persons were prosecuted; and 3,553 persons convicted (UNODC 2021: 25). The majority were adult males: 67% of those investigated/suspected or arrested; 64% of those prosecuted; and 62% of those convicted. The majority (74%) of those convicted were citizens of the country in which they were convicted; around one quarter were not, though often from the region (18% within the region, 8% other regions) (UNODC 2021: 39, 40). Those convicted in countries of origin (of victims) were even more likely to be from that country than among those convicted in counties of destination (of the victims).

The UNODC (2021, 2022a, 2023) collates a dataset of narratives of court cases, since 2010, which offers more detailed data for analysis, though they concern only the cases of those who are convicted. By 2022, there were 800 court case summaries in the dataset (UNODC 2023: 10).

Traffickers use a variety of means to control their victims, from explicit violence to deception. The range of forms varies between the stages of recruitment of the victim and that of their exploitation, typically involving deception during recruitment and violence during the later period of exploitation. During recruitment, the means used by traffickers are deception (45%), abuse of vulnerability (29%), mix of abuse of vulnerability and deception (20%), explicit violence (4%), and other (2%). During the period of exploitation, the means are explicit violence (59%), other forms of control (16%), threats (13%), abuse of vulnerability (10%), and other (2%). The information on recruitment is from 207 court cases and on exploitation from 213 court cases in the UNODC dataset on court cases (UNODC

2023: 52). There was use of extreme and/or sexual violence at some point for 22% of victims, use of explicit violence for 32%, use of threats and physical restrictions for 20%, and no violence or threats for 26%. This is information from an analysis of 2,382 victims in 387 court cases (UNODC 2023: 53).

Trafficking for labour exploitation is more common in some industries than others. There are different estimates from the UNODC court cases and from ILO/Walk Free/IOM population estimates. According to UNODC court data, the distribution of victims is agriculture and farming 28%, fishing industry 28%, domestic work 10%, cleaning services 8%, street selling 7%, construction work 6%, entertainment sector 3%, mining 3%, catering hospitality 3%, nursing 1%, and garment manufacture 1%. This is the share of victims found in the collection of court case narratives, 2010–20, based on 290 victims of trafficking for forced labour in 89 cases that concluded with a conviction (UNODC 2023: 37). According to estimates from the ILO, Walk Free, and IOM (2022: 32), the largest share of forced labour is in services excluding domestic work (32%), followed by manufacturing (19%), construction (16%), agriculture (12%), domestic work (8%), mining and quarrying (1%), and other (11%).

The UNODC (2023: 48–9) identifies four different forms of trafficking structure, two of which are organized and two opportunistic, and counts the proportion of traffickers in each: governance type of organized crime groups 'who wield security governance in a community or territory by means of fear and violence and may be involved in multiple illicit markets' (23%); business-enterprise type of organized crime groups 'involving three or more traffickers systematically working together to traffic persons as a core component of their criminal activities' (46%), opportunistic associations of traffickers 'working together, where two traffickers operate together, or more than two traffickers who do not systematically work together beyond a single criminal act' (21%), and individual traffickers 'who typically operate on their own' (10%). The proportions are based on 3,778 victims and 2253 traffickers reported in 686 cases that resulted in conviction, 2012–20.

In trafficking cases, there are usually several victims and several traffickers, rather than as in conventional crime cases where there is one victim and one offender for each case. The numbers vary by the type of trafficking organization: governance (11.4 victims and 9.7 traffickers per case), business (8.6 victims and 4.5 traffickers per case), opportunistic associations (3.3 victims and 2.3 traffickers per case), and individual traffickers (2.5 victims and 1.1 trafficker per case); based on 713 court cases 2012–20 (UNODC 2023: 49).

In trafficking cases, there is not a single action at one moment in time, but rather a prolonged duration of activity. The duration of trafficking varies by form of trafficking organization: governance (42 months), business (19.7 months), opportunistic associations (14.7 months), and individual traffickers (22.6 months) (UNODC 2023: 50).

Traffickers who come to the attention of the authorities are only part of the relevant population since others will not have had such contact. An increase in the numbers of recorded traffickers may mean one or both of two things: increased activity by the criminal justice system in relation to trafficking; and an increase in the 'real' population of traffickers. These data alone are not sufficient to adjudicate whether it is an increase in criminal justice system activity or in trafficking itself.

Population estimates of victims of modern slavery

The International Labour Organization, Walk Free, and the International Organization for Migration (ILO, Walk Free, and IOM 2022) provide global estimates of modern slavery. Modern slavery refers 'to situations of exploitation that a person cannot refuse or cannot leave because of threats, violence, deception, abuse of power or other forms of coercion' (ILO, Walk Free, and IOM 2022: 2, 13). This definition of modern slavery is not used in international legal instruments, but components of modern slavery are. Modern slavery 'is comprised of two principal components – forced labour and forced marriage'. Forced labour is sub-divided into privately imposed forced labour and state-imposed forced labour. Privately imposed forced labour is sub-divided into forced labour exploitation and forced commercial sexual exploitation of adults and commercial sexual exploitation of children (ILO, Walk Free, and IOM 2022: 13). However, 'other main concepts of modern slavery … trafficking in persons … are not included explicitly in the global estimates' (ILO, Walk Free, and IOM 2022: 13–15). The core methodology is a set of surveys in over 70 countries, supplemented with information from administrative sources on victims (from the IOM and CTDC), expert judgement supported by secondary literature, and statistical modelling.

ILO/Walk Free/IOM estimates that there were 49.6 million people in modern slavery on any given day in 2021. This is divided into 27.6 million in forced labour and 22 million in forced marriages. This means that 0.35% of the global population are in forced labour and 0.28% of the global population are in forced marriages (ILO, Walk Free, and IOM 2022: 2).

Of the 27.6 million in forced labour, 11.8 million (43%) are women and girls, while 3.3 million (12%) are children (see Table 4.3). There were 6.3 million people in situations of forced commercial sexual exploitation, which is 23% of all forced labour, among whom 80% were women and girls. All regions of the world have forced labour; the highest proportion of the population is in the Arab States (5.3 per thousand people), followed by Europe and Central Asia (3.5 per thousand), and Africa (2.9 per thousand). Most (86%) of the forced labour occurs in the private economy. Of the 3.9 million people in state-imposed forced labour, over half (55%) involve the abuse of compulsory prison labour, 27% involve conscription, and 17%

Table 4.3: Trafficking/modern slavery: number and proportion of persons by sex and age – ILO/Walk Free/IOM

	Male no. in '000s	Male %	Female no. in '000s	Female %	Adult no. in '000s	Adult %	Child no. in '000s	Child %	Total number in '000s	Total % in world population
Privately imposed forced labour excluding FCSE	11,303	0.29	6,022	0.16	16,017	0.29	1,308	0.06	17,325	0.22
Private forced commercial sexual exploitation (FCSE)	1,403	0.04	4,929	0.13	4,644	0.09	1,688	0.07	6,332	0.08
State-imposed forced labour	3,072	0.08	848	0.02	3,603	0.07	317	0.01	3,920	0.05
Total forced labour	**15,779**	**0.40**	**11,798**	**0.31**	**24,263**	**0.45**	**3,314**	**0.14**	**27,577**	**0.35**
Total forced marriage	**7,060**	**0.18**	**14,933**	**0.39**	**13,020**	**0.24**	**8,973**	**0.38**	**21,993**	**0.28**
Total modern slavery	**22,839**	**0.58**	**26,731**	**0.69**	**37,283**	**0.69**	**12,287**	**0.52**	**49,570**	**0.64**

Note: Year is 2021; percentages are out of the relevant world population

Source: Adapted from ILO, Walk Free, and IOM (2022: 17)

for economic development beyond normal civil obligations (ILO, Walk Free, and IOM 2022: 2–4). Of the forms of coercion, withholding of wages is the most common form (36%), followed by threat of dismissal (20%) (ILO, Walk Free, and IOM 2022: 42). Forced labour is three times as common among migrant (13.8%) than among non-migrant (4.1%) adult workers (ILO, Walk Free, and IOM 2022: 36). Forced commercial sexual exploitation, treated as a part of forced labour, is largely (78%) female (4,929,000 out of 6,332,000 victims).

Of the 22 million people in forced marriages, 14.9 million (68%) are women and girls. All regions of the world have forced marriages; the highest proportion of the regional population is in the Arab States (4.8 per thousand people), followed by Asia and the Pacific (3.3 per thousand). Half of those in forced marriages were coerced using emotional blackmail or verbal abuse, and 19% by physical or sexual violence or threats of violence. Once forced to marry, there is increased risk of further forms of exploitation. Most (73%) were forced to marry by parents, and 16% by other relatives (ILO, Walk Free, and IOM 2022: 2–4).

The data on which the Global Estimates of Modern Slavery 2021 are based come from surveys, supplemented by administrative sources and by expert judgement. The estimates for non-sexual privately imposed forced labour and for forced marriage rest on this survey data. The estimates for commercial sexual exploitation apply a ratio derived from administrative data to this data on forced labour. The estimates for state-imposed forced labour rest on expert judgement.

Surveys were carried out in 68 countries on forced labour and 75 countries on forced marriage by the ILO and Walk Free in a Gallup poll, asking whether the respondent or any family member had been forced to work or marry. For the forced labour survey, 1,000 to 2,000 people were interviewed per country, amounting to 77,914 respondents, and, since they were asked about the experiences of other family members, potentially collecting data relevant to 628,598 people. For the forced marriage survey, 109,798 respondents were interviewed, collecting data relevant to 931,394 people, since they were asked about the experiences of their family networks (ILO, Walk Free, and IOM 2022).

Statistical modelling is used to fill the gaps in data including for countries where there are no surveys. This modelling uses additional data on vulnerability of the victims, such as their civil and political protections, social, health, and economic rights, and state responses including the identification of survivors, criminal justice mechanisms, coordination, and actions by businesses. This modelling has been developing over time, increasing in sophistication and in the range of data used to create variables. This means that each of the estimates in the time series has a slightly different underlying model (Walk Free 2018; ILO, Walk Free, and IOM 2022).

Questions have been raised as to whether some variables are omitted. For example, Chuang (2015a) argues that there is an under-specification of labour inspectors and offers additional sources of data on these from the ILO, while others have sought better comparative data on the regulation of the sex trade.

This is the procedure used to estimate sexual exploitation:

> Administrative data from IOM's databases of assisted victims of trafficking were used in combination with the 54 datasets to estimate forced sexual exploitation and forced labour of children, as well as the duration of forced labour exploitation. This involved calculating the ratio of adults to children, and also of 'sexual exploitation' cases to 'labour' cases in the IOM dataset, which contained information on 30,000 victims of trafficking around the world who had received assistance from the agency. These ratios were then applied to the estimates taken from the survey data on forced labour of adults to arrive at an estimate of the number of children in forced labour and another estimate of 'sexual exploitation'. (Walk Free 2018: 167)

The selection of the source of administrative data on the ratio of labour to sexual exploitation has implications for the ratio, since this differs between datasets. The IOM and (more recently used) CDTC datasets have a significantly lower ratio of sexual exploitation to labour exploitation than the UNODC (2009, 2012, 2014a, 2016, 2018c, 2021, 2022a). This has implications for the amount of trafficking for sexual exploitation/forced commercial sexual exploitation in the overall figure for trafficking/modern slavery. If the UNODC ratio were used, the amount of forced commercial sexual exploitation would be substantially higher. Since sexual exploitation is disproportionately against female victims, this would change the sex ratio in the estimates of the total trafficking/modern slavery. This means if the UNODC ratio of sexual to non-sexual private exploitation were applied, rather than that of the IOM/CDTC, then the proportion of victims of modern slavery who were female would also significantly increase. This would further mean a significant increase in the amount of modern slavery overall. This is discussed further in Walby and Francis (2023).

The procedure for estimates for state-imposed forced labour is different because of the difficulties in using surveys for this topic: 'As the surveys focused on the non-institutionalised population, meaning that people in prisons, labour camps or military facilities, and other institutional settings are not sampled, the surveys are not suitable for estimating state-imposed forced labour' (Walk Free 2018: 167). Instead, the estimates of state-imposed forced labour: 'were identified through a systematic review of the comments from the ILO supervisory bodies followed by a review of secondary sources' (ILO, Walk Free, and IOM 2022: 116).

The production of the ILO/Walk Free/IOM global estimates of modern slavery is a monumental undertaking. The dataset put together is extraordinary. It can also be improved. Areas for improvement include: better alignment of concepts and their operationalization between trafficking and modern slavery; more surveys to increase the range of countries and to create time-series data; changing the source of data for the ratio of labour and sexual exploitation; and, including more variables in the modelling of data gaps, including labour inspectors and the regulation of the sex trade. There are ongoing developments including: cooperation between the IOM and UNODC on the First International Classification Standard for Administrative Data on Trafficking in Person (ILO, Walk Free, and IOM 2022: 97); and a partnership between ILO, Walk Free, IOM, and UNODC on a bespoke survey module on forced labour (ILO, Walk Free, and IOM 2022: 97).

Policy development

Collecting data on policy developments matters. It is useful for analysis that compares the outcomes of different policy interventions, of what works, under what circumstances. This data is being collected in several ways.

Data on the development of policies in countries around the world is collected for ILO, Walk Free, and IOM (2022). Regional entities monitor policy developments and their implementation, including the EU (European Commission 2018a), and the Council of Europe, through the Group of Experts on Action against Trafficking in Human Beings (GRETA). Some states monitor their own developments, for example in the UK whether companies monitor their supply chains for trafficking/modern slavery as required by the 2015 UK Modern Slavery Act.

The US State Department produces an annual summary of state responses to trafficking (US Department of State 2017, 2022a). This rests on its interpretation of trafficking in the light of its counter-trafficking law, which is close to the UN 2000 Protocol, with the addition of a sub-category of more severe trafficking. On the basis of specially collected and published qualitative and quantitative data on each country around the world, the US produces a three-fold ranking of state efforts to prevent trafficking. States in the third tier are sanctioned through economic and trade policy. The assumption is that state responses make a difference to the amount of trafficking. Further, the US Labor Department generates reports on the products most likely to have been produced by child or forced labour in different countries of the world (US Department of Labor 2022).

There is data on the development of the criminalization of trafficking. The UNODC (2021: 62), using its elaboration of national data, investigated whether each country had criminalized trafficking in persons as a specific offence covering all or some forms of trafficking, using the UN definition. They found an increase in the percentage of 181 countries that had specific criminal offences for trafficking for most or all of its forms, from 54% in November 2012 to 93% in August 2020. The percentage of countries with no criminalization fell from 27% to 2% and those criminalizing only some forms fell from 19% to 5% over the same period, 2012–20. Further, the UNODC (2021: 62–4) found that the average conviction rate for a trafficking offence per 100,000 population increased globally from around 0.1 in 2003 to 0.3 in 2018. The highest conviction rate was for Europe throughout the period 2002–18. Europe began the process of the criminalization of trafficking earlier than other regions. Yet, most of the increase between 2002 and 2018 was accounted for by regions other than Europe, with the most rapid increase being in the Americas.

Correlations and causes

Some studies have investigated the correlations between trafficking/modern slavery and a range of societal phenomena to test theories about causation. They face challenges because of the weakness of the comparative data on the distribution of trafficking/modern slavery across time and place. Nevertheless, there are some important innovations and contributions.

Economic inequality is associated with trafficking/modern slavery, both interpersonal (Rao and Presenti 2012; Cho 2015) and interstate (Cho 2015). The actions and structure of the polity matter (Cho 2015), including deregulation (Peksen et al 2017), rule of law (Cho 2015; ILO, Walk Free, and IOM 2022), corruption (Bales 2007b; Global Initiative against Transnational Organized Crime 2021), and the depth of democracy (Global Initiative against Transnational Organized Crime 2021). The links between migration and vulnerability to trafficking/modern slavery are found in several studies (Rao and Presenti 2012; Cho 2015; ILO, Walk Free, and IOM 2022). Trafficking/modern slavery is associated with several dimensions of structural gender inequality (Cameron et al 2023). War is associated with higher rates of trafficking/modern slavery (UNODC 2018b; UNODC 2023: 52).

Cost of trafficking/modern slavery for society

What is the impact of trafficking/modern slavery on society? One way of measuring this is through the concept of cost, to put a monetary value on the damage it causes. There are other, perhaps more important, ways to think of the impact on society, in terms of pain and suffering, loss of human rights, illegality, and corruption of processes. The cost methodology accompanies these other frameworks and contributes to decisions on the allocation of financial resources to counter trafficking/modern slavery by public and governmental bodies.

Victims of trafficking/modern slavery suffer violence and coercion. This violence and coercion generate hurts to victims' physical and mental health. These hurts to victims' health generate costs to society in the use of extra public services (specialized services, law enforcement, health services, and social protection), lost economic output, lost quality of life, and coordination and prevention work. These costs are borne by the public. (This section draws on the findings of the *Study on the Economic, Social and Human Costs of Trafficking in Human Beings within the EU* (Walby et al 2020).)

These costs are borne by the public: the people who are inhabitants, workers, citizens, and employers, who pay taxes and insurance premiums to fund the services, who jointly suffer from the diverted and thus lost economic output, and who are willing to pay to avoid the lost quality of life experienced by fellow human beings.

Alternative assumptions within the methodology can lead to different estimates of the cost to society. This includes: whether the estimate of the number of victims concerns those who are registered or all victims in the population; whether the costs of criminal justice are included; and whether the long-term harms to mental health from sexual exploitation are included.

The costs presented in this section are average costs across the EU. They may be different in other world regions. They would be different if more or less services were provided to people in these circumstances, if the value of the economic output produced by the average citizen was higher or lower than the EU, and if the distribution of forms of trafficking/modern slavery were different.

Specialized services used by victims of trafficking include accommodation, medical and psychological assistance, legal assistance, education, training, job placement, reintegration assistance and return assistance (European Commission 2018a: 42–6). This assistance is legally mandated under the UN Palermo Protocol and the 2011 EU Directive. Children should receive additional services, including access to education. NGOs contribute to the provision of these specialized services (Walby et al 2016a: 33–56).

Law enforcement concerns both criminal and non-criminal law, sometimes called civil or administrative law. It includes police, prosecution, courts, prisons, regulators, and inspectors (Walby et al 2016b, Walby et al 2020; UNODC 2021). Police investigations in trafficking/modern slavery are complex, sometimes involving cross-border working in joint investigation teams. Civil or administrative law includes licensing premises for risky activities, and inspecting standards for labour, health and safety.

Health services are used for a range of physical and mental health conditions caused by the coercion and violence of trafficking/modern slavery. These services are used both immediately and to address long-term needs. The type of service use and the length of time it is used vary by the form of trafficking, since this is associated with different forms of hurts. For example, sexual exploitation tends to generate long-term harms to mental health.

Trafficking/modern slavery leads to lost wages, profits, and taxes from the loss of employment in the legal economy. Economic resources are diverted away from the legitimate economy by trafficking. When a person is being trafficked, the victim loses wages in unrewarded employment, the community and state loses the taxes that would otherwise have been paid, and employers lose the potential profits they might have made. Even though national accounts include some illegal activities (Eurostat 2015), they do not include profit from trafficking/modern slavery (Eurostat 2018: 18).

The years of life lost to trafficking/modern slavery include an adjustment for the quality of life lost. Victims of trafficking/modern slavery live lives that have lower quality than if they were not trafficked. Drawing on work in the field of health by the Global Burden of Disease project, the concept of quality-adjusted life year is used, and their measurements mobilized. It draws upon the earlier concept of a society's 'willingness to pay' to avoid pain and suffering.

Governmental agencies coordinate services, policies, training, and awareness raising, and build the knowledge base to prevent trafficking. The work of central governmental authorities and their agencies to coordinate counter-trafficking work and to address prevention is a cost. This is work to develop policy coherence and to address prevention through interventions in organizations and institutions, rather than a concern only for individuals.

Governments routinely use costing methodologies as a contribution to their decision-making on budgets. This analysis uses the conventional methodology. This is applied to the special circumstances of trafficking/ modern slavery. It uses the governmental manuals that facilitate shared, and hence comparable, practices (European Commission 2015), and draws on the methodology used for the costing of gender-based violence (Walby and Olive 2014), the cost of crime (Brand and Price 2000), and of modern slavery (Reed et al 2018). A conservative approach was taken in developing these estimates, in which costs were not included if the quality of the data was in doubt. Hence the cost is an under-estimate.

Data on the number of victims was taken from the European Commission (2018a). The scientific literature was reviewed to ascertain the extent to which victims of trafficking globally suffered physical violence, sexual violence, and threats, disaggregated by trafficking form. Surveys of populations were analysed to provide information on what harms had consequences for using health and welfare services, the extent of employment, and quality of life. The network of EU National Rapporteurs and equivalent mechanisms were asked to provide data on the use and cost of specialized services, law enforcement, and coordination. Eurostat data was obtained on the costs of health, social protection, law enforcement, and economic support. The European Commission provided documents on benchmarks for key values.

The costs are presented as the cost per victim. These are the costs over the lifetime of the victim. There are two ways of counting victims: those registered with the authorities, and survey-based estimates of prevalence in the population. This chapter uses the first approach. It is a minimal but robust estimation. If the second approach were used the costs would be much higher overall; however, for some of the victims who are not registered they would be lower since they would not be using specialized services and law enforcement.

There are different costs at different phases of trafficking: in trafficking, in services, and post-trafficking. Some costs last for many years, others are for shorter periods of time. While a victim is in trafficking, there are costs of law enforcement, lost economic output, reduced quality of life and coordination, but not specialized services or health services. While a victim is in services, all the costs occur. When a victim is post-trafficking, there are still continuing costs from health services and social protection, lost economic output, and reduced quality of life (Walby et al 2020).

The cost per victim, over their lifetime, was €312,756. This was made up of €9,614 for specialized services, €93,293 for law enforcement, €20,749 for health services and social protection, €59,537 for lost economic output, €127,504 for lost quality of life, and €2,059 for the coordination of prevention work. These figures are for 2016 (Walby et al 2020: 27).

For the EU, this is a total cost of €3,700,524,433 (Walby et al 2020: 27).

Of the three main types of cost, the use of public services was 40%, lost economic output was 19%, and lost quality of life, 41% (Walby et al 2020: 26).

The costs of trafficking for purposes of sexual exploitation are higher (€353,893) than those of labour exploitation (€219,382), largely due to the greater health costs linked to the length of time of harms due to sexual violence. The costs for females (€337,999) are higher than for males (€256,184), because females are more likely to be trafficked for sexual exploitation (Walby et al 2020: 28).

The use of the number of victims registered with the authorities rather than the estimated number of victims in the population has implications for the cost per victim and for the cost for a specific country. Registered victims use more services (specialized services, law enforcement) than unregistered victims, while the same prevention costs would be spread over a larger number of people, thus less per victim; so, the cost for each unregistered victim would be lower than for each registered victim. There are many more victims in the population than there are registered victims, so the use of this number would have increased the cost per country of trafficking, while reducing the cost per victim. An unregistered victim may not use any specialized services, law enforcement, health services, or increase coordination and prevention costs. Nevertheless, they will still lose economic output and quality of life.

The UK Home Office study on the cost of modern slavery did not have information on the cost of the criminal justice system nor on the long-term costs of sexual exploitation to mental health (Reed et al 2018). The study for the EU included these costs and found higher costs for women than for men, as a consequence of the different extent of sexual exploitation among men and women (Walby et al 2022).

Trafficking/modern slavery has an impact on society as well as on the victims across multiple dimensions. Some of these impacts can be estimated using a monetary frame of reference. This facilitates governments and public bodies taking better account of trafficking/modern slavery in financial decision-making on public policy priorities.

The cost for each registered victim in the EU of €312,756 is a sign of the huge damage that trafficking/modern slavery inflicts on economy and society.

The costing methodology offers a way of reflecting on the detriment of trafficking/modern slavery to sustainable development. It invites a reversal of the typical approach to the direction of causal pathways connecting different parts of society: from changes in the economy causing changes in coercion/violence to one in which changes in the level of coercion (trafficking/modern slavery) causes changes in the economy (sustainable development). This methodology can be used to indicate the impact of different rates of trafficking/modern slavery on society as an addition to the more usual approach of the impact of various forms of society on rates of trafficking/modern slavery.

Conclusion

There has been significant development in data and indicators to support the development of theory and policy to counter trafficking/modern slavery since 2000.

Females are the majority (65%) of the victims of trafficking/modern slavery. There is sex segregation in the types of exploitation, in that the vast majority (92%) of victims of trafficking for sexual exploitation are female, while there is less difference between genders in exploitation for forced labour and for other types. Migrants are more than three times more likely than non-migrants to be in forced labour. They make up one third (35%) of victims globally, varying from 25% to 65% in different global regions.

Trafficking/modern slavery has a huge impact on society as well as on its victims. The cost for each registered victim in the EU of €312,756 indicates the tremendous damage that trafficking/modern slavery causes to society.

The key indicator is in the UN Sustainable Development Goals: SDG Indicator 16.2.2, the 'Number of victims of human trafficking per 100,000 population, by sex, age and form of exploitation'. However, the data to populate this indicator is still under development. There are major developments by international bodies and academics to improve the knowledge base to achieve the data needed to support this indicator. There are substantial achievements by the UNODC in coordinating the counting of registered victims in UN member states and by the ILO, Walk Free, and IOM in developing survey-led estimates of the proportion of victims of modern slavery in the population. There is some data collection on policies by both UNODC and the ILO/Walk Free/IOM. There are debates as to next steps.

There have been two approaches to conceptualization, one centred on trafficking in human beings (UNODC), and one centred on forced labour and modern slavery (ILO/Walk Free/IOM), although there is substantial and recognized overlap and growing convergence. The more effective merging of these two would aid the further development of data to support the SDG measurement framework. This would entail a typology that has less internal hierarchy and more explicit translation between categories. This would concern a single field of trafficking/modern slavery with sub-categories of 'forced labour exploitation', 'sexual exploitation', 'other exploitation (including organs, forced begging)', 'state-forced labour exploitation', and 'forced marriage'. This treats sexual exploitation as a specific field rather than a sub-field of labour exploitation and includes forced marriage as a visible category rather than part of 'other'.

The ILO, Walk Free, and IOM (2022) estimate that there are 49,570,000 people in modern slavery. There are 49,032 registered victims around the world in 2018, according to data collated by the UNODC (2021). This suggests a ratio of registered victim to estimated victims in the population is thus 1:1000, in which only one in a thousand victims of trafficking/modern slavery are registered with the authorities.

The choice of administrative dataset to support the ratio of labour to sexual exploitation by ILO, Walk Free, and IOM (2022) has significant consequences for the amount of trafficking/modern slavery involving sexual exploitation and thus, because these victims are disproportionately female, for the relative proportion of women and men among victims. If the UNODC rather than IOM data were the basis of the ratio, then the estimate of the amount of trafficking for sexual exploitation/forced commercial sexual exploitation would significantly increase, the number of female victims of modern slavery would increase, and the overall number of victims of modern slavery would increase.

The UNODC (2021, 2023) and ILO, Walk Free, and IOM (2022) have estimates at a global level and for global regions for registered victims and for victims in the population respectively. There are remaining challenges in producing robust data for the SDG Indicator, which would mean programmes of research for the development of data. This would mean producing more empirical data to reduce the reliance of estimates on expert judgement and statistical modelling, which would include the regular repetition of surveys over time.

The available quantitative estimates have been used to investigate the correlation of trafficking/modern slavery with its potential causes. Trafficking/modern slavery correlates with economic inequalities, suggesting the varieties of modernity make a difference. War increases trafficking/ modern slavery, both directly and indirectly through migration as people flee war zones, suggesting that relations of coloniality contribute to trafficking/ modern slavery. Variations in gendered inequality correlate with trafficking/ modern slavery, especially for sexual exploitation and forced marriage. The intersection of these regimes of inequality generates specific situations of vulnerability to trafficking/modern slavery.

The UN has been establishing itself as the key platform for indicators of trafficking/modern slavery in the SDGs. Historically, there have been multiple developments in indicators, definitions, and data among diverse epistemic systems in this field. The definitions used by the UNODC are anchored in an international legal instrument, the 2000 UN Palermo Protocol to Prevent, Suppress and Combat Trafficking in Persons (UN 2000a). The term 'modern slavery', used by ILO/Walk Free/IOM, is not defined in an international legal instrument; however, several of its components are defined legally, including forced labour and practices similar to slavery, including forced marriage. These two major UN agencies have had different trajectories of development centred on the different international legal instruments for which they are responsible guardians, generating slightly different epistemic systems. The development of the UN as a platform for indicators and data for the SDGs offers an opportunity for narrowing the differences and generating the data for the indicator for a single field of trafficking/modern slavery.

5

Policy

Introduction

Policy relevant to trafficking/modern slavery sits at the confluence of multiple debates and agendas, including the strategy for economic development (led by GDP or SDGs), security (the extent to which the criminal justice system is prioritized), human rights (the extent to which these trump migration restrictions), and the nature of globalization. There have been claims that trafficking/modern slavery policy is narrow, carceral, and a distraction from larger issues, focusing on individuals, on prosecuting 'a few bad apples', and on 'rescuing victims'. The argument here is that recent developments now do address the 'whole of government', including policy on economic development, although this depends on context including the variety of modernity. However, policy rarely sufficiently addresses the profit-taking that drives trafficking/ modern slavery, nor the exclusions from welfare and democratic participation that create situations of vulnerability for women and migrants.

Multiple policy areas are engaged as relevant to anti-trafficking, including financial investment, industrial policy, business regulation, employment regulation, welfare, security, criminal justice, human rights, specialized welfare, migration, gender equality, and research. The strategic policy areas of economic development, security, and human rights are balanced in different ways in different contexts. Whether the coercive and carceral power of polities (military, criminal justice) is at the forefront or is a residual power as compared with economic regulation shapes the outcomes of interventions (Chapter 1). But the argument that the use of criminal law to reduce trafficking/modern slavery is intrinsically carceral for society is rejected; it can make a positive contribution when used in a targeted and proportionate manner. The balance between the use of security and criminal justice or regulation of the economy and welfare depends on the variety of modernity, which includes the depth of democracy.

Can trafficking/modern slavery policy detract from policies to support migrants? Policies to reduce trafficking/modern slavery can become entangled with other policies with unintended consequences. Policies aimed at another goal can have the unintended outcome of increasing trafficking/modern slavery. The entanglement with contestations over policy towards migration can twist the implications of anti-trafficking/modern slavery policy. The analysis is always intersectional. Migrants and women are disproportionately the victims of trafficking/modern slavery. The analysis requires not only consideration of policies to address the class inequalities of capitalism, but also the inequalities associated with coloniality, and gender regimes. While extreme economic exploitation is a feature, trafficking/modern slavery is more than this because it includes coercion. Restrictions on the capacity to exit abusive situations means that policies to address market-based inequalities are not enough.

Whether trafficking/modern slavery policy is global or national concerns the extent of effective state sovereignty over matters of law and order as well as political economy. There are multiple policy actors and levels of governance. Policy is global, through the activities of the UN and its agencies, and national, in that states interpret and selectively implement laws and policies. It is significantly affected by the varieties of modernity, which are shaped by the depth of democracy and by regional powers, including the US, EU, and China. All policy actors are shaped by their environment, including the depth of democracy, economy, violence, and civil society.

The 'whole of society' is relevant for the analysis, since these policies intervene across all the institutional domains of economy, violence, polity, and civil society. Multiple regimes of inequality shape and are shaped by these policies, including capitalism, colonialism, and gender regimes.

Policy actors

Policies on trafficking/modern slavery are developed and implemented at multiple levels of governance, including the global (the UN and its agencies), regional including continental states (US, EU, China), and other states (for example, the UK and Germany). The analysis challenges the assumption that national states have effective sovereignty over policies concerning law and order. The UN is a powerful policy platform, which shapes and is shaped by its environment of other polities, global economy, violence, and global civil society. The depth of democracy shapes these polities and their policies (Chapter 2). This is not a simple hierarchy of power, rather the environment that shapes each polity is made up of the other polities, as well as economies, violence, and civil society. The existence of a policy is not the same as its implementation.

UN and its agencies

The UN is a key source of legitimation for the international legal and policy instruments on trafficking/modern slavery, with 191 of its 193 member states ratifying the Palermo Protocol (UNODC 2023). The UN General Assembly passes resolutions (UN General Assembly 2020a) and receives reports on trafficking/modern slavery from the UN Secretary-General (UN General Assembly 2018b, 2022a, 2022b), the UN Special Rapporteur on Contemporary Forms of Slavery (UN General Assembly 2018c, 2019b, 2020c), and the UN Special Rapporteur on Trafficking in Persons (UN Special Rapporteur on Trafficking in Persons 2023). Several of the UN's agencies have adopted multi-component policy packages to reduce trafficking/modern slavery.

The World Bank Group (2020, 2022), which supports the development of lower-income countries, has adopted the Sustainable Development Goals (World Bank Group 2016), which includes Targets to reduce trafficking/modern slavery. The International Labour Organization (ILO), a tripartite body of employers, governments, and trade unions, is the guardian of the 1930 Convention on Forced Labour, developing policy (ILO 2005, 2006, 2018, 2019, 2021a, 2021b, 2022a, 2022b, 2022c) and measurement (ILO 2012a, 2012b, 2022b; ILO, Walk Free, and IOM 2022). The UN Security Council (UNSC 2022) has a remit to secure peace, including to mitigate trafficking/modern slavery in times of war (UNSC 2017). The United Nations Office on Drugs and Crime (UNODC) is the 'guardian' of the 2000 Palermo Protocol, producing reports on policy and measurement (UNODC 2009, 2012, 2014a, 2016, 2018c, 2021, 2022b, 2023), on interpreting legal concepts (UNODC 2013, 2014b, 2015), and on specific situations (UNODC 2011, 2018a, 2018b, 2018c, 2022a). The UN Office of the High Commissioner for Human Rights (UN OHCHR 2011, 2014, 2023a, 2023b) has a programme of work on human rights and human trafficking. UN Women, the UN's lead agency on gender equality, has a programme of work that contests trafficking/modern slavery as an aspect of violence against women (UN Women 2021, 2022), engaging with the UN General Assembly (UN General Assembly 2020a) and reporting on the role of climate crises, the pandemic, and conflict (including Ukraine), in the trafficking of women and girls (UN General Assembly 2022b). The UN Inter-Agency Coordination Group against Trafficking in Persons (ICAT) was created in 2007 to improve the coordination of UN agencies, by systematizing cooperation and multi-stakeholder partnerships (ICAT 2018, 2022), addressing concerns about coordination (Cockayne 2015). The International Organization on Migration (IOM) leads for the UN on migration, including the 2019 UN Global Compact (IOM 2023a), which includes combatting trafficking/modern slavery (IOM 2007, 2012, 2022, 2023a, 2023b). The UN and its agencies have a wide policy range.

Regional

While the UN offers a wide range of policies at the international level, there is significant variation in interpretation and implementation. Each of the major polities of the US, EU, and China has responded differently, each having a strategy not only for their own country, but also towards the rest of the world. The US utilizes trade sanctions and funding to implement policy on trafficking/modern slavery around the world. The EU offers funding for development and civil societal organizations and other forms of influence. China has its own distinctive investment and development approaches, which bring accusations by some of state-driven trafficking. There are other groupings of states from the OECD and NATO to the Global South.

The US passed an anti-trafficking law, The Trafficking Victims Protection Act (TVPA), in 2000 based on the Palermo Protocol (US 2000). It deploys an annual *Trafficking in Persons Report* as its 'principal diplomatic tool to engage foreign governments on human trafficking', using sanctions through trade and aid policy (US Department of State 2017). The US State Department monitors countries for their anti-trafficking measures (US Department of State 2017, 2022a, 2023) and ranks these into three tiers. Tier 1 are those governments that fully comply with US TVPA minimum requirements; Tier 2 includes governments that do not fully comply with TVPA minimum requirements but are making efforts; while Tier 3 do not fully comply with the minimum standards and are not making significant efforts to do so. Tier 3 is sanctioned by the loss of access to easy trade with, and non-humanitarian aid from, the US. While the Report reviews three aspects – prosecuting traffickers, protecting victims, and preventing trafficking – there has been a tendency to prioritize the criminal justice system during some administrations, though this shifted under the Obama (O'Brien and Wilson 2015) and Biden administrations (US Department of State 2023). The US understands anti-trafficking policy as a contribution to national security against organized crime (Bigio and Vogelstein 2019), though with controversial effects (Chuang 2006; Brennan 2014). To combat trafficking for purposes of sexual exploitation, countries are expected to follow the US preference for criminalizing the sex trade (Yen 2018). Under the Bush administration, anti-trafficking was used to further criminalize all persons in the sex trade, while under the Clinton and Obama administrations, a broader understanding of exploitation and human rights used anti-trafficking to support and fund policies to improve women's and migrant's victim rights and services (O'Brien and Wilson 2015). Most recently, anti-trafficking has been mobilized in trade competition with China, with US bans on textiles originating from the Xinjiang Autonomous Region (Cockayne 2021: 49; US Department of State 2022c, 2023).

The European Union adopted its own legal instrument, the Anti-Trafficking Directive based on the Palermo Protocol in 2011 (European Commission 2011) and an EU Strategy to assist its implementation (European Commission 2012, 2022a). The EU created an Anti-Trafficking Coordinator, a Network of National Rapporteurs and Equivalent Mechanisms in its Member States, and an EU Civil Society Platform (European Commission 2012, 2021a). EU agencies have increasingly cooperated on anti-Trafficking measures (Europol 2014; EU 2018b). The EU funds projects to create knowledge about trafficking to inform its policies. This includes reports on the gender dimensions (Walby et al 2016b), a comprehensive review of projects funded by the European Commission (Walby et al 2016a), analyses of available data (Francis et al 2018), and an estimate of the cost of trafficking (Walby et al 2020; Walby et al 2022), which contributed to the new EU Strategy on Combatting Trafficking in Human Beings 2021–2025 (EC 2021a). EU anti-trafficking Strategy is focused on trafficking/modern slavery within the EU, though it has funded projects worldwide. The EU has a comprehensive Strategy which, though including prosecuting traffickers and assisting victims, is oriented towards prevention. In contrast to the US, the European international strategy is oriented toward cooperation rather than sanctioning, with funding directed toward assisting countries to develop comprehensive sets of policies (Walby et al 2016a; European Commission 2021a). Civil society organizations in developing countries are major recipients of funding for anti-trafficking projects, sometimes routed through UN agencies. The 2021 European Commission Strategy towards the Eradication of Trafficking in Human Beings 2021–2025 (European Commission 2021a) pledges to continue funding to: 'tackle the situation in countries of origin and transit to Europe and outside … giving special attention to (i) the gender dimension, (ii) donor coordination, (iii) local ownership and (iv) support to civil society organizations and local actors and activists, (v) addressing the special protection needs of children in migration' (European Commission 2021a: 5).

China is the only large country not to sign the UN Palermo Protocol. In 2022, however, China enacted its own Action Plan to combat human trafficking by 2030, which it states is based on both international conventions and its own domestic laws (China Law Translate 2022).

The UN agencies, the US State Department, and the EU Commission all contribute to the implementation of the UN Palermo Protocol, but in different ways. The UN has a comprehensive strategy, increasingly foregrounding a human rights approach, though its prominence varies across its agencies. The US has a comprehensive strategy, but an emphasis on encouraging the prosecution of traffickers in foreign countries through sanctions on trade and aid. The EU has a comprehensive strategy, which includes supporting civil society organizations. These differences are found in the multiple policy fields discussed in the remainder of this chapter. China has a further strategy.

Policy actors in context

Global policy actors develop their policies in a wide environment of multiple actors, not only the regional polities of the US, EU, and China, but also national states, civil society, and economic forces. States retain importance as sites where legislation is transposed into domestic law and where policy priorities are set. Judicial systems interpret and implement the laws, according to local context, as intended by the drafters of the Palermo Protocol (UNODC 2013, 2014b, 2015). There are several civil society organizations that are significant in policy construction at a global level, including Walk Free, Alliance 8.7, labour organizations, and feminist NGOs.

The depth of democracy is important for the way that global policy is shaped: this includes not only voting but also presence and the range of institutions included in democratic decision-making (Chapter 2). It is key in shaping the variety of modernity. There are competing policy goals and reducing trafficking/modern slavery is not always treated as the most important. This depends on context.

Economic development

Some policies for economic development decrease trafficking/modern slavery; others increase it. Some consequences are unintended. Diverse policies are entangled in contradictory ways. There are different strategies for development that shape the context for more detailed policies. These include finance, industrial policy, business and supply chains, regulating labour, welfare, security, criminal justice, human rights, and specialized services. There are intersecting policies for migration and gender equality.

Strategies for development

Three strategies for development can be distinguished: the 'Washington Consensus'; the Sustainable Development Goals; and the state led approach. Each has implications for trafficking/modern slavery.

The 'Washington Consensus' (discussed further in the following section) has been a strategy for economic development focused on increasing the size of the market economy, often measured as an increase in Gross Domestic Product per person, through increasing free trade and deregulating markets (Chapter 2). It prioritized economic growth in the monetized market economy, in the expectation that it would drive progress broadly. As discussed in Chapters 2 and 4, economic development has not ended trafficking/modern slavery.

The Sustainable Development Goals (UN 2015) constitute an alternative strategy for development that incorporates long-term sustainability and social inclusion into the vision of how development should be achieved and what it should look like. There are 17 Goals: (1) no poverty; (2) zero hunger; (3) good health and well-being; (4) quality education; (5) gender equality; (6) clean water and sanitation; (7) affordable and clean energy; (8) decent work and economic growth; (9) industry, innovation, and infrastructure; (10) reduced inequalities; (11) sustainable cities and communities; (12) responsible consumption and production; (13) climate action; (14) life below water; (15) life on land; (16) peace, justice, and strong institutions; and (17) partnership for the Goals. Under Goal 8, Target 7 concerns policy on trafficking/modern slavery. Target 8.7 is: 'Take immediate and effective measures to eradicate forced labour, end modern slavery and human trafficking and secure the prohibition and elimination of the worst forms of child labour, including recruitment and use of child soldiers, and by 2025 end child labour in all its forms'. Of course, adopting the SDGs' Goals and Targets is not the same as their practical implementation.

There are further strategies for development, of which the most important is that of China, because of the scale of its investment in developing countries. In its Asian investments, China has often 'transplanted' its own labour to its foreign direct investments (Xiang 2012a), but labour recruitment to China's investments in Europe (Ceccagno and Sacchetto 2020) and Africa (Lee 2018) differ, with labour conditions often congruent with local labour standards and international norms. Most recently the US TiP reports evidence of China engaged in state-driven trafficking of the ethnic Uyghur population in textile supply chains (US Department of State 2022a, see also US Department of State 2022b).

Finance

International financial investment is important for the shape as well as level of economic development. Conditions on investment for development could include policies to reduce the likelihood of trafficking/modern slavery. The World Bank Group and China are both significant providers of finance for development, especially for low- and middle- income countries (UNCTAD 2023). The conditions attached to loans can shape whether the way development takes place is conducive to the increase or decrease of trafficking/modern slavery. The World Bank Group (Kapur et al 2002) has moved away from the Washington Consensus and in 2016 adopted the SDGs as a set of principles to guide its policies for investment (World Bank Group 2016). There is a question as to whether the private providers of finance, which are increasingly important, will follow this lead. The organizational ecology of global financial governance has been changing, with an increase in private transnational regulatory organizations while the number of intergovernmental organizations has been stable (Abbott et al 2016). In 2016, the World Bank Group (2016) both increased engagement with private funds to allow private investors to finance International Development Association projects and extended its mandate to include the public goods of the Sustainable Development Goals (Heldt and Dörfler

2022). The implementation of the SDGs in practical decisions by the World Bank Group on financial investment is challenging. Is the World Bank Group able to ensure that its private investors also adopt the SDG priorities and ensure that compliance is real rather than merely rhetorical; and is a focus on 'safeguarding' against risks of funding sectors engaged in trafficking/modern slavery sufficiently ambitious (Cockayne 2021)?

Industrial policy

Industrial policy concerns decisions as to which areas of the economy are to be encouraged to increase or decrease. Policies include: an outright ban on certain types of economic activity altogether; regulation of business; and regulation of the employment relations. These can be nuanced to apply differently to different aspects. For example, it is possible to ban third-party profit-taking to curtail the growth of businesses in an area, but to allow private individuals freedom to transact at an individual level, as discussed in Chapter 6 on sexual exploitation. Policies exist in many countries to ban commercial exchanges in some areas of activities and industries where trafficking/modern slavery is common, while not preventing non-commercial exchanges (as in organ donation). Others ban particular categories of people, such as women, children, and migrants, from particular kinds of economic activity. As discussed in the following examples, trade in organs is universally illegal; trade in sex is fully illegal in some countries and partially illegal in some others; the trade in the supply of labour was historically illegal and has been legalized and is usually subject to regulation.

The selling of organs for transplants is illegal under the Palermo Protocol as a form of human trafficking, while it is legal to use organs from dead persons who had signed agreements and where there is no financial exchange. The WHO and transplantation professionals, such as the Transplantation Society, have formed a consensus at professional meetings that the commercial trade in organs should be banned, see for example, the Kuwait Statement (Transplantation Society and International Society of Nephrology 2008, 2018), on the grounds that most cases involve organs sourced from the poor and vulnerable in the developing world under relations that are considered coercive in the lack of alternative options (Budiani-Saberi and Delmonico 2008; Satz 2008; Budiani-Saberi and Columb 2013; Capron and Delmonico 2015). The investigation and prosecution of organ trafficking is challenging, with cases involving organized criminal networks colluding with transplant professionals (Ambagtsheer 2021), and with an estimated 5% (Capron and Delmonico 2015) to 5–10% (Budiani-Saberi and Delmonico 2008) of kidney transplants worldwide being instances of trafficking.

The trade in sex is banned in the US; some aspects of it are illegal in countries such as Sweden and the UK; it is legal and regulated in others such as Germany. International bodies, such as the ILO, have complex positions on whether the sex trade is within their remit, or only those forms that reach the threshold of coercion that constitutes trafficking/modern slavery (Boris et al 2010). The justification of the bans and regulations are that the sex trade is risky (Barry 1995; Sanders 2004), and further that it is a route to trafficking/modern slavery, which causes harms to the victims (Zimmerman et al 2008; Oram et al 2012, 2016), generates costs to economy and society (Walby et al 2020; Cockayne 2021), and creates moral harms (Satz 1995, 2010). These justifications are contested in the name of freedom and the agency of women (Aradau 2008; Bernstein 2010; O'Connell Davidson 2015). There are complex debates as to the appropriate response (Boris and Parreñas 2010; Boris et al 2010; Matthews et al 2014). As shown in the Introduction, there are several potential sites of regulation: the profit-taking by third parties running a business, the person selling sex, and the person buying sex. The contested regulation of the sex trade to reduce trafficking/modern slavery is discussed in detail in Chapter 6 on sexual exploitation.

Fee-charging private employment services have historically been banned on the grounds that they led to excessive exploitation of workers, especially migrant labour in vulnerable situations (Vosko 2010). With ILO 1997, fee-charging private employment services are again permitted in international conventions, and now typically regulated. The people whose labour is being sold in this way are disproportionately migrants and women (Gottfried 2013; Strauss 2014; Coe and Ward 2014; Forde et al 2015). ILO 1997, however, permits charging employers but not workers for employment placement, but states ratifying the Convention can mandate exceptions, and charging workers is widely practised for recruiting migrant labour. The link between fees charged to workers for access to jobs and the generation of situations of vulnerability through debt is one of the well-recognized mechanisms through which traffickers control their victims, especially migrant labour (UNODC 2022a; Fabbri et al 2023). The dependence of licensed recruitment on informal brokers, common in migrant recruitment (Lindquist 2010, 2012; Rodriguez 2010; Xiang 2012b, 2017), can mean that fees are charged multiply by different recruiters, further exacerbating situations of vulnerability.

When intrinsically risky economic sectors are permitted to operate for profit, people get hurt and some die. When there are no effective economic regulations of the economy to prevent such abuse, the response of the state can be the reactive use of criminal justice. This is illustrated in the example of the 19 cockle pickers who died in Morecambe Bay, UK. They were recruited from China and organized by a gangmaster to work gathering cockles (seafood) at low tide (a risky business in a large bay with quicksands, gulleys, and tides that locals know come in quicker than a person can run away from them); they drowned when the tide came in because they kept working too long to get to safety (The Guardian 2005). The gangmaster was charged with manslaughter and imprisoned for 14 years (BBC 2006). The UK adopted the UK Gangmasters' (Licensing) Act (UK 2004) creating an Authority to regulate the suppliers of labour, including a criminal sanction for non-registration. However, ten years later, the local verdict was that the risky situation was worse not better (BBC 2014). In 2016, the legislation and the powers of the Authority were extended to include further labour abuses (UK Gangmasters and Labour Abuse Authority 2023).

The ILO has developed Conventions and advice on these matters (Boris 2023). ILO Conventions in 1933 and 1949 (ILO 1933, 1949) prohibited fee-charging employment services because of a 'growing concern with the unscrupulous activities of for-profit private employment agents placing migrant workers' (Vosko 2010: 54), thereby largely removing labour intermediation from the economies of ratifying industrial societies. In 1997, ILO Convention 181 ended this prohibition, though fees should only be charged to those buying labour (ILO 1997). This facilitated the growth of a profitable recruitment industry. The ILO readjusted its recommended policy in the 2014 Fair Migration Agenda (ILO 2014), and its 2018 Definition of Recruitment Fees and Related Costs (ILO 2018, 2019, 2021a). The ILO includes 'fair recruitment' in its policy recommendations to stop forced labour (ILO 2018). ILO policy is now to 'introduce and enforce laws to prohibit charging of recruitment fees to employees, register and monitor recruitment agencies for deceptive practices, and ensure contracts are made available in a language migrants can understand' (ILO, Walk Free, and IOM 2022: 7). More than 90 countries have laws governing recruitment agencies, though the ILO finds that few of these are comprehensive, thus leaving room for abuse. The ILO notes that a further policy is to develop government-to-government recruitment mechanisms, bypassing private employment agencies (ILO 2018: 6–7).

The private recruitment industry takes profits from supplying labour, particularly affecting migrants. The ILO has addressed the issue of the private recruitment industry by a range of policy recommendations over the years, including a full ban, a partial ban (of charging fees to workers), side-stepping it by developing government mechanisms, and by monitoring and regulation. The effect of policies varies by context, depending on access to justice and other support. When economic regulation does not prevent trafficking/modern slavery, criminal justice is a responsive residual response.

Regulating supply chains

A trafficking chain will often have a mix of coercive links, free but illegal links, and free and legal links, as discussed in Chapters 1 and 2. The mixture of legal and illegal links and border-crossing makes it hard to police (Kirby and Penna 2010; Penna and Kirby 2012). The business model in supply chains is to deliberately separate the legally bounded entity accumulating profits at the top of the chain from responsibility for the performance of the productive work elsewhere in the chain (Fudge 2012, 2018; Crane 2013; LeBaron 2021; Crane et al 2022a; LeBaron and Lister 2022). The coercive practices, the ones that cross the threshold of the exploitation of vulnerability to constitute trafficking/modern slavery, are – given legacies of coloniality – more likely to be in lower-income countries in the South, or, if in the North, engaging migrant labour (as in the cockle harvesting example in the UK). The profits, while taken from every link of the chain, are disproportionately accumulated at the top of the chain.

Can policy be developed to make the (indirect) beneficiaries at the top of the chain legally responsible for abuses elsewhere in the chain? Several are under development. One approach is to block flows of illicit money at the top of the chain. This has variously involved increasing transparency, to make it easier for authorities stopping the movement of illicit profits into the legal economy, known as 'money laundering', by stopping the privacy surrounding illicit flows in secrecy jurisdictions, known as 'tax havens', and making visible the beneficial owners of property (Levi 2002; Shaxson 2012). A second approach is to make the companies at the top of the chain legally responsible for the activities of the companies lower down their supply chains. This involves transparency, such as monitoring and reporting in annual company reports, as well as sanctions. It can involve identifying the products made by victims of trafficking/modern slavery (see for example the list produced by the US Department of Labor 2022) and associated producer and consumer boycotts. Transparency alone has been found to be insufficient, leading to arguments for sanctions (LeBaron 2020a; Rogerson et al 2020). Policies based on codes of conduct relating to transnational supply chains require governance mechanisms within firms, as well as external audit mechanisms including 'kitemarks'. These can be part of a firm's corporate social responsibility claims. The UN Global Compact (UN 2021) is a voluntary association of companies that agree to meet standards to prevent abuses including trafficking/modern slavery. In LeBaron's (2020a) assessment, existing voluntary mechanisms fail because of the absence of sanctions.

State regulations to ensure companies take responsibility for removing trafficking/modern slavery from their supply chains are under development, using either transparency or sanctions. Reporting on due diligence to ensure no modern slavery in a company's supply chain was included in the 2015 UK Modern Slavery Act. California has a similar Act, the California Transparency in Supply Chains Act (State of California 2012). The OECD has non-binding guidelines on due diligence in supply chains that have been adopted by 50 countries (OECD 2018). Similar laws, but with sanctions, have been proposed or enacted in France (2017 French Duty of Vigilance), Germany (2023 German Supply Chain Act), and the Netherlands (Child Labour Due Diligence Act) (tradebeyond 2023). An EU supply chain Directive has been proposed for companies in the EU, though pressure from companies has restricted this to those few companies with over 1,000 employees (European Commission 2022d).

Regulating labour

State regulation of markets in labour to prevent abuse and coercion can reduce trafficking/modern slavery. It offers a route for complaint and redress against employers in specialized, non-criminal tribunals and courts. However, not all work is regulated in this way, since not all workers have direct employers who can be made accountable. The exceptions and exclusions are situations of vulnerability to trafficking/modern slavery. Migrants and women disproportionately gain their livelihoods in unregulated activities. Policies to reduce the exclusion of migrants and women from legal protections in work would reduce trafficking/modern slavery. However, there are contested policy priorities concerning immigration, gender equality, and trafficking/modern slavery.

The legal regulation of work is focused on situations where there is a direct relationship between employer and employee. This concerns issues such as unfair dismissal, discrimination, and harassment. These regulations have developed over many decades and vary significantly between global regions and individual countries. Trafficking/modern slavery is less likely in contexts of regulated direct employment relations and open markets in labour in which a wronged worker can make a complaint through institutionalized routes to obtain redress or freely move to another job, though this depends on regulations being implemented and enforced. Alternative forms of enforcement include licensing and inspection, as discussed earlier.

However, the heyday of such regulation is gone, even in the more social democratic world regions such as Europe, though there are still more regulations in the EU than in the more neoliberal US. These changes are both because of processes of deregulation in the Global North since the 1990s (Vosko 2010; Emmenegger et al 2012), and because of the disproportionate growth in employment in sectors that do not have direct employment relations, including self-employment and other forms of nonregular work (Apitzsch et al 2015), including that organized through platforms (Gillespie 2010; Gawer 2014; Plantin et al 2018; Poell et al 2019; Scoular et al 2019). The policy of deregulation has been part of the neoliberal project, institutionalized, for example, by the OECD (1994) and IMF in the structural adjustment programmes under the 'Washington Consensus' (Reich 2016). The experience of precarious employment makes workers less likely to complain because of fear of losing their jobs. Migrant workers are less likely than citizen workers to complain because of fear of deportation if they were to lose their job. Wronged, abused, coerced workers are among those who are less likely to have a direct employer who can be held to account through state-sponsored tribunals and courts.

The rise of platforms as brokerage of jobs in the digital economy reduces the proportion of workers who have a direct employer from whom they can claim employment rights (Gillespie 2010; Poell et al 2019). Further, these deterritorialize work (Ettlinger 2017), and introduce new sets of profit-takers into supply chains. Self-employment dissolves the status of the person expending their labour or services as an employee and those engaging them from any obligations as employers; platforms dissolve the status of those taking profits from labour and service from any obligations of contract beyond a single gig. Platform work increases the power of the platform to control those delivering service (Huws 2020) and expands the scope for the exploitation of those performing services (Chicchi 2020). Virtual platforms have become the most important way in which the sex trade is organized (Scoular et al 2019). The UNODC views the regulation of platforms as one of the central challenges to the prevention of trafficking/ modern slavery, especially prevalent in trafficking for purposes of sexual exploitation (UNODC 2023).

Migrants are more than three times as likely to be victims of trafficking/ modern slavery than non-migrants (ILO, Walk Free, and IOM 2022) and make up one third (35%) of registered victims, though varying from 65% to 25% by global region (UNODC 2021: 10, 55) (see also Chapter 4).

There are connections between the expansion of non-regular labour and unfree forced labour (Fudge and Strauss 2014). These intersect with migrant status. Migrant workers are often in employment that is non-regular and where regulations are not well-implemented (Fudge and Strauss 2014; Rijken and Lange 2018; Wagner and Shire 2019). Irregular migration often situates migrants in informal work, without recourse to protections. Policies to reduce irregular migration can be in tension with policies to reduce trafficking in human beings, as victims fear deportation if they turn to authorities (Aradau 2008; Hathaway 2008). These competing priorities have generated debates (Andrijasevic 2007) about the culpability of states in contributing to the situations of vulnerability of migrants to exploitative and abusive employers (Anderson 2014a).

The intersection of migration policy with economic policy creates further aspects of vulnerability (Anderson and O'Connell Davidson 2003; van der Leun 2011; Follis 2012; Fudge 2012; Surak 2013; Xiang et al 2013; Shire 2020). Employment deregulation interacts with migration controls to situate migrants in work settings in which they are particularly vulnerable to exploitation (Waite et al 2015). The creation of specific categories of labour migration in immigration controls, common to guest-worker programmes (Surak 2013) and forms of managed migration designed to prevent settlement (Xiang et al 2013) block migrant workers from accessing standards and redress available to citizen workers. Some migrants have 'tied visas', which means that they cannot leave one employer for another; they are less able to make complaints since this makes them vulnerable to deportation; and if they leave the employer to whom their visa is tied, they are obliged to leave the country (Thomas 2013; Demetriou 2015). Tied visas make legal migrants vulnerable to abusive and coercive demands from their employers. Migrants usually have less access to forms of welfare support than citizens, which makes them further vulnerable to abusive and coercive demands from their employers. The fear of deportation generated by the forms of regulation of international migration has the effect of regulating labour markets.

Situations of vulnerability are especially acute for migrants without regular status, as they lack access to welfare and justice, and can face criminalization for illegal presence. The treatment of illegal migration as a criminal rather than administrative matter (Bowling 2020) makes non-documented migrants more vulnerable. This has a gender dimension, in that women migrants have fewer available routes for regular migration or formalized work opportunities than men. In informal and less secure work settings like domestic labour, precarious service jobs, and the sex trade, labour standards either do not apply or are not upheld, while forms of control can be personalized and despotic (Andrijasevic and Anderson 2009; Anderson 2014b; Kofman and Raghuran 2015). In informal settings, practices such as employers holding workers' passports and personal documents exacerbate vulnerability (Sorrentino and Jokinen 2014). Migrants who are in some way irregular are less willing and able to avail themselves of the services of the welfare and criminal justice systems if they are abused, exacerbating their vulnerable situations. Non-documented migrants have even less access to justice and to welfare; seeking help may well lead to their deportation.

There are attempts to develop practices and policies to mitigate these risks for migrants and women. Practices that build networks matter (Ryan 2011; Yuval-Davis et al 2018). At the international level, on migration, the UN Global Compact on Migration (UN General Assembly 2019a), coordinated by the International Organization for Migration, promises assistance to migrants that could reduce trafficking/modern slavery (IOM 2023a, 2023b), though there are hesitations over its effectiveness (Chuang 2020, 2021; Fudge 2023). Gender equality is advanced through the programmes of UN Women and the UN Convention on the Elimination of Discrimination against Women (UN 1979). At a regional level, the EU Directives offer protections for workers who are part-time (European Commission 1997), temporary (European Commission 2008), posted workers (European Commission 1996), and against sex discrimination and harassment at work

(European Commission 2006). However, there are concerns about the implementation and prioritization of such policies for non-citizens, and especially if a deregulatory strategy of economic growth is followed, and if efforts are mainly focused on voluntary self-governance (LeBaron 2020a).

Welfare and social protection

There is considerable variation in the extent to which welfare and social protection is available. The provision of welfare, of social protection, provides an alternative source of livelihood to help people exit or never accept jobs or activities that are abusive and coercive. This includes income support and services including health care, reproductive care, and education. Such provision mitigates situations of vulnerability to trafficking/modern slavery that are associated with lack of access to a safe livelihood. There is consensus among policy entities and practitioners of the importance of the provision of social protection (ILO, Walk Free, and IOM 2022: 6; UNODC 2023).

There are variations in welfare provision between countries and variations in access to welfare within countries. The general differences between states can be aligned with varieties of modernity in which there is more welfare in social-democratic regimes, low public spending on welfare in neoliberal regimes, and least in authoritarian regimes (Esping-Andersen 1990; Castles 2012). The inclusion of women independently from men has been a recent development, and, for women in some countries, access to income support is still restricted to positions as dependents of wage-earner husbands and fathers, and is not available for single, lone or independent women (Orloff 1996; Orloff and Laperrière 2021). Migrants are often excluded from some, if not all, forms of social protection, even when they are legally entitled to work, while migrants without documents are almost universally excluded. The coverage of migrants depends on residence and migration status, which in most cases means that only migrants with long-term or permanent residence become eligible for welfare coverage, while irregular migrants or those in uncovered employment statuses (informal, self-employed) are excluded from welfare coverage (Sönmez et al 2011; Bruzelius 2019; Niño-Zarazúa et al 2019; Scarpa et al 2021). This is exacerbated by the concentration of women and migrants in the informal sector, where social protection is less common. Exclusions from welfare social protection generate situations of vulnerability that are more common for women and migrants than others.

The removal of these exclusions has been called for by policy bodies:

> Extend social protection, including floors, to all workers and their families, to mitigate the socio-economic vulnerability that underpins much of forced labour, and to provide workers with the basic income security to be able to say no to jobs that are abusive and to quit jobs that

have become so. Extending social protection coverage to the informal sector is a priority. It is important that social protection also provides inclusive, equitable and non-discriminatory coverage to migrants. (ILO, Walk Free, and IOM 2022: 6)

Security

Security policy concerns violence and coercion, and the shaping of the social relations and institutions that increase or decrease it. The security policy actors are largely polities (global, hegemon, national, local). Security policy is traditionally split between external (international, security, war) and internal (domestic, criminal justice) but is increasingly engaging with both at the same time (Buzan et al 1998; Bigo 2006; Vaughan-Williams 2015). This is the case for trafficking/modern slavery, due to the consequences of interstate and civil war for vulnerabilities to trafficking/modern slavery, processes of migration that can create vulnerabilities, and the sometimes transnational organization of this crime. One set of international policy actors (in concert with hegemons and states) is concerned with security to prevent war and to mitigate the vulnerabilities of migration. A second set of policy actors (states in concert with international actors and hegemons) is concerned with security to prevent violent and coercive crime (including across borders), with a focus on criminal justice and other bodies of law.

There are challenges. There are various ways in which policy is being improved or might be improved. There can be contradictory or unintended effects of policy. There are issues about the balance and relationship with other forms of policy intervention in economic development and in human rights and humanitarian settings. They have implications for wider theory and policy.

International agencies for security

The international security policy agencies relevant to trafficking/modern slavery include several agencies of the UN, including the General Assembly, Secretary-General, UN Security Council, Tribunals to implement the Rome Statute, UN Rapporteurs on Contemporary Slavery and on Trafficking, the UNODC, UN Women, and associated bodies including the International Organization for Migration. They operate in an environment in which states are important, especially those that are regional hegemons, such as the US and EU, as well as the global economic system, violence, and global civil society.

These bodies address trafficking/modern slavery by identifying the issue for public attention, and attempting to prevent and end war, to reduce enslavement by military victors of conquered populations, and to mitigate the vulnerabilities to trafficking/modern slavery of those fleeing war (whether considered migration, internal or external 'displacement', 'refugees', or asylum seekers). These may be described as security issues, and also as peace, humanitarianism, and human rights issues.

The UN Secretary-General and the UN General Assembly offer oversight and impetus for action (UN Secretary-General 2020; UN General Assembly 2020b), Resolutions of the UN General Assembly (UN General Assembly 2019a, 2020a), initiation of research studies, and by providing a platform for the UN Rapporteurs on Contemporary Forms of Slavery and on Trafficking (UN General Assembly 2018b, 2018c, 2019b, 2020b, 2022a, 2022b).

The UN Security Council offers targeted oversight and impetus for action. This includes Resolutions, calls for UN peacekeeping, and for the mobilization of the Rome Statute on war crimes through establishing special Tribunals. UN Security Council Resolution 2388 in 2017 condemned trafficking, particularly by 'Islamic State' (ISIL, Da'esh), and called for this to be included when considering sanctions (UN Security Council 2017). Security Council Resolution 2331 in 2016 recognized that offences associated with trafficking might constitute war crimes and, in some contexts, crimes against humanity (UN Security Council 2016). The UN Security Council Resolution 2388 noted the connections between trafficking and wider issues: 'the Council stressed that trafficking undermined the rule of law and contributed to other forms of transnational organized crime that could exacerbate conflict and foster insecurity and instability, thereby undermining development' (UN Security Council 2017).

UN Women offers specific contributions on the position of women and girls in trafficking/modern slavery (UN Women 2021), including to the UN General Assembly via the Secretary-General (UN General Assembly 2020b, 2022b).

The UNODC provides data on registered victims and traffickers (2009, 2012, 2014a, 2016, 2018c, 2021, 2023) and specialized studies of trafficking, including in times of conflict (UNODC 2018a, 2018b, 2022b). It offers possible policies, including humanitarian support to populations in and fleeing conflict areas, the integration of anti-trafficking measures in emergency situations with displaced populations, and counter-trafficking training for military and peacekeeping personnel (UNODC 2023).

There are challenges. UN actions take place in the context of states, regional powers (US, EU, China), military alliances (for example, NATO), and warfare. A call for action by the UN does not mean that action will necessarily be taken. Further, the introduction of peacekeepers can have contradictory and unintended effects on trafficking since, despite intentions, the introduction of foreign soldiers can increase demand for commercial sex, which may generate trafficking (Smith and Miller-de la Cuesta 2011).

The UN agencies have put the development of policies to counter trafficking/modern slavery in conflict zones on the agenda. The best policy, of course, is to prevent war.

Criminal justice systems

The rule of law reduces the crime of trafficking/modern slavery. Enforcing criminal law through the criminal justice system is important, alongside the enforcement of other bodies of law, for example, those regulating the economy. The mobilization of criminal and other forms of law varies between countries, regimes of inequality, and varieties of modernity (Ayers and Braithwaite 1992; Black 2002, 2008; Ashworth and Zedner 2012; Braithwaite 2023). It has been variously argued that there is too much coercive and carceral intervention into trafficking/modern slavery (Bernstein 2010; O'Connell Davidson 2015), that criminal justice needs more development before it is sufficient to deliver justice for women (MacKinnon 2011; McGlynn 2022), and that this varies by the context of the variety of gender regime (Walby 2023a). Could better economic regulation and provision of welfare mean there are less traffickers to apprehend and to whom to apply criminal justice (Spapens et al 2015)? These issues are addressed by considering: what criminal justice is and how it works to prevent trafficking/modern slavery; how it is being and might be improved; its contradictory unintended effects; and its wider implications.

The criminal justice system is intended to reduce impunity, remove traffickers from circulation, provide deterrence and a sense of justice to victims and community, enforcing the law through police, prosecution, courts, and sanctions. Most countries have criminalized trafficking in alignment with the Palermo Protocol. By August 2020, 169 countries had legislation that was broadly in line with the UN Palermo Protocol. Others have partial legislation. There has been an increase over time in this legislation, from August 2012, when 10% of countries had no specific TiP offence, falling to 2% in August 2020, when 76% of countries had a specific TiP offence criminalizing most or all forms of TiP, increasing to 93% in August 2020 (UNODC 2021: 61). The global average conviction rate has been increasing; early adopters, such as many European countries, have higher conviction rates (UNODC 2021: 62–3).

There are challenges. The interpretation and implementation of the Palermo Protocol vary significantly between countries and groups. There can be gaps in the legislation; differences in the interpretation of legal concepts; difficulties in enforcement; uneven enforcement; the expansion of the online world faster than regulations can follow; and contradictions arising from intersections with other bodies of law, especially concerning the sex trade and migration.

There can be gaps in the domestic legislation (Haughey 2016), so that it does not cover well all links in the trafficking chain, in particular, due to money laundering, but also generally in the cases of forced marriage, state forced labour, and new cyber developments. There can be gaps in legislation that enable illegal profits to be moved through institutions into the legal economy or stored offshore in secrecy jurisdictions (tax havens) (Shaxson 2012); this is compounded when trafficking/modern slavery is a form of organized crime (Europol 2015b, 2016) that requires corruption to be addressed (UNODC 2011; Penna and O'Brien 2018; Global Initiative against Transnational Organized Crime 2021, 2023), though not all movement of illegal profits from trafficking/modern slavery use the formal banking system (Broad et al 2022). There can be gaps in the scrutiny of supply chains to remove the links that depend on trafficking/modern slavery (LeBaron 2015, 2020a, 2021; LeBaron et al 2017; Crane et al 2019; LeBaron and Rühmkorf 2019). Trafficking/modern slavery activities can move to online forms to which criminal regulations, designed for the offline world, may not fully apply (Europol 2020). An example is the development of online platforms to facilitate the sale of sex and take profits from this service (Scoular et al 2019). The development of the EU Digital Services Act is a first step towards closing the gap between online and offline regulations.

Some of the concepts used in trafficking/modern slavery legislation can be subject to varying interpretation, including exploitation (UNODC 2015), vulnerability (UNODC 2013), and consent (UNODC 2014b). Difficulties for the policing of trafficking/modern slavery include lack of clarity and understanding of practical definitions (Farrell et al 2020).

Enforcement is challenging. There are relatively few successful prosecutions (Chapter 4). There are challenges in policing human trafficking/modern slavery (Chantavarich 2020; UK National Crime Agency 2023) when the victims do not trust the police and thus do not seek their assistance (Farrell et al 2019), and vulnerable victims may be unwilling to testify in court out of fear. There are challenges in providing access to the protection of the criminal justice system for people who are minoritized through race and sexuality, and through gender identity (Fehrenbacher et al 2020). There are difficulties for policing in identifying child victims, for example, those exploited to transport drugs, and to appropriately manage the discretion that they have (Espeute and Lanskey 2023). While traffickers may work across borders, most policing is contained within national boundaries (Penna and Kirby 2012), and the development of international criminal justice is challenging (Cockayne and Panaccione 2015; Cockayne et al 2016). Traffickers may be protected by corrupt practices (UNODC 2011; Penna and O'Brien 2018; Global Initiative against Transnational Organized Crime 2021, 2023). The entwining of illegal activities with legal markets makes it hard to catch the financial flows and the beneficiaries at the top of the trafficking chain (European Commission 2021b). There can be weak state capacity to enforce the law in times of crisis, war, and disaster. Vulnerabilities associated with migration, both legal and illegal, mean victims are reluctant to participate since they face, or think they may face, deportation. Those arrested, prosecuted, and convicted may be disproportionately from low levels of the trafficking chain (Broad and Gadd 2023), and the proportion (33–38%) of these who are female may indicate that those subject to criminal justice are disproportionately low-level recruiters rather than higher-level organizers (Kangaspunta et al 2016).

There are challenges when law enforcement for trafficking/modern slavery becomes entangled with other bodies of law, including those on migration and those on the sex trade, with competing priorities for law enforcement. While in the EU selling sex is not illegal, there can be challenges for the police in the US, where all aspects of prostitution are criminalized, in distinguishing between a person who is voluntarily selling sex and a victim of human trafficking (Reis et al 2022), especially where the same entity is required to enforce the law on both (Farrell and Cronin 2015). The distinction between smuggling (illegal entry into a country) and human trafficking (control over a human being) is important, but the implementation of the distinction can harm victims (Campana and Varese 2016).

There are initiatives to develop legislation to close the gaps identified (European Commission 2016a, 2016b), to clarify, and to aid enforcement. The European Commission proposes legislative reform using a new Directive to address gaps in the 2011 Trafficking Directive (European Commission 2022b), which addresses the following issues. It would: criminalize those who use the services of people who are trafficked, especially when they had a reasonable probability of knowing a person is a victim or with reckless disregard; make companies responsible for carrying out due diligence to stop trafficking/modern slavery in their supply chains; and, develop additional legislation and provide resources to close down routes for illegal financial flows (tax havens, secrecy jurisdictions, hiding beneficial ownership in trusts), and extend offline laws to online contexts.

There are developments to improve policing. There is some progress in law enforcement when the police engage with multiple civil society agencies (Elliot et al 2020), including those that have specialized expertise, rather than proceeding alone (Pajon and Walsh 2023). There is improved identification of victims when the police receive training (Reis et al 2022).

There are contradictory and unintended effects concerning the intersection of criminal activities to stop trafficking/modern slavery with laws and policies on migration and on the sex trade. These bodies of law are entangled in complex ways. There is concern that laws and policies on migration and the sex trade have taken inappropriate precedence over the needs of victims of trafficking/modern slavery. There is concern that the mobilization of the actions to prevent trafficking/modern slavery has been to the detriment of migrants and those selling sex (Anderson 2010, 2013, 2014b; O'Connell Davidson 2015; Molodikova 2020; Clemente 2022; Romero et al 2023). This concern is especially articulated in the analysis of representations and discursive aspects (Aradau 2004, 2008; Andrijasevic 2007; Andrijasevic and Anderson 2009; Andrijasevic and Mai 2016). Article 7.1 of the Palermo Protocol states that each 'State Party shall consider adopting legislative or other appropriate measures that permit victims of trafficking in persons to remain in its territory, temporarily or permanently, in appropriate cases', which means that it is a matter of national policy whether victims of trafficking are deported or given leave to remain.

The analysis of these complex and problematic intersections is continued in more detail in Chapter 6 on sexual exploitation. This identifies the importance of the specifics of the contexts of these intersections in different times and countries.

A key issue in the analysis of policy on trafficking/modern slavery is the balance of the use of different bodies of law. This concerns whether the use of the criminal justice system is proportionate and targeted or if it is excessive. If trafficking/modern slavery were suppressed by other interventions regulating the economy with non-criminal sanctions, removing exceptions to social protection to make victims more resilient through access to livelihoods, then there would be less of it to be suppressed by criminal justice. The balance between the use of criminal justice or other forms of law to address trafficking/modern slavery tends to depend on the wider societal context, whether social democratic, neoliberal, or authoritarian. This context includes the varieties of modernity. Europe (especially but not only the EU) tends to use a relatively dense set of regulations and welfare provision. The US tends to use more criminal justice. This might be considered a contrast between a more social democratic as compared with a more neoliberal variety of modernity. A further contrast is with countries in which states use forced labour, which might be considered to be a more authoritarian variety of modernity.

The complexity of the intersection of the policies concerned with trafficking/modern slavery, and with migration and the sex trade, illuminates the need to consider intersecting regimes of inequality. Policies mitigating class inequalities are not sufficient to address the intersections with other inequalities, including those linked to gender and migrant status. This requires addressing coloniality and gender regimes in addition to capitalism and class.

The targeted and proportionate use of criminal justice at the apex of the trafficking chain currently insufficiently addresses the impunity of offenders. It requires the filling of legislative gaps, including for the movement and hiding of illegal profits, and more effective law enforcement involving the police in cooperation with other agencies whose concern is the well-being of the victims. Criminal justice aimed at traffickers can be entangled with policies on migration and the sex trade (when the selling of sex is criminalized as in the US, but is not in Europe), so varies between countries.

Human rights

'Human rights' is a principle of justice that informs international and national legal instruments and policies to eradicate trafficking/modern slavery. At the international level, it undergirds claims for freedom of association, for specialized services for victims, and for gender equality.

Human rights machinery

The most powerful statement of human rights is the UN Universal Declaration of Human Rights (UN 1948). In the UN these principles are given effect in the activities of the UN Office of the High Commissioner for Human Rights (2011, 2023), the Human Rights Council, and UN Special Rapporteurs as well as more broadly across the UN system. The UN Special Rapporteur on Contemporary Forms of Slavery (2023) (Bhoola and Panaccione 2016) and UN Special Rapporteur on Trafficking in Persons (2023) gather data, research, and information about specific instances, and provide annual reports, which are reviewed by the UN General Assembly. There are regional bodies, including the Council of Europe and its associated court, the European Court of Human Rights, and monitoring agencies (GRETA 2019; Council of Europe 2023).

The human rights framing of policy on trafficking/modern slavery is different from those based on sustainable development and on security. The focus is on every individual, who is entitled to rights as a human being, whether a refugee, asylum seeker, or otherwise fleeing war, disaster, and persecution. The aim is that there is 'no one left behind'.

While 'human rights' is rhetorically strong, it is institutionally weak. In recent UN developments concerning trafficking/modern slavery, the human rights project has formed alliances with others, including development and security/crime. It is the stronger for it.

The principle of human rights frames claims for a range of practical policies. These include the freedom of association, to form organizations in civil society, including trade unions. These collective efforts can be considered to draw from principles of human rights.

The ILO/Walk Free/IOM frame the issue in this way:

> Respect for the freedoms of workers to associate and to bargain collectively is indispensable to a world free from forced labour. These

fundamental labour rights enable workers to exert a collective voice to defend their shared interests and to bargain collectively for secure and decent work, thus creating workplaces that are inimical to forced labour and workers who are resilient to its risks. These rights are essential prerequisites for social dialogue, which in turn is critical to building lasting, consensus-based solutions to the challenge of forced labour. Currently, workers in much of the world, and the majority of workers in the informal economy – migrants as well as nationals – lack a representative and collective voice. (ILO, Walk Free, and IOM 2022: 6)

Specialized services

Specialized services are provided to victims of trafficking who are registered with the authorities. These services for registered victims are mandated at a global level by the UN 2000 Palermo Protocol and supported by entities at UN and regional levels. Implementation at national level, however, is uneven in several regards.

Registered victims of trafficking should receive specified services, according to the UN 2000 Palermo Protocol and further developed in regional legal instruments such as those of the Organization for Security and Cooperation (OSCE) (2004), Council of Europe Convention (2005), the EU 2011 Anti-Trafficking Directive, the EU 2021 Strategy for Eradicating Trafficking, and the national legislation of states. The Palermo Protocol Article 6 specifies that these services include information on the legal process, assistance with the legal process concerning the prosecution of offenders, appropriate housing, counselling, medical, psychological, and material assistance, employment, educational and training opportunities, and compensation. These should take account of special needs of the victim, including those concerning their age and gender. There are some services that must be provided, and some that states should consider providing. The 2005 Council of Europe Convention on Action against Trafficking in Human Beings developed a more detailed account of the services to be provided by its 47 Member States, including that they should take account of principles concerning human rights, gender mainstreaming, and be child-sensitive (Article 5.3).

The National Referral Mechanism (NRM) was introduced to improve and standardize the procedure for the identification of victims of trafficking, so that they could be assisted and receive their entitlements. The purpose of the NRM was to identity, refer, and to make sure the rights of victims were protected (Silkner 2008). The concept was introduced by the Organization for Security and Cooperation (2004) in 2004. It included a significant role for non-governmental organizations. The EU mandated the mechanism for its Member States, intending there to be a clear pathway to look after victims.

Although the provision of some services is a legal duty on states, their practical provision has often involved civil society bodies (Hoff 2011), including NGOs, trade unions, and diasporic organizations (Heiss and Kelley 2017). This is sometimes to fill a gap in state activities, and, sometimes in collaboration with state entities, such as the police, to support victims of trafficking who might be vulnerable witnesses (Walby et al 2016a).

These services for victims are unevenly provided by states. Challenges in the delivery of these services have been found in studies around the world (Lazzarino et al 2022), including the US (Romero et al 2023), Australia (George et al 2017; Raby et al 2023), Malaysia (Abdul 2023), Ghana (Balfour et al 2022), and in statistics collected by the European Commission (2018a, 2020) about the use of these services by registered victims in EU Member States. These challenges include the functioning of the NRM, the identification of victims, the length of time of support, the treatment of children, and the treatment of migrants.

There is concern over the working of the NRM. Only a tiny proportion of victims in the population are registered with the authorities (see Chapter 4). Effective identification and registration form a necessary gateway to access specialized services. The UNODC (2023: vi) reports that most victims are 'self-rescued', in that more escape and reach authorities by their own actions (41%) than by the initial action by law enforcement (28%), by those of the community or strangers (11%), victims' families (10%), or by other institutions or civil society (9%). There is concern over the process of identification and referral into the NRM system, with variations related to the nature of the case in the UK (O'Brien et al 2022). There are efforts to improve its working, for example in the UK reforms were piloted and evaluated (Ellis et al 2017), and a recommendation to lengthen the period of support and to move to needs-based support (Roberts 2018). Identification of victims appears more likely in environments where international instruments are upheld (Young and Chua 2023).

There has been concern over services for child victims of trafficking (O'Connell Davidson 2011; Donger and Bhabha 2018; Rafferty 2021). For example, there was a problem of fragmentation between the several agencies that needed to cooperate (Harvey et al 2015). There have been attempts to develop special child-sensitive practices, and to appoint 'children's guardians' to support unaccompanied children (Fundamental Rights Agency 2022), though these have been variably addressed across EU Member States (Walby et al 2016a: 62; Palmer 2019).

There is concern over access to the NRM and associated specialized services, especially for migrants. Victims of trafficking/modern slavery may prefer to stay in the country in which they have been victimized, but national state rules on immigration may block this preference. There is concern about the extent, conditions, and harms of forced repatriation of victims (Aradau 2008; O'Connell Davidson 2015; UK Home Affairs Select Committee 2023). The NRM process is particularly challenging during asylum processes (GRETA 2015). The International Organization for Migration (2007), an organization closely linked to the UN, assists states in the process of repatriation of victims of trafficking to their countries of origin and develops practices and protocols to minimize and mitigate the harms. The Global Compact for Safe, Orderly and Regular Migration, endorsed by a Resolution of the UN General Assembly (2019a), provides principles and practices to improve the situation of migrants, while recognizing the authority of national states to determine their own borders. Nevertheless, the forced deportation of victims of trafficking/modern slavery who do not have documented citizenship is a focus of substantial concern (Chuang 2021; Fudge 2023). Further, there are risks of re-trafficking in the so-called 'rescues' of migrant victims returned to situations of vulnerability (Lindquist 2013a; Donger and Bhabha 2018; Paasche et al 2018), which are potentially greater where countries of origin have not signed or sufficiently implemented the UN Protocol (Balfour et al 2022).

The specialized services provided to registered victims of trafficking/ modern slavery offer important mitigations to the harms they have suffered but are accessed by a small proportion of all victims, and the identification and registration process in the NRM can be entwined with processes of forced deportation of migrant victims.

Gender equality

Gender inequality increases the situations of vulnerability to trafficking/ modern slavery, especially to trafficking for sexual exploitation and to forced marriage, which disproportionately concern women and girls (see data in Chapter 4). Hence, multiple policy bodies, including the UN General Assembly, UNODC, ILO, and UN Women, suggest that reducing gender inequality is likely to reduce trafficking/modern slavery.

Variations in gender regimes, in modernity, shape the context for policy development (Walby 2020, 2023a; Gottfried et al 2023). The removal of sex discrimination in the economy and of exceptions to access to welfare and social protection are more likely in more democratic societies, especially in social democratic forms of public gender regimes (Shire and Walby 2020).

Policies for gender equality range across all institutional domains and include: economy (livelihood, economic and financial autonomy, equal pay and conditions); violence (ending violence); polity (laws, discrimination, inheritance, representation); and, civil society (beliefs, education). The policies include removing discrimination in pay, access to employment, inheritance, and political representation. Policies to remove discriminatory bans on women's access to independent livelihoods, to education, and to female property ownership are likely to reduce trafficking/modern slavery (UN Women 2021; ILO, Walk Free, and IOM 2022) including forced marriage (UN OHCHR 2014). Discriminatory bans on owning property can increase vulnerability to trafficking/modern slavery, since in some locations and economic sectors, ownership of assets, such as agricultural land, is significant for the capacity to access an autonomous livelihood and resist coercion (Panda and Agarwal 2005). The gender equality policies in SDG5 are all relevant to reducing the trafficking/modern slavery of women and girls.

Conclusion

Criticisms of anti-trafficking policy have sometimes interpreted it as narrow, carceral, and a distraction from more strategic policy issues concerning economic exploitation and migration policy. However, this chapter shows that anti-trafficking policy goes well beyond a concern with criminal justice, and that recent developments include a full spectrum of interventions across multiple sites. However, there remain weaknesses in addressing the profit-taking that drives trafficking/modern slavery, and in removing the exclusions from welfare and democratic participation of women and migrants that create situations of vulnerability. Anti-trafficking policy is most effective when deployed across numerous legal and regulatory fields, spanning sustainable development, economic regulation, and democratic reforms, as well as criminal justice.

This chapter has shown that multiple policies reduce (or increase) trafficking/modern slavery across the whole of government and the whole of society. In each policy area, there are ongoing debates as to potential reforms, in the context of differences in strategic priorities between the multiple policy actors. There can be tension between policies on economic development, security, and human rights, and a tension between different strategies to achieve goals. A focus on the top of the trafficking chain, including profit-taking, is relevant to further developing effective policy. The resources to stop trafficking/modern slavery are often limited by prioritization of other policy goals in the context of multiple regimes of inequality (capitalism, coloniality, and gender).

There are numerous active sites of discussion of improvement of policies. These are a summary of the emerging recommendations. Strategies for policy reform have been proposed by several bodies, including the UNODC, ILO/ Walk Free/IOM, the US, and the EU, and are being debated, developed, and implemented, albeit unevenly, concerning areas in the economy, security, civil society, and polity. China is developing its own approach, stating that it is building on international as well as its own policy pathways.

In the economy, issues concern the overall strategy, global financial investment, industrial policy, business policy, supply chains, employment regulation, welfare provision, migration, and discrimination.

Policy for development that encompasses the full range of the Sustainable Development Goals (SDGs), and explicitly includes ending trafficking/ modern slavery, is the preferred approach, overtaking the previous focus on increasing Gross Domestic Product. This includes placing conditions on global financial investment to ensure it is in alignment with the SDGs. There are developments in this direction from the World Bank Group, though there are concerns about whether financial investment by private investors and by the Chinese state meets these standards. Increasing financial transparency – for example, eliminating tax havens and secrecy jurisdictions, and keeping public registers of property ownership and beneficiaries of trusts – would make it easier to stop corruption and money laundering at the top of the trafficking chain.

There is consideration of industrial policy. This includes the regulation of profit-taking by businesses. It also includes implementing the ban on developing a commercial trade in organs.

There is understanding of the need to increase the responsibility of companies to remove coercion from their supply chains, and debates as to how this might be implemented. This regulates their processes of profit-taking. It includes increasing transparent reporting by businesses and devising appropriate sanctions for those that do not, using appropriate bodies of law (company law, financial liability, criminal law), and extending regulations developed for the offline world to the online world, as part of the regulation of digital services.

There is ongoing discussion of the regulation of businesses in areas that generate situations of vulnerability – for example, the recruitment industry in relation to migrants, and third-party profit-taking from the sale of sex – and extending to the online world those regulations applied to the offline world, for example, criminalizing profit-taking from websites facilitating the sale of sex.

Policies to address informal and unregulated employment include reversing tendencies to deregulate employment, with its growth of precarious employment and bogus self-employment, avoidance of labour rights and social protections, and deepening processes of licensing and inspection to maintain standards for labour, health and safety.

Policies to improve the resilience of potential victims include removing exclusions from the provision of welfare, including those for women, minorities and migrants. These include reducing the use of tied visas, the implementation of the UN Global Compact on Migration, and removing discrimination against women and minorities in the economy, both in employment and in inheritance. Opening pathways for migrant victims to regularize their migration status in the destinations where they experience exploitation would both support prosecutions and improve the situations of vulnerability that make migrants available for exploitation.

In security, there are developments concerning the UN Security Council, migration, and the targeted and proportionate criminalization of trafficking/ modern slavery. This involves strengthening the UN capacity to broker peace and regulate conflict zones, to prevent war, to shorten and mitigate periods of conflict, and to mitigate the vulnerabilities of migrants fleeing war. It includes the proportionate and targeted application of criminal and other forms of justice, without discrimination against women, minorities, and migrants. This includes the criminalization of the knowing or reckless use of the services of a trafficked person, and – again – the extension of regulations developed for the offline world to the online world (such as, criminalizing profit-taking from websites that facilitate the sale of sex). It also includes ensuring that victims of trafficking/modern slavery are not criminalized for the activities they did when controlled by traffickers.

In the area of human rights and civil society, there is development of policy for the provision of humanitarian assistance, specialized victim services, regularization of migration status, removing discrimination, promoting gender equality, and supporting research. This involves providing adequately funded specialized victim services to ensure victims are given services to mitigate harms and to restore lives, whatever their migration status.

More generally, policies are needed to reduce the situations of vulnerability associated with migration and to implement the Global Compact, to remove discrimination against women, minorities and migrants, to eliminate gender inequality in employment and inheritance, to promote gender equality across economy, violence, polity, and civil society, and to support research and the improved collection of data.

In the polity itself, there are issues in ensuring free associations and deepening democracy, to ensure free associations in civil society (including trade unions), to facilitate resilience and resistance, and to contribute to democratic debate.

A significant difference in strategy towards policy to reduce trafficking/ modern slavery is between a focus on the regulation of the economy (including profit-taking and the provision of welfare) as a preventative approach and a focus on the use of the criminal justice system and state coercion as a mainly reactive approach. This is aligned with the wider context of the varieties of modernity. The more democratic varieties tend to make greater use of economic regulation to prevent trafficking/modern slavery rather than the more carceral forms of state response after it has taken place. These policy practices are shaped by histories of regimes of inequality.

6

Sexual Exploitation

Introduction

Trafficking for purposes of sexual exploitation operates as profit-driven chains at the intersection of coercion, the economy, and multiple regimes of inequality. The sex trade is the industrial context for coerced sexual exploitation. The sex trade is based on the commodification of bodies for sexual services and the commercialization of the exchange of sex for money. Not all persons who sell sex are coerced and trafficked, nor are they all women and girls. Sexual exploitation is the largest single form of trafficking/modern slavery, according to UNODC data. This is a gendered form of trafficking/modern slavery: more than 90% of the registered victims of trafficking for sexual exploitation are women and girls; while three-quarters of trafficked women and girls are coerced in sexual exploitation (Chapter 4). The situations of vulnerability enabling trafficking for sexual exploitation are deeply rooted in how gender inequalities intersect with legacies of coloniality and migration status.

Debates about trafficking/modern slavery in sexual exploitation are entangled in debates about the sex trade These have tended to over-simplify and over-polarize into abolition (criminalize) or empowerment (decriminalize) (O'Connell Davidson 1998, 2015; Jeffreys 2008). A more nuanced approach is developed here. As shown in Chapter 3, anti-trafficking law in the UN Palermo Protocol (UN 2000a) criminalizes coercion in the sex trade (pimping, forced prostitution, the sexual exploitation of children and youth under age 18). The criminalization of violence and coercion in the sex trade is nearly universal. The Palermo Protocol, however, goes beyond the criminalization of coercion to mandate that states prevent trafficking and protect victims. States do so through a myriad of civil laws to regulate the economy and to provide welfare and specialized services (Chapter 5). The balance between criminal sanctions and regulation/ welfare differs broadly along the varieties of modernity: the more social democratic countries providing the most economic regulation and welfare as compared with the more security-oriented approach of the neoliberal and authoritarian regimes. As shown in the following, the attempt to abolish the sex trade through criminal law (as, for example, in the US) deviates from the norm internationally. The questions for more social democratic modernities are whether persons selling sex are empowered through civil legal regulations of the economy, such as industrial policy, business and employment regulations, and whether victims are protected in ways that reduce situations of vulnerability.

States vary in their balance of security (criminal law) and regulation/welfare (civil law, social protection) to prevent trafficking for sexual exploitation. There are multiple sites at which states can regulate the causes of trafficking/ modern slavery in relation to the sex trade. It is not as simple as criminalize or decriminalize. Some parts of the sex trade may be criminalized while others are not. As part of industrial policy, polities may attempt to reduce or eliminate the sex trade entirely, or they may instead regulate businesses and employment relations. As part of welfare, states may include all people, or leave minorities, migrants, and women unprotected. Drawing on the concept of trafficking chains, relations of sexual exploitation and other forms of trafficking/modern slavery are understood as multi-sided (Figure 1.1). States vary in whether they attempt to regulate selling, buying, or profit-taking from sex. These different approaches are the source of significant variations in outcomes.

Can trafficking/modern slavery be eliminated from the sex trade by economic regulation rather than by criminalization? The question is addressed empirically with the example of Germany, which has pursued the economic regulatory approach, justified by the anticipation that this will empower persons selling sex. This chapter analyses the development of the multiple legal and policy instruments that Germany has mobilized to attempt to remove coercion from the sex trade, while still allowing it to be a profitable business. The German practices are compared with other countries that also do not criminalize the sale of sex but regulate the trade differently (Sweden and Great Britain) and one that criminalizes all aspects of the sex trade (the US).

Studies, terms, and concepts

There are a range of terms in this field, including sex trade, sex work, selling sex, prostitution, persons in prostitution, and persons who are prostituted. A person who is trafficked should not be described as 'selling sex' since their sexual services are being sold. The use of one term or another is sometimes held to position the speaker/writer within a specific framework, theoretical position, or political stance. Here, the attempt is to use the most neutral and technical terms available to contribute to the debate in a scientific manner. However, if an article or law uses a particular term, it will also be used here. In practice, this means the preferred use of 'selling sex' and the 'sex trade', while following German legislative practice of referring to prostitution as an economic activity and sellers of sex as persons active in prostitution. Prostitution has been defined as 'the exchange of sex or sexual services for money or other material benefits ... as a social institution which allows certain powers of command over one person's body to be exercised by another' (O'Connell Davidson 1998: 9).

Within the sex trade, the location of the boundary that makes some activities legal and others illegal for purposes of sexual exploitation is contested. The definition of trafficking in law is centred on coercion, but much analysis of regulating the sex trade centres on harm or consent rather than coercion.

Barry (1979, 1995) focuses on harm. The extent of harm is widely recognized (Sanders 2004; Sanders et al 2017). Many of the attempts to regulate the sex trade have focused on reducing harm to the people selling sex. O'Connell Davidson (2015) focuses on consent. While it is common for criminal law to give a privileged position to consent, this is not the case for the UN Palermo Protocol on trafficking. Jennings et al (2020) consider that coercion and consent can coexist in trafficking/modern slavery. Others (Du Bois 1998 [1935]; Bales 1999; Brass 2016) have given more emphasis to coercion in their analyses.

The question here concerns trafficking/modern slavery. Hence, the focus is on the coercion that is core to the definition of trafficking/modern slavery. It does not focus on either harm or consent. In the legal definition of trafficking, consent is irrelevant. The UN 2000 Palermo Protocol Article 3(b) states:

> The consent of a victim of trafficking in persons to the intended exploitation set forth in subparagraph (a) of this article shall be irrelevant where any of the means set forth in paragraph (a) have been used.

Coercion is the focus of the definition of trafficking in the UN 2000 Palermo Protocol, as at Article 3(a):

> 'Trafficking in persons' shall mean the recruitment, transportation, transfer, harbouring or receipt of persons, by means of the threat or use of force or other forms of coercion, of abduction, of fraud, of deception, of the abuse of power or of a position of vulnerability or of the giving or receiving of payments or benefits to achieve the consent of a person having control over another person, for the purpose of exploitation. Exploitation shall include, at a minimum, the exploitation of the prostitution of others or of other forms of sexual exploitation, forced labour or services, slavery or practices similar to slavery, servitude or the removal of organs.

The issue for trafficking is whether the legal and policy interventions reduce the coercion of those in the sex trade. There is research on global comparisons of prostitution and trafficking as to whether more prostitution means more trafficking (Danailova-Trainor and Besler 2006) and whether legalizing prostitution correlates with more trafficking (Jakobsson and Kotsadam 2013, 2016; Cho et al 2013). Jakobsson and Kotsadam find sufficient evidence to conclude 'that the trafficking of women for commercial sexual exploitation is least prevalent in countries where prostitution is illegal, most prevalent in countries where prostitution is legalised, and in between in those countries where prostitution is legal but procuring is illegal' (2016: 468). This has been subject to debate (Weitzer 2015). There are data challenges. The data on the extent and nature of prostitution and on its regulation are not well developed (Matolcsi et al 2021). Ideally, the analysis of the impact of regulating the sex trade on trafficking would be investigated using data on changes in the sex trade, its regulation, and the amount of trafficking for purposes of sexual exploitation. These are addressed here in relation to evidence on changes in Germany.

There are multiple bodies of relevant law, not only criminal law. Some assume that the use of law usually means the use of criminal law (LeBaron 2020a; O'Connell Davidson 2015). Analyses will, for example, refer to criminalizing or decriminalizing trafficking, without referring to non-criminal law. This underestimates the range of bodies of law available, which contain multiple forms of non-criminal, civil law (Ayers and Braithwaite 1992; Kelly et al 2009; Van Daele 2015; Matthews 2018). The UN 2000 Palermo Protocol mandates use of several bodies of law and policy to counter trafficking. It is not restricted to criminal law. In this analysis, multiple bodies of law are distinguished. As a shorthand, a dichotomy is sometimes made between criminal and non-criminal civil law. The further, finer-grained, distinctions are made within the category of non-criminal, civil law, where several bodies of law are relevant. In addition, welfare is also considered to be a body of law. All the areas of policy addressed in Chapter 5, and in this chapter, have become or are rooted, ultimately, in a body of law.

Regulations operate on the global as well as national and local levels. Coercion and force in the sex trade is prohibited globally; the sex trade is criminalized and regulated in various ways (selling, buying, profit-taking) and localities may enact further restrictions based on public order and public health (banning street prostitution).

Regulations

The sex trade is often treated as a single entity for regulation – either as something to be abolished or decriminalized. The concept of trafficking chains brings all sides of transactions into focus. When applied to coerced

Figure 6.1: Trafficking for purposes of sexual exploitation

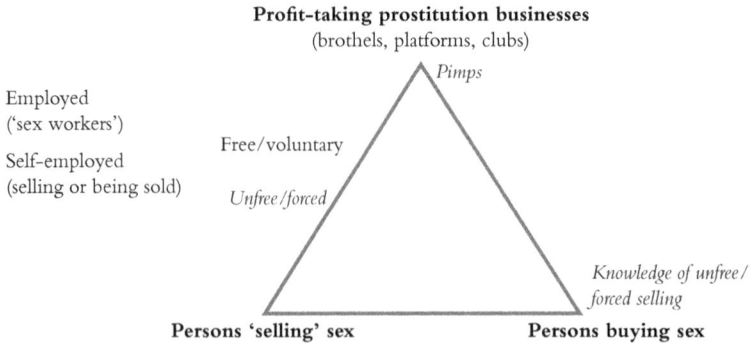

Profit-taking prostitution businesses
(brothels, platforms, clubs)

Pimps

Employed
('sex workers')

Self-employed
(selling or being sold)

Free/voluntary

Unfree/forced

*Knowledge of unfree/
forced selling*

Persons 'selling' sex   **Persons buying sex**

sexual exploitation in the sex trade, the concept of trafficking chains illuminates profit-taking, a dimension that is rarely addressed in policy debates more narrowly focused on whether sellers or buyers are criminalized or not.

Figure 6.1 illustrates the three sides of transactions from which profits are extracted either legally or illegally in relation to how regulations aim to eliminate sexual exploitation: selling; buying; and in prostitution businesses, that is, the person, group or entity, organizing and taking profits from the sale of sex to clients. There is great variation however, in what is criminalized, and how legal dimensions of the sex trade are regulated. A trafficking chain is less likely to arise where transactions are purely bilateral without third-party profit-takers. In such cases, the top of the triangle in Figure 6.1 would not exist at all.

Figure 6.1 includes both variations in what may be legalized in the sex trade, and the practices that are explicitly criminalized through anti-trafficking (italicized text in Figure 6.1). Anti-trafficking law for over a century has criminalized pimps on the side of profit-taking and forced prostitution (on the side of selling sex in Figure 6.1) (League of Nations 1921, 1933; UN 1949; 1956). Thus a distinction is made between forced prostitution and voluntary prostitution. In the EU on the buying side, the 2011 Anti-Trafficking Directive suggests that Member States criminalize the knowing use of persons forced to sell sex (italicized text in Figure 6.1). Figure 6.1 includes further regulatory complexities in the sex trade: whether sellers of sex are employed and covered by employment and labour protections, as implied by the term 'sex worker', or, as is far more usual, self-employed, and thus not generally covered by labour standards or social protections. A further complexity concerns whether the self-employed sell sex to clients directly (in a bilateral relation) or are being sold as illustrated in the triangle with prostitution businesses brokering the sale of sex. These further distinctions within the sex trade are discussed in the following for the German and other European regulatory approaches.

Anti-trafficking law, but also other laws aim at either prohibiting or regulating the sex trade, and are variously directed at sellers, buyers and/ or profit-takers. These other legal instruments include both criminal and non-criminal laws, and are variously implemented by the police, criminal justice system, civil legal system, administrative authorities, state and non-governmental welfare agencies, and civil society organizations. The US, UK, Sweden, and Germany exemplify variations in the attempts to eliminate sexual exploitation from the sex trade.

Regulating the sex trade in the US, Great Britain, Sweden, and Germany

The US, Great Britain, Sweden, and Germany all criminalize coercion and violence by prohibiting pimping and forced prostitution in any form. It is also criminal to engage children (defined as under 18 years in most countries) in the sex trade. The similarities between these cases, however, end here.

The US is very different in criminalizing all components of prostitution, force/coercion, profit-taking by third parties, selling sex, and buying sex, as well as sex trafficking. There are limited exceptions to the criminalization of the selling of sex, for example, the city of Las Vegas, and one state – Maine – where, since 2023, buying, but not selling is criminalized. There is little provision of welfare towards those criminalized for selling sex. Whether in situations of vulnerability or not, sellers are subject to prosecution and, if migrants, deportation. There is, however, specialized welfare for identified victims of trafficking for purposes of sexual exploitation, as mandated by the UN Palermo Protocol.

In Europe, selling sex is legal. This is the major difference to the US. Those selling sex or being sold are not criminalized. However, in most countries or municipalities, street prostitution is restricted. Several countries (Sweden, Finland, France, Iceland, Ireland, Norway, and Spain) criminalize buying sex, but in most of the EU this is legal.

In the case of Sweden, both the profit-taker and the purchaser are criminalized, while the seller is not. Buying sex is, however, considered a misdemeanour and treated in a manner similar to a road traffic offence. The policy goal is to suppress the sex trade because it is seen as incompatible with gender equality, which is an important political priority. The suppression of the sex trade is also intended and expected to reduce trafficking in human beings for purposes of sexual exploitation. There is substantial provision of welfare, but only for citizens, so migrants have little access (Askola 2007; Yttergen 2012; Bucken-Knapp et al 2012; Turner 2013).

In Great Britain (England, Wales and Scotland) profit-taking from the organization or operation of the sale of sex is criminalized. The criminalization of profit-taking by third parties to prostitution has long existed. This legal practice was consolidated in the mid-20th century during the liberalization of the regulation of selling sex (UK Parliament 1957) and remains today (UK 2003). Individuals can sell sex and buy sex without criminal or other legal sanction in Great Britain. The purchase of sex was made illegal in Northern Ireland (part of the UK, but not Great Britain) in 2015.

In Germany (and Austria, the Netherlands, and Switzerland), like elsewhere, coercion is illegal, but all sides of the sex trade are legal: selling, buying, and profit-taking. The sale of sex is treated as an occupation. Rarely, however, do brothels or other places of prostitution assume the role of employers, and rarely are sellers of sexual services employees. Estimates in Germany are that 70–80% of persons selling sex are 'solo self-employed' (BMFSFJ 2007) who, under German law, are not covered by labour standards, are not wage workers, and do not benefit from social insurance for employees, to which employers are mandated to contribute. In most countries, self-employed people bear all of the economic and social risks of their economic activities themselves. Brothel owners typically rent space, at rates well above normal rental prices, to persons selling sex. Brothel owners also typically provide other services to clients for fees (alcohol, food). Thus, brothel owners and persons selling sex are in a renter-tenant, not an employment relation. The employment relation implied by the term 'sex worker' is the basis for the claim that legalization 'empowers' those selling sex. In fact, they are better classified as precarious and bogusly self-employed (Apitzsch et al 2015). The four patterns of regulation of the sex trade are summarized in Table 6.1.

The abolition approach is practised in the US. Policy variations in Europe, and the debates that inform them tend to revolve around the Swedish case, often referred to as the 'Nordic model' of criminalizing buyers, versus the legalization of the trade in Germany, often referred to as empowerment of those selling sex. From the perspective of trafficking chains, however, the important variation is whether policies criminalize profit-taking by third parties. Both Sweden and Great Britain do so, Germany does not.

Table 6.1: Patterns of regulation in the sex trade

	Sides of the sex trade which are legal (yes or no)			
	Force/coercion	Profit-taking	Selling	Buying
US	No	No	No	No
Great Britain	No	No	Yes	Yes
Sweden	No	No	Yes	No
Germany	No	Yes	Yes	Yes

German practices and developments

The German case offers an opportunity to explore the claim that legalization is a pathway to preventing coerced sexual exploitation, unlike in Sweden where this is done by removing demand, but also unlike in Great Britain (and Sweden) where this is done by removing profit-taking.

Germany formally legalized prostitution in 2001 with the 'Law to Regulate the Legal Relations of Prostitutes' referred to as the 'Prostitution Law' (BGB 2001). This law did little except legalize prostitution. The assumption behind the 2001 law was that persons in prostitution would gain legal rights, for example, to claim wages and seek redress in labour courts.

A major reform of this law in 2016 was tied to Germany's transposition of the 2011 EU Anti-Trafficking Directive. On 11 October 2016, the German parliament passed the 'Law for Improving the Fight against Human Trafficking' (BGB 2016b) to bring Germany in line with EU law, then ten days later, the 'Law for Protecting Persons Engaged in Prostitution' (BGB 2016a). Why this was necessary is the subject of this section.

In Germany, the criminalization of the use of coercion against persons in prostitution, and, for a short time, also of profit-taking (defined as deriving economic advantage from prostitution), both preceded the development of the civil legal regulation of the sex trade. Selling sex was never criminalized per se in Germany, though it was defined in law as an immoral act of taking advantage of another person (BGB 2002). The first explicit mention of trafficking for purposes of sexual exploitation in the criminal code was in 1973, when a code originally criminalizing the use of coercion to force a person into any form of fornication was revised into a code defining and criminalizing human trafficking, which at that time was synonymous with trafficking for purposes of sexual exploitation (that is, other forms of exploitation were not considered, StGB 1973). The 1973 code defines trafficking as the use of violence, coercion, or cunning to lead a person into prostituting themselves, and explicitly defines the 'exploitation of vulnerability' as a criminal act (*Ausnutzung der Hilflosigheit*) in relation to a person being in a foreign country. This focus on foreign persons selling sex was reiterated in a 1992 reform of this code which defined 'severe human trafficking' as any commercial recruitment of foreign persons into prostitution that takes advantage of their vulnerability as foreigners (StGB 1992).

Two other codes outlawing coercion were reformed in 1998 to outlaw profit-taking. The §180a of the criminal code covered persons 'commercially operating an enterprise within which persons prostitute themselves'. This included both rendering persons prostituting themselves personally or economically dependent and also 'promoting prostitution through measures which go beyond the mere provision of an apartment, lodging or stay and the service connected to this' (translation by Shire, StGB 1998a). The code on pimping (*Zuhälterei*) was similarly extended in 1998 to include any profit-taking, by defining procurement as the promotion or exploitation of a prostitute for purposes of 'deriving an economic advantage (*Vermögensvorteil*), or of promoting the commercial mediation of sex by determining the place, time, extent or any other aspect of the exercise of prostitution or of preventing a person from stopping to prostitute themselves' (StGB 1998b). In sum, the codes criminalized all forms of promoting or procuring the prostitution of others that were either coercive or undertaken for profit. Thus, up until the 2001 law, Germany – like most other countries in Europe – outlawed profit-taking in the sex trade.

The 2001 law legalizing prostitution was claimed to remove the moral stigma of selling sex, and to give sellers legal status, 'empowering' them to claim rights in labour courts, for example, for unpaid wages. The law includes three articles summarized in Table 6.1. The first states that: 'Sex acts undertaken with an agreed upon payment are agreements with a legal standing. The same holds for employment relations of persons for sexual services for a determined time in exchange for payment' (BGB 2001, translation by Shire). The second article established the right of prostitutes to make legal claims in cases when agreed-upon payments were not upheld. The third declared that persons in employment relations in prostitution had full entitlement to make and claim social insurance contributions and benefits.

What went unrecognized, as shown in Table 6.2, was how the legal change led to removal of the codes in criminal law that prohibited profit-taking. In the code covering the promotion of prostitution, the title was changed from 'promotion of prostitution' to 'exploitation of prostitutes'; the section prohibiting promotion beyond facilitation was deleted (StGB 2002); within the section covering pimping (which remained a crime), the prohibition of ongoing profit-taking was deleted (StGB 2001b). These changes were made on the day the Prostitution Law was enacted (1 January 2002), effectively legalizing all forms of third-party profit-taking, while continuing to criminalize coercion in the sex trade.

The growth in the industry since legalization has been enormous, with observers often claiming that Germany has become the 'brothel of Europe' (Klein 2021).

German federal states had the right to ban prostitution for reasons of public order and protection of youth, and to delegate this capacity to local authorities, in a clause introduced into the 1974 German code. Typically, this was used to shut down street prostitution (Walby et al 2016b; EGStGB §297 2022). A new code was introduced into the civil law at the same time as the 2001 Prostitution Law was enacted to permit and encourage federal states to monitor prostitution, and to encourage localities to suppress crimes of pimping and trafficking (EGStGB 2022). The case of Dortmund, a municipality that made strong use of this regulatory possibility, is discussed

Table 6.2: Civil and criminal laws regulating prostitution in Germany, as of 2002

Civil law	Criminal law
Law to regulate legal relations in prostitution (Prostitution Law, ProstG) enacted 1 January 2002 (Bundesgesetzbuch) (BGB 2001) §1 and §2 established that the sex trade was legal form of commerce, and that employment in the sex trade was also a legal status. §3 guaranteed prostitutes in employment relations access to social insurance.	§180 *Förderung sexueller Handlungen Minderjähriger* (Promotion of sexual act of minors) (StGB 2001) Criminalized the prostitution of any persons under 18 years of age (this code was already established, though some detail was taken out in the 2001 version). §180a *Ausbeutung von Prostituierten* (Exploitation of Prostitutes) (StGB 2002) In the 1998 version of the code, the title was 'Promotion of Prostitution'. The 2002 revision changed this to 'Exploitation of Prostitutes' and removed a section criminalizing any actions promoting prostitution beyond the mere facilitation on premises. §181 *Schwerer Menschenhandel* (Severe Human Trafficking) (StGB 1992) Was not changed, thus continuing the criminalization of the exploitation of the vulnerability of others through cunning, coercion, or violence in prostitution. §181a *Zuhälterei* (pimping) 2002 Paragraph 2 in the 1998 code for imprisonment of persons who 'promote the prostitution of another person commercially by mediating sexual intercourse or who maintains a relationship with a person in prostitution beyond a single transaction' was changed in the 2002 revision to the imprisonment of persons 'who restrict the personal or economic freedom of mobility by promoting the commercial prostitution of another person through mediating sexual intercourse and maintaining a relationship with the person beyond a single transaction'.

Note: All translations by Shire

later in this chapter. Since such regulations were voluntary, wide variations existed across the 16 German federal states. The City of Dortmund (discussed in the following) is exemplary in how it made use of commercial law to regulate and monitor the urban sex trade.

The legalization of prostitution in Germany coincided with preparations in the EU to support and adopt the 2000 UN Protocol on trafficking (UN 2000a), a process which began to draw attention to possible links between the sex trade and sexual exploitation. Germany did not seek to reduce demand, in fact, the industry grew. The UN Protocol was important for emphasizing protecting and supporting victims. In Germany, the public imagery of persons in the sex trade was of 'empowered workers' and not victims of sexual exploitation. Yet, most sellers of sex were not in an employment relationship, but self-employed, and thus had no recourse to labour law, labour standards, employees' social insurance, or any of the other benefits of a dependent employment relation. By the mid-2000s in Germany, it had become clear that such solo self-employment was in fact a precarious employment relation (Apitzsch et al 2015).

In 2005, Germany ratified the Palermo Protocol, necessitating again a round of reforms in the German criminal code, this time adding rather than removing clauses. The code outlawing severe human trafficking (StGB §181 2001a) was eliminated, and a new code (StGB §232 2005a) was introduced, outlawing human trafficking for purposes of sexual exploitation, defined as 'the exploitation of a situation of force or vulnerability in relation to being in a foreign country for the purpose of taking up or continuing prostitution'. Thus, again, Germany signalled that trafficking/modern slavery was something relevant for migrants, not for German citizens. A second code was added to outlaw trafficking for purposes of labour exploitation (StGB §23 2005b; BKA 2009).

The ratification of the UN 2000 Palermo Protocol required attention to the status of victims in German law, especially those who were irregular migrants. Laws covering witness protection were extended to 'victim-witnesses' of human trafficking. A 2004 EU Directive required Member States to extend stays of residence to victims to enable prosecutions (Council of Europe 2005). German immigration law was changed to permit residence for persons cooperating with authorities for the duration of criminal proceedings. Yet, as elsewhere, victims without residence permits were subject to deportation at the end of court proceedings (BKA 2009, 49–59).

As noted previously, a new code was introduced in the civil law at the time of the 2001 Prostitution Law to encourage federal states to monitor prostitution, and to encourage localities to suppress crimes of coercion – pimping and trafficking (EGStGB 2022). Ultimately this was delegated to the local level of public administration, where a few regulatory interventions were introduced to prevent coercion, identify, and protect victims of trafficking/modern slavery. The City of Dortmund was among the most active municipalities to do so.

Regulating prostitution in the City of Dortmund

How was the distinction between a legal sector of prostitution and the criminalization of trafficking for purposes of sexual exploitation enforced? How did the status of persons selling sex as solo-self-employed, and their relation to brothel owners as tenants rather than employees, affect the legal sector of prostitution, especially its resilience to crimes of sexual exploitation? Within the German federal system, the responsibility for enforcement was held by the 16 federal states, which varied in their regulation of places of prostitution; within those states that did enact regulations, responsibility fell to the local municipal authorities and police. Some federal states, most notably North Rhine Westphalia (NRW), undertook to facilitate the monitoring of legal commercial prostitution by mobilizing existing commercial laws. The City of Dortmund was one such case.

Dortmund drew on existing laws covering the restaurant and hotel sector to require all commercial prostitution enterprises (bars, brothels, clubs) to register and be licensed (in as far as they served alcohol and food). As discussed in Chapter 5, licensing is a form of commercial law used to control economic activities that may pose a risk to the public or consumers. Places of prostitution typically serve food and alcohol, making it possible to extend licensing and monitoring of bars and restaurants to prostitution establishments. Local ordinances passed by the City of Dortmund required all places of prostitution with three or more persons selling sex to register as a commercial enterprise, and with eight or more such persons to apply for licensing under the regulations governing the restaurant and bar sector (*Gaststättengesetz*). Self-employed prostitutes were encouraged to register their commercial activity (Minzel 2006; Schäfer 2012), but this remained voluntary and without clear benefits. Commercial licensing is enforced in Germany through local authorities in the 'Public Order Office' (*Ordnungsamt*). Thus, licensing brought civil servants in local government into the task of monitoring places of prostitution.

The state of North Rhine Westphalia enacted a new law in the wake of the 2002 legalization permitting law enforcement to monitor and control places of prostitution. The Public Order Office was responsible for commercial law, while the police gained access to control violations concerning pimping and trafficking. A further function, especially after the ratification of the 2000 Palermo Protocol, concerned support for victims identified through public and police monitoring. An innovative practice was developed in the City of Dortmund in which public order officials and the police cooperated with a local non-governmental organization dedicated to supporting persons in prostitution. Monthly inspections of the City's brothels were carried out together. In cases where sellers were identified by inspections as possible victims of trafficking, income and other support rested on their citizenship status and willingness to cooperate with authorities in prosecutions. In some cases, NGOs advised irregular migrants to make claims for income support under asylum laws, while residents could apply for social transfers. In Dortmund, advice about social support and direct services, such as safe houses and legal aid, were not provided by public officials, but by the non-profit NGO, the *Mitternachtsmission* (Midnight Mission), which had long been engaged in supporting victims of trafficking and advocating for the legal rights of persons selling sex.

The local Public Order Office officials, the police, and members of the *Mitternachtsmission* carried out regular inspections of places of prostitution in Dortmund jointly, but each with a specific function – the Public Order Office for compliance with licensing obligations, the police for evidence of crimes of sexual exploitation, and the *Mitternachtsmission* for providing social support for possible victims or persons wishing to exit the sex trade. The Public Order Office and the police were part of the federal state and local municipal budget, while the NGO depended on state grants and charity to fund its operations. In cases where victims of human trafficking were identified, the NGO provided counselling and emergency support, while the Public Order Office and police carried out investigations of places of prostitution and attempted to identify the perpetrators or those aiding them. In the balance of things, criminal prosecution and commercial monitoring were more strongly supported than non-governmental social support.

The study of the City of Dortmund yields insights into the dynamics of legalized profit-taking and business models under the Prostitution Law (Walby et al 2016b). None of the 18 brothels operating in Dortmund in 2015, when interviews were conducted (reported in Walby et al 2016b: 107), directly employed persons selling sex. Local authorities thought this was the case for almost all the 1,500 persons estimated to be selling sex in 2015 in Dortmund. Self-employment status matters for welfare provision, including health and pension provision, since self-employed persons in Germany pay their own social insurance for their health and pensions. Proprietors of brothels and other commercial prostitution enterprises instead acted as landlords renting space to sellers. Thus, the employment status some lawmakers assumed would provide social protections did not exist. Their status as self-employed also meant that persons in prostitution had no recourse to labour and employment rights, since they were not dependently employed. Persons selling sex in the 'legitimate/legal' prostitution sector were tenants paying fees to landlords, not employees. Their 'work' selling sex brought no employment benefits, labour, or social protections. Thus, none of the social costs of selling sex were borne by operators of places of prostitutions, making the sex trade a highly profitable undertaking in Germany.

The expansion eastwards of the EU from 2004 on increased the number of migrants in the German prostitution industry. The proportion of Eastern European persons recruited into prostitution in Germany expanded rapidly.

Reports indicate that 80% of all registered persons selling sex today are not German, and that most are EU citizens from Romania, Bulgaria and Hungary (Statistisches Bundesamt 2020, 2021, 2022). The changes affected the activities of the *Mitternachtmission* and other NGOs providing support to persons in prostitution. Increasingly their activities focused on migrant support activities, and later, as Germany accepted large numbers of refugees, on asylum aid (Walby et al 2016b: 108; KOK 2021).

The increase of persons selling sex who were not German citizens in Dortmund led to new dynamics in the commercial prostitution sector, which made monitoring all but impossible. As a police officer interviewed recounted:

> 'Until a few years ago we almost always met women in brothels whom we knew already and who have worked there for a longer period. At the moment, however, there is something like "traveling prostitution" and more and more women travel through Germany and adjoining countries, for a week in Dortmund, then 10 days in Cologne, then moving on to Frankfurt, then Munich, then Hamburg. So it is more difficult for us to get into contact with them. To establish trustful relations is almost impossible because they are here only for a short time. This makes it more difficult to identify victims of trafficking because a trustful relationship is a necessary condition.' (Interview, Police Prostitution Division Dortmund, 1 April 2015 and 26 June 2015, in Walby 2016b: 109)

Overall, the City of Dortmund became a model for its systematic licensing of places of prostitution, and cooperation developed between local authorities, the police, and NGOs in monitoring prostitution, identifying, and supporting victims. The fact that prostitutes are self-employed rather than directly employed, however, removed the intended extension of labour and employment rights and social insurance, placing them in unprotected and precarious situations. The movement of persons who were not German citizens between commercial establishments further undermined the ability of local officials to monitor effectively.

While the Dortmund case shows how law enforcement, commercial licensing and monitoring, and NGO support services could cooperate to identify victims in the context of legal profit-taking prostitution businesses, the intersectional inequalities that developed with the expansion of the non-German population in prostitution increased rather than mitigated vulnerabilities to exploitation, while challenging capacities for identification and, with this, the legal and welfare support offered to victims of human trafficking. Government and NGOs documented the failure of the law to extend rights and protections to persons in prostitution (SoFFi.K 2005: 55; BMFSFJ 2007; Kavemann 2009; Doelemeyer et al 2010; Kelly et al 2014).

The 2011 EU Anti-Trafficking Directive and the 2016 reform of German prostitution

In 2011, the EU enacted its own Anti-Trafficking Directive to better bring its Member States in alignment with international law on trafficking/modern slavery. The German criminal code was changed significantly in 2016 to transpose the 2011 EU Directive (see Table 6.3). The changes expanded the forms of trafficking, added a specific category of forced prostitution, and, for the first time in German law, criminalized those buyers of sex who do so knowingly from persons forced to prostitute themselves (StGB §232 2016b). A further change in the criminal code removed constitutional rights protecting citizens' private residences and communication from surveillance, allowing police to inspect prostitution for trafficking crimes in private homes for the first time. Trafficking violations potentially involved imprisonment from six months to five years. Violations of forced prostitution could lead to up to ten years of imprisonment. These prison sentences, however, were already available in earlier laws on crimes of sexual exploitation.

Then, days after these changes, a new Prostitution Law was passed acknowledging for the first time since legalization of the sex trade in 2001 the link between the prostitution industry and trafficking, between prostitution and gendered power imbalances, and that 'sex work' was 'not

Table 6.3: Changes in the German criminal code to transpose the EU 2011 Anti-Trafficking Directive

2005: Criminal codes on trafficking for purposes of sexual exploitation	2016: Criminal code changes on trafficking for purposes of sexual exploitation (15 October 2016)
StGB (2005) §232: *Menschenhandel zum Zweck der sexuellen Ausbeutung* (Human trafficking for purposes of sexual exploitation) Criminalizes: persons who traffic, the facilitation of all prostitution of persons under 21, and, all forms of violence and commerce specifically for the purpose of trafficking.	StGB (2016a) §232 *Menschenhandel zum Zweck der sexuellen Ausbeutung* (Human trafficking for purposes of sexual exploitation) The definition of trafficking is extended to 'slavery, servitude, debt bondage or other relations corresponding to these or similar to these'. StGB (2016a) §232a *Strafgesetzbuch (StGB): Zwangsprostitution* (Forced prostitution) Paragraph 6 criminalizes buyers of sex from persons who have been trafficked as defined in §232. Article 5 poses limits on the constitutional rights to secrecy of communications and to the protection of residences.

work like any other' (Bundesgesetzbuch 2016a). Still, the reform assumed that the prostitution industry could operate without coercion. As stated in the preamble to the law, not prostitution itself, but the 'absence of legal standards for prostitution ... enable ... non-transparent and criminogenic structures, making it more difficult to combat trafficking and hinder the implementation of minimum health, work safety and security requirements' (Deutsche Bundestag 2016: 32).

Though called the 'Law to Protect Persons Active in Prostitution', the new law actually included extensive regulations and obligations on commercial prostitution operations, rather than direct protections (like health insurance) for persons in prostitution. The assumption was that regulating the industry would protect persons in it from exploitation. Little of this was new, however. The City of Dortmund had undertaken similar measures under the other laws voluntarily. What was new was that they were now federally mandated. The 2016 Law to Protect Persons Active in Prostitution includes eight parts, most of which regulate commercial establishments (see Table 6.4).

While headlined as a law to protect persons in prostitution, the law emphasizes the regulation, licensing, documentation, and monitoring of commercial operations – of the profit-taking aspect of prostitution. The stated intention of this combination of criminal and civil law is to remove and keep crime out of the economy of the sex trade. The reformed Prostitution Law introduced 49 new obligations on operators of prostitution enterprises, with implications for how they take profits and interact with sellers of sex, and to render operators responsible for preventing forced prostitution, underaged prostitution, and to act on evidence of procurement or trafficking in their operations (Deutsche Bundestag 2016).

The 2016 Prostitution Law integrates prevention of trafficking into civil law by making public officials responsible, during the consultation with persons registering to sell sex, for acting on evidence that such persons are being procured, forced, in a vulnerable position, in a position of economic or personal dependence or exploitation, and for enforcing the ban on selling sex for persons under 18 years of age. The reformed law denies licensing to any person who appears to be unreliable for the role of interacting with persons selling sex, to anyone convicted of a crime in the last five years, or whose business concept fails to rule out exploitation of persons selling sex. The law obliges operators of prostitution businesses to only permit adults (18 years of age and older) to sell sex. It obliges operators to monitor for pimps, or any other evidence of force, exploitation, vulnerability, personal or economic dependence. Operators may only engage sellers who have registered with authorities.

In these ways, the 2016 Prostitution Law makes local officials, consultation services and operators of prostitution businesses responsible for the identification of possible victims, and liable for trafficking crimes under

Table 6.4: German 2016 Law to Protect Persons Active in Prostitution (StGB 2016b)

Part 1
General provisions

§1 Defines the purview of the law to cover the exercise of prostitution by persons 18 years or older, and the operation of commercial prostitution.

§2 Sexual services are defined as sex acts on or before at least one other present person for pay, or the allowing of such acts on oneself for pay. Performances in which no other person is sexually active are not considered sexual services.

Prostitutes are defined as persons providing sexual services.

Operators of commercial prostitution are those who offer the sexual services of at least one person or who provide the space for such services by operating a place of prostitution, a prostitution vehicle, a prostitution event, or the brokering/mediation of prostitution.

Part 2
Prostitutes

§3 Registration obligation with local authorities regardless of whether persons are self-employed or employed.

§4 With proof of official ID with work or residence permission, name, birthdate, citizenship, residence and the place of prostitution. The completion of health checks and consultations specified under §10 (below) are also required. Extensions of registration for persons 21 years of age and above require a yearly health check, for persons under 21, a health check every six months.

§5 Registration is issued within five days if the provisions of §4 are met, and the person is not under 18 years of age, and is not an expectant mother within six weeks of delivery date, or if 21 years of age and above there are no signs of having been procured, exploited or forced, or of pursing prostitution due to helplessness due to being in a foreign country, or due to personal or economic dependence, or of being exploited by a third person.

§6 The registration certificate includes a picture and the information required in §4. A certificate with an alias is possible, with a picture, the alias name, date of birth and other information provided in §4.

§7 The registration requires officials to provide information and consultation. Information is to be provided about the law, the legal exercise of prostitution, and the role of local authorities, about health and social protections including consultations on pregnancy, on sourcing help in emergencies, and about tax and financial obligations, with information provided in a language the prostitute understands.

§8 The consultations must take place in a trustful environment. Recognized consultants may accompany the prostitute, and third parties may also participate if all agree. Translators may also be used if necessary.

§9 If further consultation is deemed necessary in regard to health or social situation, further consultation should be arranged, especially if there is evidence of procurement, force, helplessness, personal or economic dependence, or exploitation, or if in the case of persons under 21, if there is evidence of someone having facilitated their prostitution.

§10 Health consultations mandated yearly, or twice yearly for persons under 21.

§11 If local authorities have evidence of an unregistered person engaging in prostitution, or the failure to complete health checks, they order the registration within a reasonable time. Local authorities can order a person to stop engaging in prostitution if this is justified by the safety of clients or presents a danger or threat to freedom and sexual determination of others, to protect youth, or in cases where this is a disturbance to the public.

Table 6.4: German 2016 Law to Protect Persons Active in Prostitution (StGB 2016b) (continued)

Part 3

Permission for operating commercial prostitution

§12 requires licensing by local authorities (§13 allows licensing through a representative). The terms of the license can be limited, and subject to extension application. The license covers a specific place or form of prostitution, with a specific business concept, for a specific building structure or facility. Licenses for prostitution events also require a business concept and are either one-time or multiple. Prostitution vehicles also require business concepts and are for a specific vehicle with a specific interior, for a maximum of 3 years, with the possibility to extend.

§14 Licensing is not permitted for persons under 18 years of age, and may be denied if the authorities believe the person or their representative not to be reliable enough to operate commercial prostitution, if the business concept in any way violates sexual freedom or suggests exploitation of prostitutes, or if the obligations to prostitution (laid out in §26 below) are not upheld, etc.

§15 Reliability of the person: persons are not considered reliable to operate commercial prostitution if in the past 5 years they have been convicted of a crime, or sexual misdemeanours, proven to have engaged in any form of fraud, violated residence laws, posting laws or black market employment, or have been found guilty of drug use with a prison sentence of at least two years, if a licence to operate commercial prostitution has been revoked in the past five years, or if they are a member of an association that has been banned or disbanded. Local authorities are required to obtain police reports and a statement from state police or the state crime office at the operators registered place of residence about the reliability of the operator. In cases where evidence of unreliability is older than five years, the authorities have the right to make individual licensing decisions. The local authorities are required to re-check the reliability of the operator regularly, no later than after three years.

§16 Outlines the business concept for the facility or event and requires that the operators have measures in place to ensure that sexual services are not provided by persons under 18 years old, or who are victims of trafficking or procurement. Also required are measures to prevent sexually transmitted diseases, to promote the health and safety of prostitutes and their clients.

§17 Allows authorities to place specific obligations on commercial prostitution facilities.

§18 Outlines minimum standards for facilities, to protect prostitutes and youth, including that the rooms used are not visible from outside, include an emergency call system, that doors can be opened from inside, that sanitation facilities are plenty, that prostitutes have separate break rooms, private lockers, and that rooms used for prostitution are not at the same time for sleeping or living, with exceptions allowed for prostitution in private residences (further specific rules are laid out for prostitution vehicles in §19 and §21 and prostitution events in §20).

§22, §23 Licenses are rejected if the operations are not taken up within a year, or not continued for a year during licensing, or revoked if any conditions are no longer met.

Part 4

Obligations of commercial operators

§24 Makes operators generally responsible for all matters of safety and health of persons selling sex.

(continued)

Table 6.4: German 2016 Law to Protect Persons Active in Prostitution (StGB 2016b) (continued)

§25 Covers the selection of persons active in prostitution in the commercial operation, and the prohibition of prostitution for persons under 18, under 21 where there is evidence of third parties facilitating the activity, of persons with any indication of force, exploitation, helplessness, personal or economic dependence, or of persons without the required registration. Operators have the power to monitor the registration, including of self-employed. Operators can refuse prostitutes who they deem are unreliable for the activity.

§26 Lays out the obligation of operators to prostitutes, and grants prostitutes the sole right to determine how sexual services will be performed. Any agreements about services performed must be written and provided to the prostitute. Operators are prohibited from collecting excessive profits from rents or mediation of services. Prostitutes have a right to see the business concept, and operators are required to record all payment made by prostitutes to the operators, or by operators to prostitutes.

§27 Operators are obliged to require prostitutes to show their registration and health certifications before engaging in any services.

§28 Operators are required to record the names (or aliases) of prostitutes who are providing services on their premises, including the date of registration validity, health certification, days when the prostitute will be providing services on their premises, and to record any payments, and to provide this information to local authorities on demand, to store it safely on their premises, and to keep the records for two years.

Part 5
Monitoring

§29, §30, §31 Monitoring of commercial prostitution: local authorities have the power to monitor premises, carry out inspections of business spaces during opening times, to access business documents and records, and to control persons at any time, and where necessary, to also do so outside of operating hours, also when the place of prostitution is a private residence, for which constitutional rights to privacy of residences are suspended for this purpose. Inspections are also permitted when local authorities expect the operation of prostitution without a license.

Part 6
Prohibitions and fines

§32 Clients of prostitutes are required to use condoms, and operators are obliged to require so and to inform about this through posted announcements. It is prohibited to advertise or even suggest the possibility of sexual services without condoms or with pregnant persons.

§33 The following are considered misdemeanours: violations of obligations to register prostitution, for failing to register after being ordered to do so, for clients who do not observe the condom use obligation, places of prostitution operating without licenses, or operating against regulations specified in Part 3 on commercial operations, who violate in any way the health and safety requirements on operations specified in Part 4.

Part 7
Personal data and federal statistics

§34 Covers data protection provisions, and §35 the collection of statistics on registration, including rejections, extensions, licensing, and rejections and revocations thereof. Local authorities are required to report to the federal statistical office.

Table 6.4: German 2016 Law to Protect Persons Active in Prostitution (StGB 2016b) (continued)

Part 8
Other
§36, §37 Cover enactment and transitionary measures.
§38 Covers evaluation of the law – the Federal Ministry for Family, Seniors, Women and Youth, which is responsible for the law, is designated to carry out an evaluation based on scientific as well as practice experiences, commencing in July 2022 and submitted to the German parliament by 1 July 2025 at the latest.

Source: BGB 2016a, translations by Shire

civil law. Anti-trafficking is handled in German law as a crime, but also as a business regulation.

Sellers of sex received new obligations to register, to undergo annual health checks (or twice annual, in the case of persons under 21), and were given rights to determine their own services, to have written contracts on services, to have records of payments, and to see the business concepts of the commercial operators where they were active. All of these attempt to compensate for the absence of an employment relation and impose employer-like obligations on operators, but fall short of extending labour standards and social insurance.

Buyers of sex are mentioned in the law as persons deserving of protection, and in their responsibility for observing the obligation to use condoms. However, they are implicated in the revised criminal code on forced prostitution as committing a crime of trafficking if they knowingly buy sex from a victim of trafficking.

The welfare-relevant provision for persons selling sex in the new Prostitution Law covers health checks (but not health care) and consultations provided to registered persons in prostitution. NGOs, under the category of 'expert consultation services' (*Fachberatungsstellen*), are given a role in identifying and supporting victims, thus codifying the role played by the *Mitternachtsmission* in the City of Dortmund and bringing Germany into compliance with the obligation in international law to provide special services to victims. NGOs generally, however, are dependent on renewals of public grants, and remain underfinanced and thus often unable to provide the expert consultation services expected of them (Rabe 2019; KOK 2021).

The law created 33 new tasks for the public administration of the law, most of which were at the local level of government. The projected costs of the new law for commercial operators of prostitution were estimated to be €71.6 million per annum (Deutsche Bundestag 2016: 39). The estimated cost for the government was a one-time cost of €11.3 million (only €33,000 of which would be covered by the national budget, the rest by the federal states) plus an estimated €13.4 million annually for local implementation (Deutsche Bundestag 2016: 49).

The collection of statistics required in Part 7 of the 2016 Prostitution Law (see Table 6.4) provides the basis for some assessment of how successful the regulations have been in marshalling the prostitution industry behind a barrier of regulation, protection, and prevention. Statistics from 2019 (when reports were available for all federal states, and before the pandemic) give the most reliable insights into implementation so far. Most people selling sex did not register as prostitutes. Taking the conservative estimate of 200,000 persons active in prostitution in Germany, registrations in 2019 covered only 20% of those active (own calculations from Statistisches Bundesamt 2020). Effectively this means that the 80% of persons who were not registering were in violation of the law. Among those not registered are migrants without residence permits, who are unlikely to register due to their illegal status (KOK 2021). Requiring registration creates a new category of illegal prostitution, and double illegality for irregular migrants, exacerbating rather than mitigating vulnerabilities to exploitation.

Situating German developments

Crime statistics on trafficking provide another insight into the effectiveness of the regulation of the prostitution industry for preventing trafficking. Criminal statistics showed very low levels of trafficking prosecutions in Germany under both the 2001/2002 and the 2016/2017 Prostitution Laws. These figures only include victims registered with the police, not victims identified by NGOs that are active in supporting persons in prostitution. The Coordination Organization against Human Trafficking, Germany (KOK), in a report on a consortium of 19 NGOs engaged in victim support in Germany, estimates double the number of identified victims, less than 20% of whom are known to have been identified in crime reports (KOK 2021). The crime statistics and KOK reports both locate most of the registered victims in non-licensed commercial prostitution, in private apartments and homes, and, in the case of the NGO reports (different from the crime statistics), among migrants from West Africa who, unlike EU member state citizens, often have irregular migration status and thus face exacerbated vulnerabilities (BKA 2020, 2021, 2022; KOK 2021). KOK reports 44% of the victims identified by its consortium of NGOs as being from the African continent; the crime statistics report is 5% (KOK 2021: 8; BKA 2022: 9). However, registered persons in prostitution and persons prostituting themselves in licensed brothels and bars are also among those identified by the police and NGOs as victims of trafficking. In 2020, 19% of the victims identified in crime statistics were registered prostitutes, and 22% of all victims were active in brothels and bars, the core of the legal sector (BKA 2022: 11). These statistical reports suggest that the law has not removed crime from the prostitution economy.

There was significant growth in the number of persons selling sex in Germany after the 2001 legalization, from 200,000 in 2002 to 400,000 by 2016 (BBC 2016) with some estimates of the increase as high as one million (Klein 2021). Such a large and growing prostitution industry was not evident in countries where profit-taking from prostitution was not legal. A report by the UK Home Affairs Committee (2016) estimated about 70,000 persons selling sex in Great Britain, with Swedish estimates based on advertisements at a maximum of 7,000 offers, but with much lower estimates of persons selling sex (Mujaj and Netscher 2015). The countries where profit-taking is not legal have less sex trade than Germany. For most of this same period, in Sweden the number of victims of human trafficking for purposes of sexual exploitation was under 50 persons, and the number of persons procuring ranged between 70 and 120 (Walby et al 2016a: Table 5.7, 72). In Sweden, where buying sex is illegal, the number of persons apprehended for buying sex was higher overall, with large yearly swings, which by the 2010s ranged between 500–1,000 (Walby et al 2016a: Table 5.7, 72). In Great Britain, where selling and buying sex is legal, but profit-taking from the sale of sex is illegal, the numbers of presumed victims were higher than in German NGO reports (in 2011–13, between 600 and 1,100), suggesting better enforcement within a much smaller sex trade (Walby et al 2016a: Table 5.8, 73).

Does the extensive regulation of prostitution in civil and criminal law in Germany reduce trafficking for purposes of sexual exploitation? Does the fully legal model have less trafficking than those that prohibit profit-taking?

Germany has a large sex industry, probably the largest in Europe, and is colloquially referred to as the 'brothel of Europe'. In comparison, prostitution appears to be lowest in Sweden, though not eradicated. Better data is required, but based on available evidence, a preliminary assessment of the link between legalized profit-taking and trafficking/modern slavery suggests a relation. The regulations introduced in 2001 and 2016 failed to extend labour rights and general welfare protections to persons in prostitution. The share of persons in prostitution who register is low, and the most vulnerable populations of sellers – migrants without residence permits – cannot register without a risk of deportation. Registered sellers and licensed businesses are estimated well below the actual populations of persons in and places of prostitution. Within the legal sector, new business practices moving persons between brothels evade the monitoring and law enforcement practices in place.

The problems with the sex trade in Germany have led to debates about adopting the 'Nordic model' in Germany, now supported by persons who have exited prostitution (such as Sandra Hucke), a coalition of over 40 movements against legalized prostitution (*Bündnis Nordisches Modell*), the popular feminist magazine *Emma*, and members of the Social Democratic Party of Germany (ASF 2021a, 71), including the current German Minister of Health, Karl Lauterbach. The women's caucus of the Social Democratic Party of Germany remains focused on debates about the Nordic Model rather than the key driving factor of profit-taking (ASF 2021b: 72–4).

Conclusion

Trafficking chains are driven by profits. Trafficking chains profiting from sexual exploitation mainly victimize women. A large share of victims are migrants; an unknown number of victims are irregular migrants, reluctant to report to authorities.

Each link in a trafficking chain has three sides – sellers, buyers, and profit-takers. This structure applies to the operation of prostitution – persons selling sex/being sold, persons buying sex, and businesses transacting the sex trade. Sellers of sex are rarely employees of brothels, but self-employed. Brothels are rarely their employers but provide facilities and services for fees. Law regulates the sex trade in one or more of these three dimensions. Coercion, in the form of pimping and forced prostitution, and the prostitution of children are criminalized nearly universally.

The regulation of the sex trade varies in whether and, if so, which sides of the sex trade are criminalized or legalized or regulated using non-criminal laws and policies.

The US deviates in its criminalization of all three sides of the sex trade. The consequence is that persons selling sex, whether they are in situations of vulnerability or not, are criminalized.

Regulations of the sex trade in Europe do not criminalize the sale of sex. Polities vary in the extent to which they offer welfare services to persons in situations of vulnerability who sell sex. Anti-trafficking law requires all countries to do so, when those selling sex are identified as victims of trafficking/modern slavery. Extensive public provision of welfare guarantees that women and other disadvantaged groups will have choices other than selling sex for livelihoods. Development policies – especially those directed towards including equity with sustainable forms of economic growth – potentially reduce the sex trade, including migration into this sector.

The most important regulatory variation from the perspective of anti-trafficking concerns profit-taking in prostitution. The criminalization of all third parties taking profits from the sex trade prevents its growth as an industrial sector. This is the policy pathway of most European states, but they pursue this in one of two ways.

The first, characteristic of Great Britain, is the direct criminalization of third parties and of profit-taking from the prostitution of others. The sex trade is prevented from growing as an industrial sector, but it is not removed from the economy. Selling and buying sex are tolerated when enacted between private individuals.

The second pathway to criminalizing profit-taking is characteristic of Sweden and often referred to as the Nordic model. Sweden criminalizes buying and profit-taking, and does so as part of gender equality policy. Usually however, only the criminalization of buying is associated with the Nordic model; this misunderstands the breadth of its policy interventions, including welfare and criminalizing profit-taking.

The main contrast within Europe is between states that criminalize versus those that legalize profit-taking. Germany is the largest EU Member State legalizing profit-taking. Prostitution in Germany is an industrial sector, the size of which is reported annually in statistics on enterprises and persons. Prostitution is regulated extensively through commercial law, as are persons in prostitution. Coerced sexual exploitation in prostitution is illegal under criminal law. Multiple bodies of law implemented at different levels of public administration regulate prostitution. In public discourses, prostitution law is often associated with the empowerment of 'sex workers'. Persons selling sex in Germany, however, are mainly self-employed and thus not covered by employment law and labour standards. Access to health checks and social consultations is contingent on registering as sellers in the sex trade. Evidence suggests high rates of non-compliance, meaning even these protections are not available. Business regulations impose extensive obligations on commercial prostitution services, including those that take place in private residences. The statistics on licensed businesses suggest that a large segment of the industry does not comply. It is probably the case that most profits are taken in the unlicensed settings of the sex trade, such as in private homes, and facilitated through platforms.

This chapter has examined the different policy pathways in the prevention of trafficking/modern slavery for purposes of sexual exploitation in relation to prostitution as an industry. All the countries examined have fully criminalized coercion in the sex trade. The US diverges from Europe by criminalizing the sex trade altogether. The main variation is the criminalization of profit-taking. The question in anti-trafficking policy is not whether to criminalize, but what to criminalize and in doing so, how to balance criminal justice with other policy fields that can make trafficking/modern slavery as business models less profitable.

7

Conclusion

Introduction

Trafficking/modern slavery is a single field with multiple sub-types. Trafficking chains are structures of exploitation, legal and illegal, localized and global, that exist to generate profits from the exploitation of the vulnerabilities of others. The theory of trafficking/modern slavery developed in this book identifies the root causes of trafficking/modern slavery in systems of inequality and coercion, encompassing the whole of society and differing across varieties of modernity. Multiple regimes of inequality are relevant in how trafficking chains emerge and operate: colonialism and gender as well as capitalism. The 'whole of society' is implicated in trafficking/modern slavery, spanning the institutional domains of economy, violence, polity, and civil society. The 'whole of government' is needed to address policy adequately. The extent and operation of trafficking/modern slavery differs in varieties of modernity: social democratic, neoliberal, and authoritarian.

Laws addressing trafficking/modern slavery have been built cumulatively over two centuries, with multiple legal concepts, including but not limited to crime. While global in scope, laws are unevenly implemented in national and regional contexts.

Data on trafficking/modern slavery includes the UN SDG Indicator on trafficking, which sets productive standards for a measurement framework. The trafficking/modern slavery of women, and of trafficking/modern slavery for purposes of sexual exploitation are underestimated in the estimates by ILO/Walk Free/IOM. An improvement lies in integrating data from the UNODC.

Policy fields for ending trafficking/modern slavery build on anti-trafficking law and evidence, encompassing all institutional domains. Policy pathways span the promotion of sustainable development, deepening democratic institutions, industrial policy, business and employment relations, welfare including special services for victims, security, and criminal justice. While trafficking/modern slavery is a crime, criminal justice is not enough to prevent it and protect its victims. A strategically important policy pathway is the prevention of third-party profit-taking from multi-sided transactions, with a focus on the top of the trafficking chain.

This comprehensive approach to informing policy to end trafficking/modern slavery directs attention not only to fighting crime, itself important, but also to mitigating the inequalities that generate and exacerbate situations of vulnerability upon which profit-taking and exploitation in trafficking chains prey. The complexities of a comprehensive approach are demonstrated in the comparative analysis of the regulation of prostitution: the industry producing the most registered victims, and the largest concentrations of women, including significant shares of migrant women.

This book contributes to scientific knowledge about the root causes, structures, and policies to end trafficking/modern slavery, and the forms of modernity where this is possible. It aims to move beyond polarized debates, as on the sex trade, and single-discipline concerns with one dimension (economy or crime), with an analytical focus on root causes and comprehensive solutions to advance knowledge and inform action. Where research proceeds in siloed disciplines, the knowledge generated remains too narrow. This book develops a comprehensive and multidisciplinary approach to generating knowledge and informing policy.

The following conclusions are offered.

On 'what is it?' There is a single field of trafficking/modern slavery, with multiple sub-types. The concept of trafficking chain with multi-sided transactions is developed.

The 'root causes' lie in systems of inequality and lack of democracy. Multiple regimes of inequality are relevant, colonialism and gender as well as capitalism. The analysis concerns the 'whole of society' analysis, including institutional domains of economy, violence, polity, and civil society. Trafficking/modern slavery exists to different extents and forms in different varieties of modernity – social democratic, neoliberal, and authoritarian.

On 'law', a single field of trafficking/modern slavery has been built cumulatively over two centuries, with multiple legal concepts – not solely that of criminality – which, while global in scope, are uneven in their national and regional implementation.

On 'data', the UN SDG Indicator on trafficking is a productive setter of standards for a measurement framework. There is an underestimation of the amount of trafficking/modern slavery against women and for sexual exploitation in the estimates by ILO/Walk Free/IOM; this can be remedied by integrating data from the UNODC.

On 'policies', the 'whole of government' approach to comprehensive policy development is the way forward. A narrow carceral approach is not inevitable. A key policy is the prevention of third-party profit-taking from multi-sided transactions, with a focus on the top of the trafficking chain.

On 'trafficking for sexual exploitation', a comprehensive approach is the way forward. The German approach that reduced restrictions on the taking of profits from the sex trade has not reduced trafficking/modern slavery. The differences between the US and the EU should not be underestimated.

On 'disciplines', multiple disciplines are contributing to the analysis as well as the building of an interdisciplinary field.

What is it?

Trafficking/modern slavery is the control of another person for the purpose of exploitation. It is coercion to extract a material benefit. Consent is not relevant. The legal definition has developed over time, building on the ending of chattel slavery to encompass practices similar to slavery, including trafficking in human beings (Chapter 3). The most recent international legal instrument is the UN Palermo Protocol of 2000 (UN 2000a) which provides the following definition:

> 'Trafficking in persons' shall mean the recruitment, transportation, transfer, harbouring or receipt of persons, by means of the threat or use of force or other forms of coercion, of abduction, of fraud, of deception, of the abuse of power or of a position of vulnerability or of the giving or receiving of payments or benefits to achieve the consent of a person having control over another person, for the purpose of exploitation. Exploitation shall include, at a minimum, the exploitation of the prostitution of others or other forms of sexual exploitation, forced labour or services, slavery or practices similar to slavery, servitude or the removal of organs.

Trafficking/modern slavery is a single field. There are sub-types. The debates on priority categories for the sub-types are complex because they stem from the accumulation of multiple legal instruments following two path-dependent traditions: first, forced labour (ILO 1930) and practices similar to slavery (UN 1956), of which the ILO is 'guardian'; and second, trafficking (UN 2000a), of which the UNODC is guardian (Chapter 3). The earlier forced labour tradition includes categories of forced labour, subdivided into state and private commercial, with commercial subdivided into labour and sexual; further additional categories are of state forced labour and forced marriage. The later trafficking tradition has categories of trafficking for purposes subdivided into labour, sexual, and other (within which is trafficking for organs, forced begging, and forced marriages, and potentially more), with little visibility for forced marriage and state forced labour, though they are not definitionally excluded (Chapter 4).

There has been some movement towards integrating these two traditions, and to giving precedence to the categories embedded in the later legislation, but legacies of the first tradition are still significant. This has implications for the collection and presentation of quantitative data (Chapter 4). This move towards integration and the further steps to advance it is embraced here. This means: treating as equivalent trafficking for labour exploitation and private commercial forced labour; treating as equivalent trafficking for sexual exploitation and private (forced) commercial sexual exploitation; using the category of state forced labour; using the category of forced marriage (rather than treating it as a sub-set of 'other' forms of trafficking); using the category of 'other' forms of trafficking to encompass that for organs, forced begging, and further miscellaneous forms. These categories are treated as parallel rather than as hierarchically nested: trafficking for labour exploitation (private commercial forced labour); trafficking for sexual exploitation (private commercial (forced) sexual exploitation); state forced labour; forced marriage; trafficking for other purposes, including organs. This merges the various fragments and traditions into a single field of trafficking/modern slavery.

The concept of third-party profit-taking from multi-sided transactions in trafficking chains is developed to cover the commercial forms of trafficking/modern slavery (but not the less frequently monetized forms of forced marriage or state forced labour).

Trafficking/modern slavery is not a market, even when monetized. The person being exploited does not have agency because of the coercion, thereby contradicting concepts of markets as voluntary exchanges. Profit is taken by third parties from these multi-sided transactions in which the victim is treated as if they were an object for sale. This is represented visually as a triangle (see Figure 1.1, Chapter 1).

The concept of 'trafficking chains' is developed to capture the links between multiple connected processes from recruitment to movement to procuring the sale of a service, which can make up trafficking/modern slavery. This builds on earlier concepts of commodity chains, supply chains, and care chains, which recognize that there are multiple points of profit-taking along the way (Chapters 1 and 2).

Root causes

The root causes of trafficking/modern slavery are to be found in inequality, lack of democracy, and war. They are based in social systems, not a few bad individuals. Trafficking/modern slavery is rooted in regimes of inequality, of capital, coloniality, and gender across the institutional domains of economy, violence, polity, and civil society, which result in varied patterns of modernity (social democratic, neoliberal, authoritarian). Understanding the root causes of trafficking/modern slavery requires a whole of society approach.

Trafficking/modern slavery varies over time and place: it is not inevitable. It is shaped by resilience and resistance, negotiation and struggle, projects

· to deepen democracy and oppose war. Trafficking/modern slavery
likely where there is more inequality, corruption, and war, and less
 ̤iy where there is a greater depth of democracy (Chapter 2).

Regimes of inequality

Trafficking/modern slavery is caused not just by inequality in general, but
specific forms – capitalism, coloniality, and gender – each interconnected
and mutually shaping, but not reducible to, each other. Addressing the logic
and practice of capitalism is not enough; this also requires understanding
coloniality, both past and present, and gender regimes, as follows:

- Capitalism: The class relations of inequality are central to capitalism. The
  extraction of profit is the purpose of trafficking/modern slavery. These
  profits accrue to the traffickers, so trafficking/modern slavery benefits
  the criminal minority who illegally obtain material benefits rather
  than capitalism as a whole. However, the opportunity for this criminal
  exploitation is made possible by wider systems of political economy that
  generate situations of vulnerability and opportunities for exploitation.
  Variation in these forms of regulation of the economy affect the extent
  and nature of trafficking/modern slavery. Trafficking/modern slavery is
  not a form of primitive accumulation that speeds capitalist development,
  but a detriment to economic growth and to sustainable development by
  its diversion of human resources, and damage to human beings.
- Coloniality: The legacies and contemporary forms of coloniality have
  implications for situations of vulnerability, as they shape access to
  citizenship, by migration status, ethnicity and minoritization. Victims
  of trafficking/modern slavery are often migrants from lower-income
  regions of the world (Chapter 4). The legacies of empire, conquest
  and war continue to reverberate through patterns of migration and the
  extraction of resources from the Global South. This is associated with
  mobility from lower income to higher income countries, to flight from
  violence and war, from disaster and famine. Migration may be driven by
  situations of vulnerability in countries of origin and migration processes
  and visa statuses can generate situations of vulnerability and exclusion in
  countries of destination. These inequalities are linked to historic global
  processes, as well as to contemporary wars.
- Gender regimes: Gender relations are shaped in a variety of gender regimes
  of inequality. The majority of victims of trafficking/modern slavery are
  female; they are especially found in trafficking for purposes of sexual
  exploitation and in forced marriage (Chapter 4). These are areas of activity
  that concern gendered livelihoods; and they are poorly regulated. There
  are differences as to the best approach to the regulation of the sex trade

to suppress coercion within it. There has been experimentation with different forms of regulation in different world regions, and within Europe. The variety of gender regime in which interventions are proposed makes a difference not only to the prospects of success for the policy but also for the nature and goals of the feminist project engaging with the issue.

Institutional domains

Trafficking/modern slavery is constituted across the whole of society – in the institutional domains of economy, violence, polity, and civil society. It is not only a matter of exploitation in the economy, nor only a crime of coercion, but much more besides.

- Economy: Situations of vulnerability to trafficking/modern slavery are shaped by the availability of livelihoods and decent work. Economic inequalities generate situations of vulnerability that can be exploited and lead to trafficking/modern slavery. Exploitation takes place along trafficking chains, which can stretch around the world. Migration flows from lower to higher income countries can generate situations of vulnerability. Poor regulation of employment, business, and financial investment increases the risk of coercion (Chapter 5). In turn, economic growth and sustainable development are detrimentally affected by trafficking/modern slavery. The coercion/violence of trafficking/modern slavery is a detriment to the economy; a cost (see Chapter 4); a detriment to both economic growth and to sustainable development by diverting resources. Unfree labour may generate profits for a few but does not assist development (Chapter 2).
- Violence and coercion: Trafficking/modern slavery is defined by the relationship between coercion and the economy. Coercion is core to trafficking/modern slavery. Violence and coercion are more frequently found in neoliberal and especially authoritarian varieties of modernity (Chapter 2). Violence/coercion shapes society as well as society shaping violence/coercion. This relationship is two-way: violence/coercion is an outcome of inequalities in the economy, polity, and civil society, and, in turn, it shapes these institutional domains.
- Polity: The polity is important for the regulation and governance of trafficking/modern slavery both directly and indirectly, taking different forms in different varieties of modernity. Law has been developing at an international level for over two centuries, outlawing the slave trade, the institution of slavery, practices similar to slavery, and trafficking, in response to pressure from global civil society and anti-slavery states (Chapter 3). There are multiple bodies of relevant law and supporting policy (Chapters 3, 5 and 6): criminal and non-criminal, of employment, of business, of capital, and of the complex relations between them; the

criminal is only one of these (Chapters 3, 5 and 6). While some forms of law and policy act to reduce trafficking and modern slavery, other changes in policies, including the deregulation of the economy, increase the potential for exploitation (see Chapters 5 and 6). Further, colonial polities use forced labour in pursuit of their goals. Polities act at multiple scales: while states were thought to have national sovereignty over issues of law and order, the global level is very important.

- Civil society: Global civil society is important in developments on trafficking/modern slavery, shaping what counts as 'common sense', and contributing to hegemonic positions. Global civil society, including global feminism, has been important in opposition to the slave trade, slavery, and trafficking, contributing to the development of international law and UN action (Chapter 3). However, there are also examples of racist, White supremacist opposition to emancipation from slavery and practices similar to slavery. Civil society is an important site of the generation of knowledge, expertise and data in universities and NGOs. Trafficking/modern slavery affects civil society, since it removes people from their capacity to act freely and form associations. There are multiple causal pathways connecting civil society and trafficking/modern slavery in both directions.

Anti-anti-trafficking critiques assume that anti-trafficking is carceral. The analysis of law and policies shows that anti-trafficking law, as established in the UN Palermo Protocol, is not carceral, but to be effective requires a comprehensive approach – including, but not limited to, criminal justice – to end profit-taking, exploitation and situations of vulnerability, involving sustainable growth and development, a broad range of economic regulations (industrial, business, employment, welfare) and deep democracies.

Varieties of modernity

Modernization has not ended trafficking/modern slavery. Rather than a single unilinear pattern of development of modernity, there are multiple modernities. There are different amounts and forms of trafficking/modern slavery associated with different varieties of modernity. In the social democratic variety, which has the most democracy and least inequalities, there is the least trafficking/modern slavery. In the authoritarian variety, which has the least democracy and the most inequalities, there is the most, including state forced labour and forced marriage. In the neoliberal variety, there is thin democracy, and high levels of inequality, but state forced labour and forced marriage are rare (Chapters 2 and 4). These varieties of modernity are gendered, with distinct variations in varieties of gender regime. The depth of democracy is key to the historical development of these differences.

Systems and society

Trafficking/modern slavery structures and is structured by the complex systems that constitute society. Each of these regimes and institutional domains is a system, affected by the other systems, each taking all the other systems as its environment. The multiple systems that make up society generate trafficking/modern slavery, and trafficking/modern slavery shapes the social systems that make up society. For example, violence and coercion are not only the outcome of economic inequalities, but also shape the nature of the economy, making it less productive, less likely to grow, and less likely to achieve sustainable development. This complexity has implications for policies that try to intervene to prevent trafficking/modern slavery. While a policy may have a direct and proportionate effect, there can be perverse effects resulting from unexpected outcomes on related systems. Trafficking/ modern slavery is best understood as a system in society.

Any theory of society needs to be able to encompass trafficking/ modern slavery. Coercion is core to the definition of trafficking/modern slavery. Violence and coercion are more important in shaping society than is recognized in most social theory, especially in political economy. Addressing the neglect of coercion in social theory is part of the challenge of demonstrating the significance of trafficking/modern slavery for theories of society. It is not only that multiple regimes of inequality generate trafficking/ modern slavery, but that trafficking/modern slavery shapes the nature of our society.

Law

Trafficking in human beings/modern slavery is a single field of law and practice, despite the multiplicity of terms. It builds on a long tradition of development of international legal instruments to combat and prevent slavery and related practices. It culminated in the 2000 UN Palermo Protocol that builds on and advances this development, extending its reach and significance. It concerns not only law to criminalize individual traffickers, but also further bodies of law to mitigate the harm to victims, and to engage in preventative actions in relation to organizations and institutions. This is a global development, challenging traditional notions of national states as sovereign on issues of law and order. The interpretation and implementation of the laws varies between global regions and countries. The most effective interventions invoke the full range of laws, not only criminal prosecutions of individuals, including regulation and governance of major institutions.

Trafficking/modern slavery is a single field of law that makes it illegal under international law to control another person for the purpose of exploitation. The legal instruments share common features, though there are differences in terminology and content, and they have been growing in reach and significance for more than 200 years. The most developed international legal definition of trafficking is in the UN 2000 Protocol on trafficking, which includes the exploitation of the vulnerability of others, and which extends the reach of the law into institutions beyond individuals.

This builds on a long history of many international legal instruments intended to stop slavery and related practices, from the 1814 Treaty of Paris onwards (see Legal Instruments). These include: 1926 Convention to Suppress the Slave Trade and Slavery; 1930 Convention Concerning Forced and Compulsory Labour; 1956 Supplementary Convention on Abolition of Slavery, the Slave Trade and Institutions and Practices Similar to Slavery; 1998 Rome Statute of the International Criminal Court; and the 2000 UN Palermo Protocol to Prevent, Suppress and Punish Trafficking in Persons, especially Women and Children, Supplementing the UN Convention against Transnational Organized Crime.

These legal instruments have been transposed into the laws of national states, sometimes mediated by the actions of regional entities such as the European Union and the Council of Europe, with some variations between states. The interpretation of the legal concepts and their implementation varies between countries.

The different legal concepts in these international instruments, while in some ways surpassed as international law has developed, nonetheless, leave legacies in organizations, shaping their activities and priorities. This can be seen in the activities of the ILO and UNODC (Chapters 4 and 5). These legacies are path-dependent developments of policy and data associated with each of these institutionally rooted legal concepts. All the legal concepts continue to be relevant, since they shape how specific actors mobilize within their remits, and they are differently mobilized in key analytic texts that theorize the relationship between trafficking/modern slavery and society.

The Palermo Protocol mandates the use of a range of forms of law and policy, including criminal and non-criminal law, economic governance, and welfare development across multiple sites and relationships. The balance between these forms of intervention, in particular, between security (including criminal justice), economic regulation, and welfare has been contested, and varies by state and region. All are relevant. Best practice in the use of criminal law includes its proportionate and targeted use. The analysis of changes in the regulation of the sex trade to reduce trafficking for purposes of sexual exploitation (Chapter 6) investigated the implications of different mixes of law and policy. The non-criminalization of the sale of sex while criminalizing third-party profit-taking from the sale of sex was found to be consistent with less exploitation than the models that either criminalized or decriminalized all relations involved. The focus on regulating institutions and practices rather than on individuals was important.

In the authoritarian variety of modernity, the state is not only relatively absent in preventing trafficking/modern slavery, but conducts forced labour itself, often of minorities. This is often associated with colonial regimes, in which there is war, conquest, empire and imperialism. The peoples defeated in war are vulnerable to trafficking/modern slavery both by the actions of the state, and as an indirect consequence of the situations of vulnerability generated by fleeing war.

The law has global effects, even though national and regional interpretation and implementation vary. This challenges notions that national states have effective sovereignty as well as legal sovereignty on issues of law and order. The international legal instruments are the outcome of the actions of global civil society and global capital as well as of states in negotiation with international institutions over more than two centuries.

Data

Women and migrants are disproportionately the victims of trafficking/human slavery, according to the estimates that have been recently developed. The selection of key numerical indicators shapes not only data but the wider field, because the categories and implied priorities are then encoded in the practices of institutions that seek to address them. The UN has become a powerful platform for indicators that have wide reverberations through policy and academic communities. The measurement framework for trafficking/modern slavery and the programme of research for its development are currently fluid, with competing alternatives. The devising and adoption of the UN SDG Indicator 16.2.2 – the 'number of victims of human trafficking per 100,000 population, by sex, age and form of exploitation' – is already shaping the field, bringing greater cooperation between UN agencies and states to deliver statistics. No dataset is yet able to deliver the information needed for the comparisons of countries over time. There is tremendous rapid ongoing development of the field of measuring trafficking/modern slavery.

According to the ILO, Walk Free, and IOM (2022), there are almost 50 million victims of modern slavery, amounting to 0.64% of the world's population. This includes 27.6 million in forced labour and 22 million in forced marriages. Females are more likely than males to be in modern slavery. Forced labour is three times as common among migrant (1.4%) than non-migrant (0.4%) adult workers. These estimates are based on population surveys in specific countries on forced labour and forced marriage, supplemented by administrative data on the ratio of labour and sexual exploitation, expert judgement, and statistical modelling. As argued in Chapter 4, the choice of the source of the administrative data, IOM/CTDC rather than UNODC, has led to an underestimation of the extent of trafficking/modern slavery of women and of sexual exploitation; this can be remedied by substituting data from the more representative UNODC. The integration of UNODC data increases the proportion of female victims and proportion of trafficking for purposes of sexual exploitation in the global estimates.

There were 49,032 detected victims of trafficking in the world in 2018, according to UNODC (2021: 25). Of these, 50% were trafficked for sexual exploitation, 38% for labour exploitation, and 12% for other exploitation. Females were 65% of these victims (46% women, 19% girls, 20% men, 15% boys). This information comes from the records of the authorities with whom the victims were registered and does not include any victims who were not registered.

There were 9,429 persons investigated, suspected, or arrested for trafficking, 7,368 persons prosecuted, and 3,553 persons convicted for trafficking in 2018, according to the UNODC (2021: 39–40). The administrative data for victims and traffickers concerns those who are registered with the authorities and is not an estimate of the number of victims or traffickers in the population, since most of these will not be in contact with the authorities.

A very small proportion of victims are registered with the authorities. There are around 50,000 victims registered with the authorities (UNODC 2021) and around 50 million victims in the population (ILO, Walk Free, and IOM 2022). The ratio of victims registered with the authorities to victims estimated in the population is 1:1,000. Around one in a thousand victims of trafficking are registered with the authorities for assistance.

The method of data collection and presentation shapes and is shaped by the different concepts used to describe sub-types of trafficking/modern slavery. Data is collected from surveys, administrative sources, and expert judgement informed by secondary sources. Surveys have been used for forced labour (trafficking for labour exploitation) and for forced marriage (trafficking for other exploitation), but not for forced commercial exploitation (trafficking for sexual exploitation) and state forced labour. Administrative data has been used for trafficking for labour, sexual, and other exploitation (including forced marriage), but not for state forced labour, and is acknowledged to underestimate forced marriage. Expert judgement informed by secondary sources has been used for state forced labour. Statistical techniques are used to fill gaps, ranging from simple extrapolation to complex modelling. The estimates produced by UNODC use administrative data concerning all registered victims in the world. The estimates produced by IOM use administrative data concerning the sub-set of registered victims that the IOM has assisted for purposes of migration and repatriation, so excluding those trafficked within a country and those trafficked outside a country that did not use IOM services. The estimates produced by ILO/Walk Free/IOM use all four methods. The estimates from ILO/Walk Free/IOM are more comprehensive in the range of categories of trafficking/modern slavery and aim to be a population estimate. The ILO/Walk Free/IOM estimates would be improved through use of the UNODC rather than IOM ratio of labour to sexual exploitation, since this is a more comprehensive dataset on registered victims. Using the UNODC data, the revised estimates indicate higher proportions of women, higher rates of sexual exploitation, and higher numbers of victims overall.

The estimates of trafficking/modern slavery are subject to debate and development. It needs a programme of development, to include, for example: collecting enough data through regular repeated high-quality surveys to make reliable estimates for each country over time; and, review and improvement of the methods of collecting and reporting administrative data on registered victims, which are currently used to estimate the extent of trafficking for sexual exploitation based on the ratio with labour exploitation. The publication of the existing raw data from surveys (such as those conducted by Walk Free) would aid these debates by enabling the normal scientific processes of peer review, investigation, and replication. There are legacies of earlier traditions in the categories used in data collected and presented today; over time, a move towards updated consistent categories is expected. This move would be faster if there were greater cooperation between UN entities, including the ILO, UNODC, and UN Women. The development of the UN SDGs has been important in encouraging the development of data and indicators.

Data is being collected on policies in each country. This potentially enables a comparison of the effect of policies on outcomes. There are gaps in this data collection, for example, the number of labour inspectors, and omission of key drivers, such as the depth of democracy, from key models (for example, ILO, Walk Free, and IOM 2022); this could be addressed in future work.

The impact of trafficking/modern slavery on society can be measured using a costing methodology. The cost for each registered victim of trafficking in the EU is €312,756. This is the cost for society for the lifetime of each victim. It provides some indication of the loss to society and economy caused by trafficking/modern slavery, and the implied benefit if it were reduced. This cost estimate for one region of the world could be revised for a global level.

It is important to build on these advances in data to improve the measurement framework that underpins scientific advances in trafficking/modern slavery. It should include the nuanced differentiation to support specific constituencies while focused on a robust unified framework. This requires further work translating between concepts and their operationalization in quantitative data, the coordination to reach agreement at a global level, and the resources to collect the relevant data, consistently, over time.

Policy

This book offers a comprehensive approach to policies to end trafficking/ modern slavery that encompass all of society, regimes of inequalities, and varieties of modernity. The international level of law and policy formation is at the foreground of policy fields and pathways, in shaping the multiple levels of policymaking and implementation. At the most abstract level, the relevant policy fields are strategies for sustainable development, security and justice, and depth of democracy. It includes the engagement of multiple stakeholders in polity, economy, and civil society. The comprehensive approach has principles that are concerned with sustainable development, democracy, international cooperation, the rule of law and due process, human rights, migration, and is gender-responsive, and child-sensitive. It draws on a whole of society approach, with multiple stakeholders aimed at reducing inequalities and increasing the depth of democracy to prevent trafficking/modern slavery.

The international level of policy development is important and builds on international law and the work of several relevant UN entities, including: the United Nations Office on Drugs and Crime (UNODC), the International Labour Organization (ILO), UN Women, UN Security Council, UN Special Rapporteur on Trafficking, UN Special Rapporteur on Contemporary Slavery, UN Women, the Inter-Agency Coordination Group against Trafficking in Persons (ICAT), and the International Organization for Migration (IOM). There are important contributions from regional powers, including the European Union and the US, and from international non-governmental entities, including the Walk Free Foundation, Alliance 8.7, and other anti-trafficking bodies.

There are multiple policy fields where proposals have been made, including the following:

Economic development: the strategy to generate decent livelihoods for all in a manner that is inclusive and sustainable, as indicated in the UN Sustainable Development Goals (SDGs).

Financial investment: to implement the principles of the SDGs in policies for global financial investment, including by the World Bank Group and other global investors.

Industrial policy: reducing (or not encouraging) industries that do not generate decent livelihoods; in relation to the sex trade, the use of sanctions to reduce the scale and riskiness of this industry; in relation to the recruitment industry, banning the taking of fees by recruiters from migrant workers and eliminating or more tightly restricting private fee-charging employment services who sell labour services cross borders.

Supply chains: due diligence in monitoring supply chains supported by sanctions; implementing all labour standards and fundamental labour rights, including rights of association and representation through independent trade unions.

Regulating labour: equal treatment in contracts and all terms of employment through the promotion of decent employment conditions for all, including reducing precarity and recognizing trade unions.

Welfare and social protection: provision of welfare to prevent situations of vulnerability, including income support, health care, and education, without exemptions for migrants, women, and minorities.

Security: reducing wars and conflicts that generate situations of vulnerability; reducing the consequences of war and conflict zones for situations of vulnerability, including for those fleeing such zones.

Migration: reducing the exclusions and vulnerabilities faced by migrants (including undocumented and irregular migrants), such as tied visas, in alignment with the UN Migration Compact.

Criminal justice: implementing the rule of law and due process to ensure that there is justice for all, including women, the minoritized, and migrants; targeted and proportionate criminal justice, focused on the upper levels of trafficking chains, including flows of illicit finance; ensuring that victims are not criminalized.

Human rights: implementing international legal agreements on human rights, including for refugees and asylum seekers, so that they are not compromised by policies on security and migration.

Specialized welfare: provision of all the specialized services mandated by the 2000 Palermo Protocol; speedy and comprehensive identification of victims.

Gender equality: reducing gender gaps in the economy and political participation, ensuring laws on inheritance are gender equal.

Democracy: deepening democracy in the polity and civil society, reducing exclusions of women and minorities including migrants from decision-making at all levels. This includes not only elections, and the proportionate presence of all in the polity, but also a free civil society, with free associations, active trade unions, and journalism.

These policies intervene across all the institutional domains of society – economy, violence, polity, and civil society. They address key aspects of the inequalities associated with migrant status and gender that generate the situations of vulnerability to trafficking/modern slavery. They are global in reach and consequence, even while there are variations at national and regional (US, EU, China) levels associated with varieties of modernity. The different combinations of policies are linked to the variety of modernity. Securitization is associated with neoliberalization. Targeting criminal justice to the top of the trafficking chain and reducing vulnerabilities through regulation and welfare are associated with social democracy. Using forced labour in support of state objectives is associated with authoritarianism.

Sexual exploitation

How and which regulations can best eradicate trafficking/modern slavery is illustrated in the detailed investigation of different policy approaches in the sex trade, and of the industrial context of sexual exploitation. Trafficking chains profiting from sexual exploitation mainly victimize women. A disproportionate share of victims are migrants. Whether and how the sex trade is regulated has implications for situations of vulnerability, the size of the sex trade, and the availability of this industry for criminal organizations to operate within and across borders.

Variations in state actions, in terms of whether the sex trade is prohibited or not, and – if not – what regulations are applied to selling, buying, and profit-taking produce different outcomes for trafficking. Coercion and force, and the procurement of children in the sex trade are criminalized under the UN Palermo Protocol, the sex trade itself is not. A large regulatory divergence is between countries that criminalize prostitution altogether (the US) and countries that legalize selling sex. The decriminalization of selling sex in Europe (including the UK, Germany and Sweden), but not in the US, has been important in facilitating access of victims of trafficking to welfare and justice services.

Yet criminalization or decriminalization is too narrow a lens through which to examine this issue. Other bodies of law, and variations in approaches to criminalize, exist among the European countries that legalize selling sex. In the UK, profit-taking is criminalized but selling and buying is not. The Nordic model criminalizes buying and profit-taking. Germany legalizes all three sides, but with a dense body of business regulations aimed at eradicating coercion from the sex trade and extending rights to those who sell sex.

The most important divergence concerns profit-taking. The UK and Sweden both criminalize profit-taking from the sex trade, while Germany does not. The emphasis in the Nordic model is on policies to promote gender inequality, such as equality in employment and the provision of state welfare, which is understood to reduce violence and coercion of women as well. Criminalizing profit-taking limits the expansion of the sex trade without the use of criminal law. Sweden goes further by criminalizing the purchase of sex. Germany regulates brothels and other places of prostitution, with the aim of eliminating criminal organizations, but a significant segment of businesses, sellers of sex, and buyers do not comply with the legal obligations. As a result, estimates suggest that most of the sex trade operates in a zone of illegality. The outcome is that the scale of prostitution is low in Sweden and, according to various estimates, enormous in Germany. Trafficking/modern slavery, as victim reports indicate, is not eliminated from the segment of prostitution businesses complying with the law in Germany. Evidence on illegal operations is scant but points to the exploitation of some of the most vulnerable groups of irregular migrants.

Criminalization plays an important role in eradicating trafficking for sexual exploitation, but not in the way practised in the US. Policy approaches that criminalize profit-taking have the potential to disrupt trafficking chains by removing profit-taking opportunities from the sex trade. Criminalizing selling sex is likely to exacerbate situations of vulnerability rather than mitigating inequalities. Legalizing selling enables welfare and special services to better prevent victimization, as well as identifying and supporting victims.

Disciplines and a new interdisciplinary field

Trafficking/modern slavery is developing as an interdisciplinary field simultaneously with developments within disciplines, including business/ management studies, criminology, data science/social statistics, economics, gender studies, geography, law, political economy, political science, post-colonial studies, social work, and sociology. Trafficking/modern slavery can be a provocation to traditional disciplines, raising new substantive and theoretical issues that are in tension with orthodoxies, potentially driving forward debates and advances in discipline. There has been much progress and there are many remaining challenges under investigation. These are some examples:

- Business/management studies. This has contributed to the analysis of trafficking chains through developments in the analysis of supply chains, production networks, and value chains. It has contributed analyses of multiple business models that go beyond simple conceptions of markets of supply and demand, to the recruitment industry, multi-sided markets, and platforms. It is challenging to move beyond voluntary compliance of companies to public authority over private authority, to address corruption, the regulation of financial investment, of businesses and of employment, and the infiltration of legal by illegal markets.
- Criminology. This has contributed to the analysis of trafficking/ modern slavery as a crime, addressing the challenges of implementing a transnational legal instrument in the criminal justice system to reduce the impunity of traffickers, including organized crime. The analysis of trafficking/modern slavery is challenging to the tradition in criminological orthodoxy that theorizes inequality as generating crime from the bottom up instead producing a focus, top-down, on the crimes of the powerful. There are challenges progressing the analysis of coercion in the economy.
- Data science/social statistics. There has been very rapid development of data, qualitative, administrative, and survey, together with the Indicator for Trafficking in the UN Sustainable Development Goals, and modelling, though the data remains contested. There are large challenges given the difficulty of obtaining reliably representative data on a phenomenon that is illegal and intrinsically hidden. Extensive work is underway to improve the quality of data, especially of comparative data over time. There needs to be regularly repeated surveys across a wider range of countries to

support the ILO, Walk Free, and IOM (2022) global estimates and the application of the higher quality administrative data from the UNODC (2021) to the Walk Free surveys to improve the accuracy of the global estimates that support the Indicator in the UN SDGs.

- Economics. Trafficking/modern slavery sits at the margins of a discipline that is centred on quantitative datasets and markets. There are contributions to shift in focus from economic growth to sustainable development, and the increasing sophistication of costing analysis. There are challenges to the discipline in the analysis of non-market mechanisms that are hard to quantify, including crime, fraud, corruption, and regulation.
- Gender studies. There have been major contributions to the analysis of the intersection of gender, ethnic, and class relations, and in the regulation of the sex trade to reduce coercion. There are challenges in resolving these debates about the role of harm as compared with agency and in addressing matters at a macro and comparative level.
- Law. There has been much cumulative development of international law, over a long time, using multiple bodies of law, to address trafficking/modern slavery. There are challenges being addressed as to the significance of agency/consent, intention and knowing in the criminalization of coercion.
- Political economy. There have been contributions to the analysis of supply chains, of the relationship between the global and national levels, of the intersection of economy and polity that are relevant to trafficking/modern slavery. There is a remaining challenge to go beyond noting to theorizing issues of coercion, coloniality, and gender.
- Political science. There have been contributions in the analysis of the significance of variations in democracy for trafficking/modern slavery, of the role of global as well as national levels of governance. There are challenges being addressed in analysing the intersection of the political with the rest of society in the shaping of trafficking/modern slavery.
- Post-colonial. There are contributions in the analysis of the legacies of coloniality in unequal global relations, ethnicity, and migration for trafficking/modern slavery. There are remaining challenges being addressed in analysing contemporary as well as historic empires, and in going beyond a focus on culture.
- Security studies. The understanding of the entwining of internal and external relations of security across conventional frontiers is an important contribution of security studies that is relevant to trafficking/modern slavery. The contestation between the human rights agenda and security is central to some important trafficking/modern slavery debates, especially concerning migration. Engaging with the challenge of integrating a gender perspective into security studies is ongoing.
- Social work. The profession of social work and its academic discipline contributes analysis of specialized services being developed to progress

practices of safeguarding and the mitigation of the harms to victim/survivors of trafficking/modern slavery. There are challenges in addressing the needs of survivors of trafficking/modern slavery for purposes of sexual exploitation; such support has sometimes been outsourced to non-governmental agencies.

- Sociology. Theories of society are a key contribution of sociology that aid the situating of analyses of trafficking/modern slavery in a wider context, and an energetic building of new concepts. Key remaining challenges being addressed include the understanding of the macro comparative level, the intersection of multiple inequalities, and the varieties of modernity. Trafficking/modern slavery requires a whole of society approach to its understanding.

The analysis of trafficking/modern slavery is developing in multiple disciplines, as illustrated in this summary of contributions and debates, and as a specific interdisciplinary field in its own right, as illustrated in a set of dedicated journals. Both disciplinary and interdisciplinary developments are productive. Traditional disciplines address new substantive and conceptual issues that stretch and develop their theories. The dedicated interdisciplinary space nurtures its development. The opposition to the concept of modern slavery on the grounds that it inevitably leads to a narrow and carceral analysis has been shown to be misplaced by the breadth of research that has developed.

Conclusion

Trafficking/modern slavery is a consequence and cause of social inequality. A lack of democracy is key to its existence. It is a violation of human rights and a serious crime. It is a detriment to sustainable development and economic growth. It is gendered in its causes and consequences. It is an outcome of coloniality, both legacies and contemporary. Trafficking/modern slavery is rooted in taking profits and material benefits using coercion: the exploitation of the vulnerability of others. Coercion matters for analyses of the economy, but coercion and economy are usually segregated into separate disciplines. Treating trafficking/modern slavery as a single field is an aid to understanding; while nuances do matter, divisions distract from the development of a theory of change, of indicators and data, and of coherent policy. Trafficking/modern slavery is global; it is not confined to either rich or poor parts of the world, while struggles against trafficking/modern slavery have been global over many decades. Trafficking/modern slavery concerns systems, not a few bad individuals. Society causes trafficking. The 'whole of government' and 'whole of society' approaches are needed to end it.

The UN seeks to eliminate trafficking/modern slavery by 2030. This book aims to be a modest contribution to that goal.

Legal Instruments

Bundesgesetzbuch (BGB) (2001) *Gesetz zur Regelung der Rechtsverhältnisse der Prostituierten (Prostitutionsgesetz – ProstG)*, 20 December 2001.

Bundesgesetzbuch (BGB) (2002) *§138 Sittenwidriges Rechtsgeschäft, Wucher*, 1 January 2002.

Bundesgesetzbuch (BGB) (2016a) *Gesetz zum Schutz von in der Prostitution tätigen Personen (Prostituiertenschutzgesetz – ProstSchG)*, 21 October 2016.

Bundesgesetzbuch (BGB) (2016b) *Gesetz zur Verbesserung der Bekämpfung des Menschenhandels und zur Änderung des Bundeszentralregistergesetzes sowie des Achten Buches Sozialgesetzbuch*, 11 October 2016.

Congress of Vienna, 1815.

Council of Europe (2005) *Convention on Action against Trafficking in Human Beings. European Treaty Series No. 197.*

Deutsche Bundestag (2016) *Entwurf eines Gesetzes zu der Regulierung des Prostitutionsgewerbes sowie zum Schutz von in der Prostitution tätigen Personen*. Drucksache 18/8556. Berlin: Deutsche Bundestag

Ergänzungsgesetz Strafgesetzbuch (EGStGB) (2022) §297 *Verbot der Prostitution*, last amended on 11 July 2022.

European Commission (1996) *Directive 96/71/EC Concerning the Posting of Workers in the Framework of the Provision of Services.*

European Commission (1997) *Directive 97/81/EC Concerning the Framework Agreement on Part-time Work Concluded by UNICE, CEEP, and the ETUC – Annex: Framework agreement on part-time work.*

European Commission (1999) *Directive 1999/70/EC Concerning the Framework Agreement on Fixed-term Work Concluded by ETUC, UNICE, and CEEP.*

European Commission (2004) *Directive 2004/81/EC on the Residence Permit Issued to Third-country Nationals who are Victims of Trafficking in Human Beings or who have been the Subject of an Action to Facilitate Illegal Immigration, who Cooperate with the Competent Authorities.*

European Commission (2006) *Directive 2006/54/EC of the European Parliament and of the Council of 5 July 2006 on the Implementation of the Principle of Equal Opportunities and Equal Treatment of Men and Women in Matters of Employment and Occupation.*

European Commission (2008) *Directive 2008/104/EC on Temporary Agency Work.*

European Commission (2011) *Directive 2011/36/EU on Preventing and Combating Trafficking in Human Beings and Protecting its Victims.*

European Commission (2017) *Council Resolution on a Model Agreement for Setting up a Joint Investigation Team (JIT).* 2017/C 18/01.

General Act of the Berlin Conference Regarding Africa, 1885.

General Act of the Brussels Conference Prohibiting the Slave Trade then Slavery, 1890.

International Labour Organization (ILO) (1930) *Convention Concerning Forced and Compulsory Labour* No. 29. Article 2. Geneva: 14th ILC session.

International Labour Organization (ILO) (1933) *ILO Convention 34 – Fee-Charging Employment Agencies.*

International Labour Organization (ILO) (1949) *ILO Convention 96 – Fee-Charging Employment Agencies.*

International Labour Organization (ILO) (1997) *ILO Convention 181– Private Employment Agencies.*

International Labour Organization (ILO) (2014) *Protocol of 2014 to the Forced Labour Convention 1930*, P029.

League of Nations (1921) *International Convention for the Suppression of Traffic in Women and Children.* Geneva.

League of Nations (1926) *Convention to Suppress the Slave trade and Slavery.* Geneva.

League of Nations (1933) *International Convention for the Suppression of Traffic in Women of Full Age.* Geneva.

State of California Department of Justice (2012) *The California Transparency in Supply Chains Act.*

Strafgesetzbuch (StGB) (1973) *§181 Menschenhandel*, 24 November 1973.

Strafgesetzbuch (StGB) (1992) *§181 Schwerer Menschenhandel*, 22 July 1992.

Strafgesetzbuch (StGB) (1998a) *§180a Förderung der Prostitution*, 1 April 1998.

Strafgesetzbuch (StGB) (1998b) *§181a Zuhälterei*, 1 April 1998.

Strafgesetzbuch (StGB) (2001a) *§180a Förderung sexueller Handlungen Minderjähriger*, 1 July 2001.

Strafgesetzbuch (StGB) (2001b) *§181a Zuhälterei*, 1 January 2002.

Strafgesetzbuch (StGB) (2002a) *§180a Ausbeutung von Prostituierten*, 1 January 2002.

Strafgesetzbuch (StGB) (2005a) *§232 Menschenhandel zum Zweck der sexuellen Ausbeutung*, 19 February 2005.

Strafgesetzbuch (StGB) (2005b) §233 Ausbeutung der Arbeitskraft, 19 February 2005.

Strafgesetzbuch (StGB) (2016a) *§232 Menschenhandel zum Zweck der sexuellen Ausbeutung*, 15 October 2016.

Strafgesetzbuch (StGB) (2016b) *§232a Zwangsprostitution*, 15 October 2016.

Treaty between the United States of America and the United Kingdom of Great Britain for the Suppression of the African Slave Trade, 1862.

Treaty of London for the Suppression of the African Slave Trade, 1841.

Treaty of Paris (1814) *First Peace of Paris*, 30 May 1814.

United Kingdom (UK) (2003) *Sexual Offences Act 2003*.

United Kingdom (UK) (2004) *Gangmasters' (Licensing) Act*.

United Kingdom (UK) (2015) *Modern Slavery Act 2015*.

United Nations (UN) (1948) *Universal Declaration of Human Rights*.

United Nations (UN) (1949) *Convention for the Suppression of the Traffic in Persons and of the Exploitation of the Prostitution of Others*, General Assembly Resolution 317 (IV). UN: New York.

United Nations (UN) (1956) *Supplementary Convention on the Abolition of Slavery, the Slave Trade and Institutions and Practices Similar to Slavery*, General Assembly resolution 317 (IV). UN: New York.

United Nations (UN) (1979) *Convention on the Elimination of All Forms of Discrimination against Women*. UN: New York.

United Nations (UN) (1998) *Rome Statute of the International Criminal Court*. UN: Rome.

United Nations (UN) (2000a) *Protocol to Prevent, Suppress and Punish Trafficking in Persons, especially Women and Children, Supplementing the United Nations Convention against Transnational Organized Crime*, 2237 UNTS 391 [also known as the Palermo Protocol].

United Nations (UN) (2000b) *Convention against Transnational Organized Crime*. 2225 UNTS 209. Opened for signature 12 December 2000; entered into force 29 September 2003.

United Nations (UN) (2003) *United Nations Convention against Corruption*.

United Nations Office of the High Commissioner for Human Rights (UN OHCHR) (2014) *International Instruments Concerning Trafficking in Persons*.

United States (US) (2000) *Victims of Trafficking and Violence Protection Act of 2000*.

United States (US) Department of Homeland Security (2022) *Uyghur Forced Labor Prevention Act (Public Law No. 117–78)*.

References

Abbott, Kenneth W., and Snidal, Duncan (1998) 'Why states act through formal international organizations', *The Journal of Conflict Resolution*, 42(1): 3–32.

Abbott, Kenneth W., and Snidal, Duncan (2010) 'International regulation without international government: Improving IO performance through orchestration', *The Review of International Organizations*, 5(3): 315–44.

Abbott, Kenneth W., Green, Jessica F., and Keohane, Robert (2016) 'Organizational ecology and institutional change in global governance', *International Organization*, 70(2): 247–77.

Abdul Hamid, H.B. (2023) 'Shelter homes - safe haven or prison?', *Anti-Trafficking Review*, (20): 111–34.

Al-Dayel, Nadia, Mumford, Andrew, and Bales, Kevin (2022) 'Not yet dead: The establishment and regulation of slavery by the Islamic State', *Studies in Conflict & Terrorism*, 45(11): 929–52.

Allain, Jean (2013) *Slavery in International Law: Of Human Exploitation and Trafficking*. Leiden: Martinus Nijhoff.

Allain, Jean, and Bales, Kevin (2012) 'Slavery and its definition', *Global Dialogue*, 14(2): 1–15.

Ambagtsheer, F. (2021) 'Understanding the challenges to investigating and prosecuting organ trafficking: A comparative analysis of two cases', *Trends in Organised Crime*. https://doi.org/10.1007/s12117-021-09421-2

Amnesty International (2016) *Amnesty International Policy on State Obligations to Respect, Protect and Fulfil the Human Rights of Sex Workers*. POL 30/4062/2016. Available at: https://www.amnesty.org/en/documents/pol30/4062/2016/en/

Anderson, Bridget (2010) 'Migration, immigration controls and the fashioning of precarious workers', *Work, Employment and Society*, 24(2): 300–17.

Anderson, Bridget (2013) *Us and Them? The Dangerous Politics of Migration Control*. Oxford: Oxford University Press.

Anderson, Bridget (2014a) 'Nation building: Domestic labour and immigration controls in the UK', in Bridget Anderson and Isabel Shutes (eds), *Migration and Care Labour: Theory, Policy and Politics*. Houndmills: Palgrave Macmillan.

Anderson, Bridget (2014b) 'Trafficking', in Elena Fiddian-Qasmiyeh, Gil Loescher, Katy Long and Nando Sigona (eds), *The Oxford Handbook of Refugee and Forced Migration Studies* , Oxford: Oxford University Press, pp 355–66.

Anderson, Bridget (2015) 'Migrant domestic workers: Good workers, poor slaves, new connections', *Social Politics*, 22(4): 636–52.

Anderson, Bridget, and O'Connell Davidson, Julia (2003) *Is Trafficking in Human Beings Demand Driven?* IOM Research Series, 15, Geneva: IOM.

Andrijasevic, Rutvica (2007) 'Beautiful dead bodies: Gender, migration and representation in anti-trafficking campaigns', *Feminist Review*, 86(1): 24–44.

Andrijasevic, Rutvica, and Anderson, Bridget (2009) 'Anti-trafficking campaigns: Decent? Honest? Truthful?', *Feminist Review*, 92(1): 151–5.

Andrijasevic, Rutvica, and Mai, Nicola (2016) 'Editorial: Trafficking (in) representations: Understanding the recurring appeal of victimhood and slavery in neoliberal times', *Anti-Trafficking Review*, 7: 1–10.

Anitha, Sundari, and Gill, Aisha (2017) 'Coercion, consent and the forced marriage debate in the UK', in Robert Leckey (ed), *Marital Rights*, London: Routledge.

Apitzsch, Birgit, Shire, Karen A., Heinrich, Steffen, Mottweiler, Hannelore, and Tünte, Markus (2015) *Flexibilität und Beschäftigungswandel.* Weinheim: Juventa Verlag.

Aradau, Claudia (2004) 'The perverse politics of four-letter words: Risk and pity in the securitisation of human trafficking', *Millennium*, 33(2): 251–77.

Aradau, Claudia (2008) *Rethinking Trafficking in Women: Politics out of Security.* London: Palgrave Macmillan.

Arbeitsgemeinschaft Sozialdemokratischer Frauen (ASF) (2021a) *Beschluss IR0009 Nordisches Modell auch in Deutschland durchsetzen! Beschlüsse der ordentlichen Bundeskonferenz der Arbeitsgemeinschaft Sozialdemokratischer Frauen,* 71. Available at: https://asf.spd.de/fileadmin/user_upload/2021_ASF-Beschlussbuch_Bundeskonferenz_Digital.pdf

Arbeitsgemeinschaft Sozialdemokratischer Frauen (ASF) (2021b) *Beschluss IR0010 Solidarität mit Sexarbeiter*innen – Nein zum Nordischen Modell Beschlüsse der ordentlichen Bundeskonferenz der Arbeitsgemeinschaft Sozialdemokratischer Frauen,* 72–4. Available at: https://asf.spd.de/fileadmin/user_upload/2021_ASF-Beschlussbuch_Bundeskonferenz_Digital.pdf

Arrighi, Giovanni (2007) *Adam Smith in Beijing: Lineages of the Twenty-First Century.* New York/London: Verso.

Ashworth, Andrew, and Zedner, Lucia (2012) 'Prevention and criminalization: Justification and limits', *New Criminal Law Review*, 15(4): 542–71.

Askola, Heli (2007) *Legal Responses to Trafficking in Women for Sexual Exploitation in the European Union.* Oxford and Portland: Hart Publishing.

Ayers, Ian, and Braithwaite, John (1992) *Responsive Legislation: Transcending the Deregulation Debate.* Oxford: Oxford University Press.

Bada, Xóchitl, and Gleeson, Shannon (2023) *Scaling Migrant Worker Rights: How Advocates Collaborate and Contest State Power.* Oakland: University of California Press.

Bair, Jennifer (2005) 'Global capitalism and commodity chains: Looking back, going forward', *Competition & Change*, 9(2): 153–80.

Bair, Jennifer (2010) 'On difference and capital: Gender and the globalization of production', *Signs*, 36(1): 203–26.

Baldwin, Robert, Black, Julia, and O'Leary, Gerard (2014) 'Risk regulation and transnationality: Institutional accountability as a driver of innovation', *Transnational Environmental Law*, 3(2): 373–90.

Bales, Kevin (1999) *Disposable People: New Slavery in the Global Economy*. Berkeley: University of California Press.

Bales, Kevin (2007a) *Ending Slavery*. Berkeley: University of California Press.

Bales, Kevin (2007b) 'What predicts human trafficking?', *International Journal of Comparative and Applied Criminal Justice*, 31(2): 269–79.

Bales, Kevin, Hesketh, Olivia, and Silverman, Bernard W. (2015) 'Modern slavery in the UK: How many victims?', *Significance*, 12(3): 16–21.

Bales, Kevin, Murphy, Laura, and Silverman, Bernard (2020) 'How many trafficked people are there in Greater New Orleans? Lessons in measurement', *Journal of Human Trafficking*, 6(4): 375–87.

Balfour, Giselle, Okech, David, Callands, Tamora A., and Kombian, Grace (2022) 'A qualitative analysis of the intervention experiences of human trafficking survivors and at-risk women in Ghana', *Journal of Human Trafficking*, 8:3, 334–48.

Ballesteros Pena, Ana, Bustelo, Maria, and Mazur, Amy G. (2023) 'The politics of the penal state: The dark side of gender regimes in the case of Spain', *Women's Studies International Forum*, 99. https://doi.org/10.1016/j.wsif.2023.102743

Banyard, Kae (2016) *Pimp State: Sex, Money, and the Future of Equality*. London: Faber & Faber.

Barrick, Kelle, and Pfeffer, Rebecca (2021) 'Advances in measurement: A scoping review of prior human trafficking prevalence studies and recommendations for future research', *Journal of Human Trafficking*, 1–21. https://doi.org/10.1080/23322705.2021.1984721

Barrientos, Stephanie W. (2013) '"Labour chains": Analysing the role of labour contractors in global production networks', *The Journal of Development Studies*, 49(8): 1058–71.

Barrientos, Stephanie (2019) *Gender and Work in Global Value Chains: Capturing the Gains?* Cambridge: Cambridge University Press.

Barrientos, Stephanie (2023) 'Global value chains and gender: Opportunities and challenges for women workers in developing economies', *Papeles de Europa*, 36, e84307. https://doi.org/10.5209/pade.84307

Barrientos, Stephanie, Bianchi, Lara, and Berman, Cindy (2019) 'Gender and governance of global value chains: Promoting rights of women workers', *International Labour Review*, 158(4): 729–52.

Barry, Kathleen (1979) *Female Sexual Slavery*. New Jersey: Prentice Hall.

Barry, Kathleen (1985) 'Social etiology of crimes against women', *Victimology*, 10(1–4): 164–73.

Barry, Kathleen (1995) *The Prostitution of Sexuality: The Global Exploitation of Women*. New York: New York University Press.

Bauman, Zygmunt (1989) *Modernity and the Holocaust*. Cambridge: Polity Press.

Bauman, Zygmunt (2000) *Liquid Modernity*. Cambridge: Polity Press.

BBC (2006) 'Cockle gangmaster gets 14 years', 28 March. Available at: http://news.bbc.co.uk/2/hi/uk_news/england/lancashire/4851194.stm

BBC (2014) 'Slavery "worse" 10 years after Morecambe Bay tragedy', 5 February. Available at: https://www.bbc.com/news/uk-england-25914594

BBC (2016) 'Germany trafficking: mass police raid on Berlin mega-brothel', 14 April. Available at https://www.bbc.com/news/uk-england-25914594

Beck, Ulrich (2002) *Individualisation*. London: Sage.

Beckert, Jens (2009) 'The social order of markets', *Theory and Society*, 38(3): 245–69.

Beckert, Jens, and Dewey, Matias (2017) 'The social organization of illegal markets', in Jens Beckert and Matias Dewey (eds), *The Architecture of Illegal Markets: Towards an Economic Sociology of Illegality in the Economy*. Oxford: Oxford University Press, pp 1–34.

Bernstein, Elizabeth (2010) 'Militarized humanitarianism meets carceral feminism: The politics of sex, rights, and freedom in contemporary antitrafficking campaigns', *Signs*, 36(1): 45–71.

Bhambra, Gurminder K. (2007) *Rethinking Modernity*. Basingstoke: Palgrave.

Bhoola, Urmila, and Panaccione, Kari (2016) 'Slavery crimes and the mandate of the United Nations Special Rapporteur on Contemporary Forms of Slavery', *Journal of International Criminal Justice*, 14(2): 363–73.

Bigio, Jamille, and Vogelstein, Rachel (2019) *The Security Implications of Human Trafficking*. Washington, DC: Council on Foreign Relations.

Bigo, Didier (2006) 'Globalized (in)security: The field and the pan-opticon', in Didier Bigo, Laurent Bonelli, Emmanuel-Pierre Guittet, Christian Olsson, and Anastassia Tsoukala (eds), *Illiberal Practices of Liberal Regimes: The (In)Security Games*. Paris: L'Harmattan, pp 5–49.

Bindel, Julie, Breslin, Ruth, and Brown, Laura (2013) *Capital Exploits: A Study of Prostitution and Trafficking in London. A Study Commissioned by the Mayor's Office for Policing and Crime (MOPAC)*. London: Eaves. Available at: https://i1.cmsfiles.com/eaves/2013/06/Capital-Exploits-June-2013.pdf-da8819.pdf

Birch, Kean, and Muniesa, Fabian (eds) (2020) *Assetization: Turning Things into Assets in Technoscientific Capitalism*. Cambridge: MIT Press.

Black, Julia (2002) 'Critical reflections on regulation', *Australasian Journal of Legal Philosophy*, 27(2002): 1–46.

Black, Julia (2008) 'Constructing and contesting legitimacy and accountability in polycentric regulatory regimes', *Regulation & Governance*, 2(2): 137–64.

Boatcă, Manuela (2015) *Global Inequalities Beyond Occidentalism*. London: Routledge.

Boris, Eileen (2023) 'Moving workers: International Labour Organization standards and the regulation of migration', in Boris, Eileen, Gottfried, Heidi, Greene, Julie, and Tham, Joo-Cheong (eds) *Global Labor Migration: New Directions*. Urbana: University of Illinois Press, pp 243–60.

Boris, Eileen, and Parreñas, Rhacel (eds) (2010) *Intimate Labors: Cultures, Technologies, and the Politics of Care*. Stanford: Stanford University Press.

Boris, Eileen, and Rodríguez García, Magaly (2010) '(In)decent work: Sex and the ILO', *Journal of Women's History*, 33(4): 194–221.

Boris, Eileen, Gilmore, Stephanie, and Parreñas, Rhacel (2010) 'Sexual labors: Interdisciplinary perspectives toward sex as work', *Sexualities*, 13(2): 131–7.

Boris, Eileen, Gottfried, Heidi, Greene, Julie, and Tham, Joo-Cheong (eds) (2023) *Global Labor Migration: New Directions*. Urbana: University of Illinois Press.

Bowker, Geoffrey, and Star, Susan Leigh (1999) *Sorting Things Out: Classification and its Consequences*. Cambridge: MIT Press.

Bowling, Ben (2020) '"A really hostile environment": Adiaphorization, global policing and the crimmigration control system', *Theoretical Criminology*, 24(2): 163–83.

Bradford, Anu (2021) *The Brussels Effect: How the European Union Rules the World*. Oxford: Oxford University Press.

Braithwaite, John (2023) *Macrocriminology and Freedom*. Canberra: Australia National University Press.

Brand, Sam, and Price, Richard (2000) *The Economic and Social Costs of Crime*. London: Home Office.

Brass, Tom (2011) 'Unfree labour as *primitive* accumulation?', *Capital & Class*, 35(1): 23–38.

Brass, Tom (2016) *Towards a Comparative Political Economy of Unfree Labour: Case Studies and Debates*. Abingdon: Routledge.

Braumoeller, Bear F. (2019) *Only the Dead: The Persistence of War in the Modern Age*. Oxford: Oxford University Press.

Brennan, Denise (2014) 'Trafficking, scandal, and abuse of migrant workers in Argentina and the United States', *The Annals of the Academy of Political Science and Social Science*, 653: 107–23.

Brenner, Neil (1999) 'Globalization as reterritorialization: The re-scaling of urban governance in the European Union', *Urban Studies,* 36(3): 431–51.

Brenner, Neil, Peck, Jamie, and Theodore, Nik (2010) 'Variegated neoliberalization: Geographies, modalities, pathways', *Global Networks,* 10(2): 182–222.

Broad, Rose, and Gadd, David (2023) *Demystifying Modern Slavery*. London: Routledge.

Broad, Rose, Lord, Nicholas, and Duncan, Charlotte (2022) 'The financial aspects of human trafficking: A financial assessment framework', *Criminology & Criminal Justice*, 22(4), 581–600.

Bruff, Ian (2014) 'The rise of authoritarian neoliberalism', *Rethinking Marxism*, 26(1): 113–29.

Bruzelius, Cecilia (2019) 'Freedom of movement, social rights and residence-based conditionality in the European Union', *Journal of European Social Policy*, 29(1): 70–83.

Bucken-Knapp, Gregg, Karlsson Schaffer, Johan, and Persson Strömbäck, Karin (2012) 'Security, equality, and the clash of ideas: Sweden's evolving anti-trafficking policy', *Human Rights Review*, 13(2): 167–85.

Budiani-Saberi, Debra, and Delmonico, Francis L. (2008) 'Organ trafficking and transplant tourism: A commentary on the global realities', *American Journal of Transplantation*, 8(5): 925–9.

Budiani-Saberi, Debra, and Columb, Seán (2013) 'A human rights approach to human trafficking for organ removal', *Medicine, Health Care and Philosophy*, 16(4): 897–914.

Bundeskriminalamt (BKA) (2009) *Palermo–Protokoll und die Folgen – Bekämpfung des „Menschenhandels zum Zweck sexueller Ausbeutung" – Materialsammlung zu nationalen und internationalen eher strategisch ausgerichteten Aktivitäten*. Wiesbaden: Bundeskriminalamt.

Bundeskriminalamt (BKA) (2020) *Menschenhandel und Ausbeutung. Bundeslagebild 2019*. Wiesbaden: Bundeskriminalamt.

Bundeskriminalamt (BKA) (2021) *Menschenhandel und Ausbeutung. Bundeslagebild 2020*. Wiesbaden: Bundeskriminalamt.

Bundeskriminalamt (BKA) (2022) *Menschenhandel und Ausbeutung. Bundeslagebild 2021*. Wiesbaden: Bundeskriminalamt.

Bundesministerium für Familie, Senioren, Frauen und Jugend (BMFSFJ) (2007) *Bericht der Bundesregierung zu den Auswirkungen des Gesetzes zur Regelung der Rechtsverhältnisse der Prostituierten. Prostitutionsgesetz – ProstG*, Berlin: BMFSF.

Bündnis der Fachberatungsstellen für Sexarbeiterinnen und Sexarbeiter (BufaS) (2017) 'Prostituiertenschutzgesetz – Kritikpunkte und Forderungen zur Umsetzung', Press release, 18 January. Available at: http://www.bufas.net/prostituiertenschutzgesetz-kritikpunkte-und-forderungen-zur-umsetzung/

Buzan, Barry, Wæver, Ole, and De Wilde, Jaap (1998) *Security: A New Framework for Analysis*. Boulder: Lynne Rienner Publishers.

Byrne, David, and Callaghan, Gillian (2023) *Complexity Theory and the Social Sciences: The State of the Art*. London: Routledge.

Callon, Michel (2021) *Markets in the Making: Rethinking Competition, Goods, and Innovation*. New York: Zone Books.

Cameron, Erinn C., Cunningham, Fiona J., Hemingway, Samantha L., Tschida Sherri L., and Jacquin, Kristine M. (2023) 'Indicators of gender inequality and violence against women predict number of reported human trafficking legal cases across countries', *Journal of Human Trafficking*, 9(1): 79–93.

Campana, Paola, and Varese, Frederico (2016) 'Exploitation in human trafficking and smuggling', *European Journal of Crime Policy Research*, 22: 89–105.

Capron, Alexander M., and Delmonico, Francis L. (2015) 'Preventing trafficking in organs for transplantation: An important facet of the fight against human trafficking', *Journal of Human Trafficking*, 1(1): 56–64.

Carvalho, Henrique, Chamberlen, Anastasia, and Lewis, Rachel (2020) 'Punitiveness beyond criminal justice: Punishable subjects in an era of prevention, anti-migration and austerity', *British Journal of Criminology*, 60(2): 265–84.

Castellani, Brian, and Hafferty, Frederic (2009) *Sociology and Complexity Science: A New Field of Enquiry*. Berlin: Springer.

Castells, Manuel (1996) *The Information Age: Volume 1: The Rise of the Network Society*. Oxford: Blackwell.

Castles, Francis G. (2012) 'The English-speaking countries', in Francis G. Castles, Stephan Leibfried, Jane Lewis, Herbert Obinger, and Christopher Pierson (eds), *The Oxford Handbook of the Welfare State*. Oxford: Oxford University Press, pp 630–55.

Ceccagno, Antonella, and Sacchetto, Devi (2020) 'A Chinese model for labour in Europe?' *International Migration*, 5(3): 73–86.

Chan, Lax, Silverman, Bernard W., and Vincent, Kyle (2021) 'Multiple systems estimation for sparse capture data: Inferential challenges when there are nonoverlapping lists', *Journal of the American Statistical Association*, 116(535): 1297–306.

Chantavanich, Supang (2020) 'Thailand's challenges in implementing anti-trafficking legislation: The case of the Rohingya', *Journal of Human Trafficking*, 6(2): 234–43.

Chase-Dunn, Christopher, and Hall, Thomas (1997) *Rise and Demise: Comparing World-Systems*. Boulder: Westview.

Chicchi, Federico (2020) 'Beyond the "salary institution": On the "society of performance" and the platformisation of the employment relationship', *Work Organisation, Labour & Globalisation*, 14(1): 15–31.

China Law Translate (2022) *China's Action Plan against Human Trafficking (2021–2030)*. Available at: https://www.chinalawtranslate.com/en/counte rtraffickingplan2021thr2030/

Cho, Seo-Young (2015) 'Modelling for determinants of human trafficking: An empirical analysis', *Social Inclusion*, 2(1), 2–21.

Cho, Seo-Young, Dreher, Axel, and Neumayer, Eric (2013) 'Does legalized prostitution increase human trafficking?', *World Development*, 41(1): 67–82.

Chuang, Janie A. (2006) 'The United States as global sheriff: Using unilateral sanctions to combat human trafficking', *Michigan Journal of International Law*, 27: 437–99.

Chuang, Janie A. (2015a) 'The challenges and perils of reframing trafficking as "Modern-Day Slavery"', *Anti-Trafficking Review*, 5: 146–9.

Chuang, Janie A. (2015b) 'Giving as governance? Philanthrocapitalism and modern-day slavery abolitionism', *UCLA Law Review*, 62: 1516–56.

Chuang, Janie A. (2020) 'Preventing trafficking through new global governance over labor migration', *Georgia State University Law Review*, 36(4): 1027–58.

Chuang, Janie A. (2021) 'Preventing human trafficking: The role of the IOM and the UN Global Compact on Migration', in Genevieve LeBaron, Jessica R. Pliley, and David W. Blight (eds) *Fighting Modern Slavery and Human Trafficking: History and Contemporary Policy*. Cambridge: Cambridge University Press. pp 179–202.

Clemente, Mara (2022) 'The counter-trafficking apparatus in action: Who benefits from it?', *Dialectical Anthropology*, 46(3): 267–89.

Cockayne, James (2015) *Unshackling Development: Why We Need a Global Partnership to End Modern Slavery*. New York: United Nations University.

Cockayne, James (2021) *Developing Freedom: The Sustainable Development Case for Ending Modern Slavery, Forced Labour and Human Trafficking*. New York: United Nations University Centre for Policy Research.

Cockayne, James, and Panaccione, Kari (2015) *Fighting Modern Slavery: What Role for International Justice?* New York: United Nations University.

Cockayne, James, Grono, Nick, and Panaccione, Kari (2016) 'Introduction', *Journal of International Criminal Justice*, 14(2): 253–67.

Coe, Neil M., and Ward, Kevin (2014) 'The creation of distinctive national temporary staffing markets', in Judy Fudge and Kendra Strauss (eds), *Temporary Work, Agencies and Unfree Labour: Insecurity in the New World of Work*. London: Routledge, pp 94–117.

Council of Europe (2023) *Country Monitoring*. Available at: https://www.coe.int/en/web/anti-human-trafficking/country-monitoring-work

Counter Trafficking Global Data Collaborative (CTDC) (2022) *The Global Victim-Perpetrator Synthetic Dataset*. Available at: https://www.ctdatacollaborative.org/

Counter Trafficking Global Data Collaborative (CTDC) (2023) *Liberty Shared Data Overview*. Available at: https://www.ctdatacollaborative.org/dashboard/liberty-shared-data-overview

Crane, Andrew (2013) 'Modern slavery as a management practice: Exploring the conditions and capabilities for human exploitation', *Academy of Management Review*, 38(1): 49–69.

Crane, Andrew, LeBaron, Genevieve, Allain, Jean, and Behbahani, Laya (2019) 'Governance gaps in eradicating forced labor: From global to domestic supply chains', *Regulation & Governance*, 13(1): 86–106.

Crane, Andrew, LeBaron, Genevieve, Phung, Kam, Behbahani, Laya, and Allain, Jean (2022a) 'Confronting the business models of modern slavery', *Journal of Management Inquiry*, 31(3): 264–85.

Crane, Andrew, Soundararajan, Vivek, Bloomfield, Michael J., LeBaron, Genevieve, and Spence, Laura J. (2022b) 'Hybrid (un)freedom in worker hostels in garment supply chains', *Human Relations*, 75(10): 1928–60.

Crenshaw, Kimberle (1991) 'Mapping the margins: Intersectionality, identity politics, and violence against women of color', *Stanford Law Review*, 43(6): 1241–99.

Danailova-Trainor, Gergana, and Belser, Patrick (2006) 'Globalization and the illicit market for human trafficking: An empirical analysis of supply and demand', *Working Paper 53 of the Special Action Programme to Combat Forced Labour*. Geneva: ILO.

David, Fiona (2017) 'Building the infrastructure of anti-trafficking, Part II: Why measurement matters', *Anti-Trafficking Review*, 8: 148–52.

Davis, Angela Y. (2003) *Are Prisons Obsolete?* New York: Seven Stories Press.

Davis, Angela Y., Dent, Gina, Meiners, Erica R., and Richie, Beth E. (2022) *Abolition. Feminism. Now.* London: Hamish Hamilton.

Davies, William, and Gane, Nicholas (2021) 'Post-neoliberalism? An introduction', *Theory, Culture & Society*, 38(6): 3–28.

Day, Sophie, Lury, Celia, and Wakeford, Nina (2014) 'Number ecologies: Numbers and numbering practices', *Distinktion: Journal of Social Theory*, 15(2): 123–54.

De Vries, Ieke (2019) 'Connected to crime: An exploration of the nesting of labour trafficking and exploitation in legitimate markets', *The British Journal of Criminology*, 59(1): 209–30.

Demetriou, Daphne (2015) '"Tied visas" and inadequate labour protections: A formula for abuse and exploitation of migrant domestic workers in the United Kingdom', *Anti-Trafficking Review*, 5: 66–88.

Dillon, Nara (2015) *Radical Inequalities: China's Revolutionary Welfare State in Comparative Perspective*. Cambridge (MA) and London: Harvard University Press.

DiRienzo, Cassandra E. (2022) 'Human trafficking: What the new IOM dataset reveals', *Journal of Human Trafficking*, 8(3): 294–308.

Dölemeyer, Anne, Pates, Rebecca, and Schmidt, Daniel (2010) 'Deviant girls, small-scale entrepreneurs, and the regulation of German sex workers', in Melissa Hope Ditmore, Antonia Levy, and Alys Willman (eds), *Sex Work Matters: Exploring Money, Power, and Intimacy in the Sex Industry.* London: Zed Books, pp 184–202.

Donger, Elizabeth, and Bhabha, Jacqueline (2018) 'Dilemmas in rescue and reintegration: A critical assessment of India's policies for children trafficked for labour exploitation', *Anti-Trafficking Review*, (10). https://doi.org/10.14197/atr.201218104

Du Bois, William E.B. (1998) [1935] *Black Reconstruction in America 1860–1880.* New York: Free Press.

Du Bois, William E.B. (2019) [1903] *The Souls of Black Folk.* London: Clydesdale.

Dunaway, Wilma (2001) 'The double register of history: Situating the forgotten woman and her household in capitalist commodity chains', *Journal of World-Systems Research*, 7(1): 2–29.

Dunaway, Wilma (ed) (2014) *Gendered Commodity Chains: Seeing Women's Work and Households in Global Production.* Stanford: Stanford University Press.

Ehrenreich, Barbara, and Hochschild, Arlie R. (eds) (2003) *Global Woman: Nannies, Maids and Sex Workers in the New Economy.* London: Granta.

Eisenstadt, Shmuel N. (ed) (2000) *Multiple Modernities.* New Brunswick: Transaction.

Elias, Norbert (1939) *The Civilising Process.* Oxford: Blackwell.

Elias, Norbert (1997) *The Germans: Power Struggles and the Development of Habitus in the Nineteenth and Twentieth Centuries.* Cambridge: Polity Press.

Elliott, Sarah, and Denise Smith, Megan (2020) 'Simulating a multi-agency approach for the protection of trafficked persons in migration and displacement settings', *Journal of Human Trafficking*, 6(2): 168–81.

Ellis, Nicola, Cooper, Christine, and Rose, Stephen (2017) *An Evaluation of the National Referral Mechanism Pilot.* Research Report 94. London: Home Office.

Emmenegger, Patrick, Häusermann, Silja, Palier, Bruno, and Seeleib-Kaiser, Martin (eds) (2012). *The Age of Dualization. The Changing Face of Inequality in Deindustrializing Societies.* Oxford: Oxford University Press.

Espeute, Serena, and Lanskey, Caroline (2023) 'An exploration of police discretion in the identification of child victims of county lines drug trafficking', *Policing and Society*, DOI: 10.1080/10439463.2023.2223341

Esping-Andersen, Gøsta (1990) *Three Worlds of Welfare Capitalism.* Princeton: Princeton University Press.

Ettlinger, Nancy (2017) 'Paradoxes, problems and potentialities of online work platforms', *Work Organisation, Labour & Globalisation*, 11(2): 21–38.

European Commission (2005) *EU Plan on Best Practices, Standards and Procedures for Combating and Preventing Trafficking in Human Beings* (2005/C 311/01). Available at: http://eur-lex.europa.eu/legal-content/EN/TXT/?uri=CELEX:52005XG1209(01)

European Commission (2012) *The EU Strategy towards the Eradication of Trafficking in Human Beings 2012–2016, COM (2012) 286, final.* Available at: http://eur-lex.europa.eu/legal-content/EN/TXT/PDF/?uri=CELEX:52012DC0286&from=EN

European Commission (2015) *Better Regulation: Guidelines and Toolkit.* Available at: https://commission.europa.eu/law/law-making-process/planning-and-proposing-law/better-regulation/better-regulation-guidelines-and-toolbox_en

European Commission (2016a) *Report from the Commission to the European Parliament and the Council: Assessing the impact of existing national law, establishing as a criminal offence the use of services which are the objects of exploitation in trafficking in human beings, on the prevention of trafficking in human beings, in accordance with Article 23(2) of the Directive 2011/36/E 722 final.* Available at: https://eur-lex.europa.eu/legal-content/EN/TXT/?uri=CELEX:52016DC0719

European Commission (2016b), *Report from the Commission to the European Parliament and the Council: Assessing the extent to which Member States have taken the necessary measures in order to comply with Directive 2011/36/EU on preventing and combating trafficking in human beings and protecting its victims in accordance with Article 23(1). COM(2016) 719 final.* Available at: https://www.europarl.europa.eu/RegData/docs_autres_institutions/commission_europeenne/com/2016/0722/COM_COM(2016)0722_EN.pdf

European Commission (2018a) *Data Collection on Trafficking in Human Beings in the EU.* Brussels: European Commission. Available at: https://ec.europa.eu/homeaffairs/sites/homeaffairs/files/what-we-do/policies/european-agenda-secu-rity/20181204_data-collection-study.pdf

European Commission (2018b) *Joint Statement of Commitment to Working Together against Trafficking in Human Beings.* Brussels: EU. Available at: https://www.eurojust.europa.eu/publication/joint-statement-commitment-working-together-address-trafficking-human-beings

European Commission (2020) *Data Collection on Trafficking in Human Beings in the EU.* Available at: https://data.europa.eu/doi/10.2837/45442

European Commission (2021a) *The EU Strategy towards the Eradication of Trafficking in Human Beings (2021–2025).* COM/2021/171, final. Available at: https://eur-lex.europa.eu/legal-content/EN/TXT/?uri=CELEX:52021DC0171

European Commission (2021b) *Mapping the Risk of Serious and Organised Crime Infiltrating Legitimate Businesses.* Final Report, Luxembourg: Publication Office of the European Union.

European Commission (2022a) *EU Strategy on Combatting Trafficking in Human Beings*, COM(2021) 171 final. Available at: https://eur-lex.europa.eu/legal-content/EN/TXT/?uri=CELEX%3A52021DC0171

European Commission (2022b) *Proposal of the Commission for the European Parliament and of the Council Amending Directive 2011/36/EU on Preventing and Combatting Trafficking in Human Beings and Protecting its Victims.* COM/2022/732. Available at: https://eur-lex.europa.eu/legal-content/EN/TXT/PDF/?uri=CELEX:52022PC0732

European Commission (2022c) *Report on the Progress Made in the Fight against Trafficking in Human Beings (Fourth Report).* SWD/2022/429 final. Available at: https://eur-lex.europa.eu/legal-content/EN/TXT/PDF/?uri=CELEX:52022DC0736&from=EN

European Commission (2022d) *Proposal for a Directive on Corporate Sustainability, Due Diligence.* Available at: https://commission.europa.eu/publications/proposal-directive-corporate-sustainability-due-diligence-and-annex_en

European Parliament (2014) *Resolution of 26 February 2014 on Sexual Exploitation and Prostitution and its Impact on Gender Equality* (2013/2103(INI)). Available at: http://www.europarl.europa.eu/sides/getDoc.do?pubRef=-//EP//NONSGML+TA+P7-TA-2014-0162+0+DOC+PDF+V0//EN

European Parliament (2020) *Towards a Mandatory EU System for Due Diligence in Supply Chains.* Available at: https://www.europarl.europa.eu/RegData/etudes/BRIE/2020/659299/EPRS_BRI(2020)659299_EN.pdf

European Union (EU) External Action Service (2022) *Guidance on Due Diligence for EU businesses to Address the Risk of Forced Labour in their Operations and Supply Chains.* Available at: https://circabc.europa.eu/rest/download/de3d9ab5-dca1-4037-aeb8-8704a379c67b

European Union Agency for Fundamental Rights (FRA) (2022) *Guardianship Systems for Unaccompanied Children in the European Union. Developments since 2014.* Luxembourg: Publications Office of the European Union.

Europol (2014) *EU Agencies Issue Report on Joint THB Actions.* Available at: https://www.europol.europa.eu/newsroom/news/eu-agencies-issue-report-joint-thb-actions

Europol (2015a) *Exploring Tomorrow's Organised Crime.* The Hague: European Police Office. Available at: https://www.europol.europa.eu/publications-documents/exploring-tomorrow's-organised-crime

Europol (2015b) *The Trafficking in Human Beings Financial Business Model.* The Hague: European Police Office. Available at: https://www.europol.europa.eu/cms/sites/default/files/documents/europol_thb_finacial_business_model_2015.pdf

Europol (2016) *Situation Report: Trafficking in Human Beings in the EU.* The Hague: European Police Office. Available at: https://www.europol.europa.eu/publications-events/publications/trafficking-in-human-beings-in-eu

Europol (2020) *The Challenges of Countering Human Trafficking in the Digital Era*. The Hague: European Police Office.

Eurostat (2015*) Trafficking in Human Beings: 2015 Edition*. Luxembourg: Publications Office of the European Union.

Eurostat (2018) *Handbook on the Compilation of Statistics on Illegal Activities in National Accounts and Balance of Payments*. Luxembourg: Publications Office of the European Union.

Fabbri, Camilla, Stöckl, Heidi, Jones, Katharina, Cook, Harry, Galez-Davis, Claire, Grant, Naomi, et al (2023) 'Labor recruitment and human trafficking: Analysis of a global trafficking survivor database', *International Migration Review*, 57(2): 629–51.

Farrell, Amy, and Cronin, Shea (2015) 'Policing prostitution in an era of human trafficking enforcement', *Crime Law and Social Change*, 64: 211–28.

Farrell, Amy, Dank, Meredith, de Vries, Ieke, Kafafian, Matthew, Hughes, Andrea, and Lockwood, Sarah (2019) 'Failing victims? Challenges of the police response to human trafficking', *Criminology & Public Policy*, 18(3): 649–73.

Farrell, Amy, Bright, Katherine, de Vries, Ieke, Pfeffer, Rebecca, and Dank, Meredith (2020) 'Policing labor trafficking in the United States', *Trends in Organized Crime*, 23: 36–56.

Fedina, Lisa, and DeForge, Bruce R. (2017) 'Estimating the trafficked population: Public-health research methodologies may be the answer', *Journal of Human Trafficking*, 3(1): 21–38.

Fehrenbacher, Anne E., Musto, Jennifer, Hoefinger, Heidi, Mai, Nicola, Macioti, P.G., Giametta, Calogero, and Bennachie, Calum (2020) 'Transgender people and human trafficking: Intersectional exclusion of transgender migrants and people of color from anti-trafficking protection in the United States', *Journal of Human Trafficking*, 6(2): 182–94.

Fineman, Martha Albertson (2008) 'The vulnerable subject: Anchoring equality in the human condition', *Yale Journal of Law and Feminism*, 20(1): 1–23.

Fioretos, Orfeo, and Heldt, Eugénia (2019) 'Legacies and innovations in global economic governance since Bretton Woods', *Review of International Political Economy*, 26(6): 1089–111.

Fligstein, Neil (2002) *The Architecture of Markets. An Economic Sociology of Twenty-First-Century Capitalist Societies*. Princeton: Princeton University Press.

Follis, Karolina (2012) *Building Fortress Europe: The Polish-Ukrainian Frontier*. Philadelphia: University of Pennsylvania Press.

Forde, Chris, MacKenzi, Robert, Ciupijus, Zyama, and Alberti, Gabriella (2015) 'Understanding the connections between temporary employment agencies and migration', *The International Journal of Comparative Labour Law and Industrial Relations*, 31(4): 357–70.

Foucault, Michel (1991) 'Governmentality', in Graham Burchell, Colin Gordon, and Peter Miller (eds), *The Foucault Effect: Studies in Governmentality*. Chicago: Chicago University Press, pp 87–105.

Francis, Brian, Walby, Sylvia, Pattinson, Becky, Elliott, Amy, Hoti, Valmira, Phoenix, Jessica et al (2018) *Data Collection on Trafficking in Human Beings in the EU*. Brussels: European Commission.

Friedman, Milton (2002) [1962] *Capitalism and Freedom*. Chicago: University of Chicago Press.

Fudge, Judy (2012) 'Precarious migrant status and precarious employment: The paradox of international rights for migrant workers', *Comparative Labor Law & Policy Journal*, 34: 95

Fudge, Judy (2018) 'Modern slavery, unfree labour and the labour market: The social dynamics of legal characterization', *Social & Legal Studies*, 27(4): 414–34.

Fudge, Judy (2023) 'Governing global labor migration: Compacts and contradictions', in Eileen Boris, Heidi Gottfried, Julie Greene, and Joo-Cheong Tham (eds) (2023) *Global Labor Migration: New Directions*. Urbana: University of Illinois Press, pp 280–96.

Fudge, Judy, and Strauss, Kendra (2014) 'Temporary work, agencies and unfree labour: Insecurity in the new world of work', in Judy Fudge and Kendra Strauss (eds), *Temporary Work, Agencies and Unfree Labour: Insecurity in the New World of Work*, Oxon: Routledge, pp 1–25.

Galbraith, John Kenneth (2009 [1954]) *The Great Crash 1929*. New York: Harper Collins.

Gallagher, Anne T. (2010) *The International Law of Human Trafficking*. Cambridge: Cambridge University Press.

Gallagher, Anne T. (2016) 'Editorial: The problems and prospects of trafficking prosecutions: Ending impunity and securing justice', *Anti-Trafficking Review*, 6: 1–11.

Gallagher, Anne T. (2017) 'What's wrong with the Global Slavery Index?' *Anti-Trafficking Review*, 8: 90–112.

Garland, David (2000) *The Culture of Control: Crime and Social Order in Contemporary Society*. Oxford: Oxford University Press.

Gawer, Annabelle (2014) 'Bridging differing perspectives on technological platforms: Toward an integrative framework', *Research Policy*, 43(7): 1239–49.

George, Emma, McNaughton, Darlene, and Tsourtos, George (2017) 'An interpretive analysis of Australia's approach to human trafficking and its focus on criminal justice over public health', *Journal of Human Trafficking*, 3(2): 81–92.

Gereffi, Gary (2014) 'Global value chains in a post-Washington Consensus world', *Review of International Political Economy*, (21)1: 9–37

Gereffi, Gary, and Korzeniewicz, Miguel (eds) (1994) *Commodity Chains and Global Capitalism*. Westport, CT: Greenwood Press.

Giddens, Anthony (1984) *The Constitution of Society*. Cambridge: Polity Press.

Giddens, Anthony (1990) *The Consequences of Modernity*. Cambridge: Polity Press.

Giddens, Anthony (1998) *The Third Way: The Renewal of Social Democracy*. Cambridge: Polity Press.

Gillespie, Tarleton (2010) 'The politics of "platforms"', *New Media & Society*, 12(3): 347–64.

Global Initiative against Transnational Organized Crime (2021) *Global Organized Crime Index*. Available at: https://ocindex.net/assets/downloads/global-ocindex-report.pdf

Global Initiative against Transnational Organized Crime (2023) 'About us'. Available at: https://globalinitiative.net/about-us/our-story/

Go, Julian (2016) *Postcolonial Thought and Social Theory*. Oxford: Oxford University Press.

Gottfried, Heidi (2013) *Gender, Work and Economy: Unpacking the Global Economy*. Cambridge: Polity Press.

Gottfried, Heidi (2023) 'Multi-scalar geographies of inequalities: Trajectories of gender regimes in a world regional perspective', *Women's Studies International Forum*, 99. https://doi.org/10.1016/j.wsif.2023.102713

Gottfried, Heidi, Walby, Sylvia, and Shire, Karen A. (2023) 'Introduction: The future of gender regimes', *Women's Studies International Forum*, 99. https://doi.org/10.1016/j.wsif.2023.102786

Gramsci, Antonio (1971) *Selection from the Prison Notebooks*. New York: International Publishers.

Group of Experts on Action against Trafficking in Human Beings (GRETA) (2015) *4th General Report on GRETA's Activities*. Strasbourg: Council of Europe.

Group of Experts on Action against Trafficking in Human Beings (GRETA) (2019) *Practical Impact of GRETA's Monitoring Work*. Strasbourg: Council of Europe. Available at: https://www.coe.int/en/web/anti-human-trafficking/country-reports

The Guardian (2005) 'Tides kill 19 cockle pickers', 6 February. Available at: https://www.theguardian.com/world/2004/feb/06/china.uk

Gupta, Rahila (2008) *Enslaved: The New British Slavery*. London: Portobello Books.

Gupta, Rahila (2016) 'Defining modern slavery out of existence: Who benefits?' Available at: https://www.opendemocracy.net/en/5050/defining-modern-slavery-out-of-existence-who-benefits/

Guth, Andrew, Anderson, Robyn, Kinnard, Kasey, and Tran, Hang (2014) 'Proper methodology and methods of collecting and analysing slavery data: An examination of the Global Slavery Index', *Social Inclusion*, 2(4): 14–22.

Hall, Peter A., and Soskice David (2001) *Varieties of Capitalism: The Institutional Foundations of Comparative Advantage*. Oxford: Oxford University Press.

Hannan, Michael T., and Freeman, John (1989) *Organizational Ecology*. Cambridge, Mass.: Harvard University Press.

Harvey, David (2003) *The New Imperialism*. Oxford: Oxford University Press.

Harvey, David (2005) *A Brief History of Neoliberalism*. Oxford: Oxford University Press.

Harvey, Jackie, Hornsby, Rob, and Sattar, Zeibeda (2015) 'Disjointed service: An English case study of multi-agency provision in tackling child trafficking', *The British Journal of Criminology*, 55(3): 494–513.

Harvey, Penny, Jensen, Casper Bruun, and Morita, Atsuro (2017) 'Introduction: Infrastructural complications', in Penny Harvey, Casper Bruun Jensen, and Atsuro Morita (eds), *Infrastructures and Social Complexity*. London: Routledge, pp 1–22.

Hathaway, James C. (2008) 'The human rights quagmire of "human trafficking"', *Virginia Journal of International Law*, 49(1): 1–59.

Haughey, Caroline (2016) *The Modern Slavery Act Review*. London: Home Office. Available at: https://www.gov.uk/government/publications/mod ern-slavery-act-2015-review-one-year-on

Hayek, Friedrich (1948) *Individualism and Economic Order*. Chicago: University of Chicago Press.

Heiss, Andrew, and Kelley, Judith G. (2017) 'From the trenches: A global survey of anti-TIP NGOs and their views of US efforts', *Journal of Human Trafficking*, 3(3): 1500–28.

Held, David, McGrew, Anthony, Goldblatt, David, and Perraton, Jonathan (1999) *Global Transformations: Politics, Economics and Culture*. Cambridge: Polity Press.

Heldt, Eugenia, and Dörfler, Thomas (2022) 'Orchestrating private investors for development: How the World Bank revitalizes', *Regulation and Governance*, 16(4): 1382–98.

Hoff, Suzanne (2011) *The Role of NGOs in Combating Human Trafficking and Supporting (Presumed) Trafficked Persons*. Strasbourg: Council of Europe.

Hopkins, Terence, and Wallerstein, Immanuel (1977) 'Patterns of development of the modern world system', *Review of the Fernand Braudel Center*, 10(3–4): 763–80.

Hopkins, Terence, and Wallerstein, Immanuel (1994) 'Conclusions about commodity chains', in Gary Gereffi and Miguel Korzeniewicz (eds), *Commodity Chains and Global Capitalism*. Westport, CT: Greenwood Press, pp.48–50.

Hörnqvist, Magnus (2020) 'Neoliberal security provision: Between state practices and individual experience', *Punishment and Society*, 22(2): 227–46.

Hulme, Shann, Disley, Emma, and Blondes, Emma Louise (2021) *Mapping the Risk of Serious and Organised Crime Infiltrating Legitimate Business*. Brussels: European Commission.

Huws, Ursula (2020) 'The algorithm and the city: Platform labour and the urban environment', *Work Organisation, Labour & Globalisation*, 14(1): 7–14.

Hyman, Richard (2022) 'Reflections on violence. Some contradictions of "Free Labour"', in Ursula Mense-Petermann, Thomas Welskopp, and Anna Zaharieva (eds), *In Search of the Global Labour Market*. Leiden: Brill, pp 64–86.

Hynes, H. Patricia (2004) 'On the battlefield of women's bodies: An overview of the harm of war to women', *Women's Studies International Forum*, 27(5–6): 431–45.

Inglehart, Ronald (1997) *Modernization and Post-Modernization*. New Jersey: Princeton University Press.

Inter-Agency Coordination Group against Trafficking in Persons (ICAT) (2014) *Preventing Trafficking in Persons by Addressing Demand*. Vienna: UNODC.

Inter-Agency Coordination Group against Trafficking in Persons (ICAT) (2018) *The Role of the Sustainable Development Goals (SDGs) in Combating Trafficking in Persons*. Vienna: UNODC.

Inter-Agency Coordination Group against Trafficking in Persons (ICAT) (2022) *Annual Report 2022*. Vienna: UNODC.

International Labour Office (ILO) (2005) *A Global Alliance against Forced Labour*. Geneva: ILO.

International Labour Office (ILO) (2012a) *Hard to See, Harder to Count: Survey Guidelines to Estimate Forced Labour of Adults and Children*. Geneva: ILO. *Alliance against Forced Labour*. Geneva: ILO.

International Labour Office (ILO) (2012b) *ILO Global Estimate of Forced Labour: Results and Methodology*. Geneva: ILO. *Alliance against Forced Labour*. Geneva: ILO.

International Labour Office (ILO) (2014) *Fair Migration: Setting an Agenda*. Geneva: ILO.

International Labour Office (ILO) (2019) *General Principles and Operational Guidelines for Fair Recruitment: Definition of Recruitment Fees and Related Costs. International Labour Office – Fundamental Principles and Rights at Work Branch, Labour Migration Branch*. Geneva: ILO.

International Labour Organization (ILO) (2002) *How the ILO Works*. Available at: https://www.ilo.org/global/about-the-ilo/how-the-ilo-works/lang--en/index.htm

International Labour Organization (ILO) (2006) *ILO Implementing the Global Employment Agenda: Employment Strategies in Support of Decent Work, 'Vision' document*. Geneva: International Labour Office.

International Labour Organization (ILO) (2018) *Ending Forced Labour by 2030: A Review of Policies and Programmes*. Geneva: ILO.

International Labour Organization (ILO) (2021a) *ILO Fair Recruitment Initiative Strategy 2021–2025: Taking Stock, Moving Forward*. Geneva: ILO.

International Labour Organization (ILO) (2021b) *Extending Social Protection to Migrant Workers, Refugees, and Their Families: Guide for Policymakers and Practitioners.* Geneva: ILO. Available at: https://www.ilo.org/global/top ics/labour-migration/publications/WCMS_826684/lang--en/index.htm

International Labour Organization (ILO) (2022a) *ILO Declaration of Fundamental Principles and Rights at Work and its Follow-up.* ILO: Geneva.

International Labour Organization (ILO) (2022b) *Details of Indicators for Sexual Exploitation.* Geneva: ILO.

International Labour Organization (ILO) (2022c) *Securing Social Protection for Migrant Workers and Their Families: Challenges and Options for Building a Better Future.* Geneva: ILO. Available at: https://www.ilo.org/gb/GBSessi ons/GB344/pol/WCMS_837401/lang--en/index.htm

International Labour Organization, Walk Free, and International Organization for Migration (ILO, Walk Free, and IOM) (2022) *Global Estimates of Modern Slavery: Forced Labour and Forced Marriage.* Geneva: ILO.

International Organization for Migration (IOM) (2007) *The IOM Handbook on Direct Assistance for Victims of Trafficking.* Geneva: IOM.

International Organization for Migration (IOM) (2012) *IOM 2011 Case Data on Human Trafficking: Global Figures and Trends.* Geneva: IOM.

International Organization for Migration (IOM) (2017) *Global Trafficking Trends in Focus: IOM Victim of Trafficking Data, 2006–2016.* Geneva: IOM.

International Organization for Migration (IOM) (2022) *IOM Migration Data Strategy. Implementation Highlights 2020–2022.* Geneva: IOM.

International Organization for Migration (IOM) (2023a) *Global Compact on Migration.* Available at: https://www.iom.int/global-compact-migration

International Organization for Migration (IOM) (2023b) *IOM Mission.* Available at: https://www.iom.int/mission

International Trade Union Confederation (ITUC) (2014) *The Role of the Internet in Trafficking for Labour Exploitation.* Brussels: FINE TUNE Project.

Jaegers, Nicola, and Rijken, Conny (2014) 'Prevention of human trafficking for labor exploitation: The role of corporations', *Northwestern Journal of International Human Rights*, 12(1): 46–73.

Jakobsson, Niklas, and Kotsadam, Andreas (2013) 'The law and economics of international sex slavery: Prostitution laws and trafficking for sexual exploitation', *European Journal of Law and the Economy*, 35: 87–107.

Jakobsson, Niklas, and Kotsadam, Andreas (2016) 'The economics of trafficking for sexual exploitation', in Scott Cunningham and Manisha Shah (eds), *The Oxford Handbook of the Economics of Prostitution.* Oxford: Oxford University Press, pp 461–81.

Jeffreys, Sheila (2008) *The Industrial Vagina: The Political Economy of the Global Sex Trade.* London: Routledge.

Jennings, Bethany, Cree, Vivienne E., and Kirkwood, Steve (2020) 'Agency and exploitation: Two sides of one coin? Women's experiences of selling sex and engaging with NGOs in Dhaka', *International Social Work*, 65(4), 761–72.

Kangaspunta, Kristiina, Sarrica, Fabrizio, and Johansen, Raggie (2016) 'Trafficking in persons: The involvement of women and children', in Helmut Kury, Sławomir Redo, and Evelyn Shea (eds), *Women and Children as Victims and Offenders: Background, Prevention, Reintegration: Suggestions for Succeeding Generations. Vol. 1.* Switzerland: Springer, pp 857–73.

Kapur, Devish, Lewis, John P., and Webb, Richard (eds) (2002) *The World Bank: Its First Half Century.* Washington, DC: Brookings Institution Press.

Kavemann, Barbara (2009) 'Das deutsche Prostitutionsgesetz im europäischen Vergleich', in Barbara Kavemann and Heike Rabe (eds), *Das Prostitutionsgesetz. Aktuelle Forschungsergebnisse, Umsetzung und Weiterentwicklung.* Opladen/Farmington Hills: Verlag Barbara Budrich, pp 13–33.

Kelley, J., Heiss, A., and Guevara, M. (2015) *Human Trafficking Non-governmental Organisations Survey: Summary.* Duke Sanford School of Public Policy. Available at: https://people.duke.edu/~ath20/human_trafficking_NGO_survey_summary.pdf

Kelly, Liz (2003) 'The wrong debate: Reflections on why force is not the key issue with respect to trafficking in women for sexual exploitation', *Feminist Review*, 73(1): 139–44.

Kelly, Liz, Coy, Maddy, and Davenport, Rebecca (2009) *Shifting Sands: A Comparison of Prostitution Across Nine Countries.* London: London Metropolitan University Child and Women Abuse Studies Unit.

Kelly, Liz, Turner, Jackie, and Coy, Maddy (2014) *Thematic Report on Approaches to Prostitution across the EU.* London: Child and Women Abuse Studies Unit, London Metropolitan University.

Keynes, John Maynard (1936) *The General Theory of Employment, Interest and Money.* London: Macmillan.

Kingston, Sarah, and Thomas, Terry (2019) 'No model in practice: A "Nordic model" to respond to prostitution?' *Crime, Law and Social Change*, 71: 423–39.

Kirby, Stuart, and Penna, Sue (2010) 'Policing mobile criminality: Towards a situational crime prevention approach to organised crime', in Kate Bullock, Ronald Clarke, and Nick Tilley (eds), *Situational Prevention of Organised Crime.* Cullompton: Willan Publishing, pp 193–212.

Kirby, Stuart, and Snow, Nicki (2016) 'Praxis and the disruption of organised crime groups', *Trends in Organised Crime*, 19(2): 111–24.

Kitchin, Rob (2021) *The Data Revolution: A Critical Analysis of Big Data, Open Data and Data Infrastructures* (2nd edn). London: Sage.

Klein, Rahel (2021): 'Bleibt Deutschland das „Bordell Europas"?' *Deutsche Welle*, 13 February. Available at: https://www.dw.com/de/bleibt-deutschl and-das-bordell-europas/a-56552309

Kofman, Eleonore, and Raghuram, Parvati (2015) *Gendered Migrations and Global Social Reproduction: Migration, Diasporas and Citizenship*. Basingstoke, Hampshire: Palgrave Macmillan.

Koordinierungskreis gegen Menschenhandel e.V. (KOK) (2021) *Datenerhebung zu Menschenhandel und Ausbeutung in Deutschland: Bericht des KOK e.V.*. Berlin: KOK.

Kotiswaran, Prabha (ed) (2017) *Revisiting the Law and Governance of Trafficking, Forced Labour and Modern Slavery*. Cambridge: Cambridge University Press.

Kotiswaran, Prabha (2021) 'The sexual politics of anti-trafficking discourse', *Feminist Legal Studies*, 29: 43–65.

Lacey, Nicola (2004) 'Criminalisation as regulation: The role of criminal law', in Christine Parker, Colin Scott, Nicola Lacey, and John Braithwaite (eds), *Regulating Law*. Oxford: Oxford University Press, pp 144–67.

Lacey, Nicola (2009) 'Historicising criminalisation: Conceptual and empirical issues', *The Modern Law Review*, 72(6): 936–60.

Lawthom, Rebecca, Kagan, Carolyn, Baines, Sue, Lo, Sandy, Sham, Sylvia, and Mok, Lisa et al (2015) 'Experiences of forced labour among UK-based Chinese migrant workers: Exploring vulnerability and protection in times of Empire', in Louise Waite, Gary Craig, Hannah Lewis, and Klara Skrivankova (eds), *Vulnerability, Exploitation and Migrants: Insecure Work in a Globalized Economy*. Houndmills: Palgrave Macmillan, pp 174–86.

Lazzarino, Runa (2019) 'Fixing the disjuncture, inverting the drift: Decolonizing human trafficking and modern slavery', *Journal of Modern Slavery*, 5(1): 1–31.

Lazzarino, Runa, Wright, Nicola, and Jordan, Melanie (2022) 'Mental healthcare for survivors of modern slavery and human trafficking: A single point-in-time, Internet-based scoping study of third sector provision', *Journal of Human Trafficking*. https://doi.org/10.1080/23322705.2021.2024043

LeBaron, Genevieve (2012) 'Rethinking prison labor: Social discipline and the state in historical perspective', *WorkingUSA*, 15(3): 327–51.

LeBaron, Genevieve (2014) 'Reconceptualizing debt bondage: Debt as a class-based form of labor discipline', *Critical Sociology*, 40(5): 763–80.

LeBaron, Genevieve (2015) 'Benchmarking global supply chains: The power of the "ethical audit" regime', *Review of International Studies*, 41(5): 905–24.

LeBaron, Genevieve (2020a) *Combatting Modern Slavery: Why Labour Governance is Failing and What We Can Do About It*. Cambridge: Polity Press.

LeBaron, Genevieve (2020b) 'Modern slavery in business: The sad and sorry state of a non-field', *Business & Society*, 60(2): 251–87.

LeBaron, Genevieve (2021) 'The role of supply chains in the global business of forced labour', *Journal of Supply Chain Management*, 57(2): 29–42.

LeBaron, Genevieve, and Phillips, Nicola (2019) 'States and the political economy of unfree labour', *New Political Economy*, 24(1): 1–21.

LeBaron, Genevieve, and Roberts, Adrienne (2010) 'Toward a political economy of capitalism and carcerality', *Signs*, 36(1): 19–44.

LeBaron, Genevieve, and Rühmkorf, Andreas (2019) 'The domestic politics of corporate accountability legislation: Struggles over the 2015 UK Modern Slavery Act', *Socio-Economic Review*, 17(3): 709–43.

LeBaron, Genevieve, and Lister, Jane (2022) 'The hidden costs of global supply chain solutions', *Review of International Political Economy*, 29(3): 669–95.

LeBaron, Genevieve, Lister, Jane, and Dauvergne, Peter (2017) 'Governing global supply chain sustainability through the ethical auditing regime', *Globalizations*, 14(6): 958–75.

Lee, Ching Kwan (2018) *The Spector of Global China: Politics, Labor and Foreign Investment in Africa*. Chicago: The University of Chicago Press.

Levi, Michael (2002) 'Money laundering and its regulation', *Annals of the American Academy of Political and Social Science*, 582(1): 181–94.

Lewis, Alexandra, and Blitz, Brad K. (2023) 'The Ru.Lag: The Kremlin's new empire of forced labour', *Journal of Modern Slavery*, 8(1): 1–32.

Lindquist, Johan (2010) 'Labour recruitment, circuits of capital and gendered mobility: Reconceptualizing the Indonesian migration industry', *Pacific Affairs*, 83(1): 115–32.

Lindquist, Johan (2012) 'The elementary school teacher, the thug and his grandmother: Informal brokers and transnational migration from Indonesia', *Pacific Affairs*, 85(1), 69–89.

Lindquist, Johan (2013a) 'Rescue, return, in place: Deportees, "victims", and the regulation of Indonesian migration', in Bao Xiang, Brenda S.A. Yeoh, and Mika Toyota (eds), *Return: Nationalizing Transnational Mobility in Asia*. Durham and London: Duke University Press, pp 122–40.

Lindquist, Johan (2013b) 'Beyond anti-anti-trafficking', *Dialectical Anthropology*, 37(2): 319–23.

Lipscombe, Sally, and Board, Jacqueline (2014) *Human Trafficking: UK Responses*. House of Commons Library Standard Note SN/HA/4324.

Lipset, Seymour Martin (1959) 'Some requisites of democracy: Economic development and political legitimacy', *American Sociological Review*, 53: 69–105.

Loader, Ian, and Walker, Neil (2007) *Civilising Security*. Cambridge: Cambridge University Press.

Lombardo, Emanuela, Kantola, Johanna, and Rubio-Marin, Ruth (2021) 'De-democratization and opposition to gender equality politics in Europe', *Social Politics*, 28(3): 521–31.

Lury, Celia (2021) *Problem Spaces: How and Why Methodology Matters*. Cambridge: Polity.

MacKinnon, Catherine A. (2011) 'Trafficking, prostitution, and inequality', *Harvard Civil Rights-Civil Liberties Law Review*, 46(2): 271–309.

Maroukis, Thanos (2016) *Demand in the Context of Trafficking in Human Beings in the Domestic Work Sector in the United Kingdom*. DemandAT Country Study No.7. Vienna: DemandAT. Available at: http://cadmus.eui.eu/handle/1814/41930

Matolcsi, Andrea (2022) 'Police implementation of the partial sex purchase ban in England and Wales', *European Journal on Criminal Policy and Research*, 28: 135–53.

Matolcsi, Andrea, Mulvihill, Natasha, Lilley-Walker, Sarah-Jane, Lanau, Alba, and Hester, Marianne (2021) 'The current landscape of prostitution and sex work in England and Wales', *Sexuality & Culture*, 25: 39–57.

Matthews, Roger (2018) 'Regulating the demand for commercialized sexual services', *Women's Studies International Forum*, 69: 1–8.

Matthews, Roger, Easton, Helen, Young, Lisa, and Bindel, Julie (2014) *Exiting Prostitution: A Study in Female Desistance*. Basingstoke: Palgrave Macmillan.

Mayntz, Renate (2017) 'Illegal markets: Boundaries and interfaces between legality and illegality', in Jens Beckert and Matias Dewey (eds) *The Architecture of Illegal Markets: Towards an Economic Sociology of Illegality in the Economy*. Oxford: Oxford University Press, pp 37 – 47.

McCulloch, Jude, and Pickering, Sharon (2009) 'Pre-crime and counter-terrorism: Imagining future crime in the "War on Terror"', *The British Journal of Criminology*, 49(5): 628–45.

McGlynn, Clare (2022) 'Challenging anti-carceral feminism: Criminalisation, justice and continuum thinking', *Women's Studies International Forum*, 93. https://doi.org/10.1016/j.wsif.2022.102614

McIlwaine, Cathy, and Moser, Caroline (2003) 'Poverty, violence and livelihood security in urban Colombia and Guatemala', *Progress in Development Studies*, 3(2): 113–30.

Merry, Sally Engle (2016) *The Seductions of Quantification: Measuring Human Rights, Gender Violence, and Sex Trafficking*. Chicago: University of Chicago Press.

Mies, Maria (1986) *Patriarchy and Accumulation on a Large Scale*. London: Zed Books.

Minsky, Hyman (2008) [1986] *Stabilizing an Unstable Economy*. New York: McGraw-Hill.

Minzel, Heiner (2006) 'Gewerberechtliche Anmeldung und Konzessionierung von Prostitutionsstätten am Beispiel: „Dortmunder Modell"', *Die Kriminalpolizei*. Available at: http://www.kriminalpolizei.de/startseite/news-detailansicht/artikel/gew

Moghadam, Valentine M. (2005) *Globalizing Women: Transnational Feminist Networks*. Baltimore: John Hopkins University Press.

Moghadam, Valentine M. (2023) 'Gender regimes, polities, and the world-system: Comparing Iran and Tunisia', *Women's Studies International Forum*, 98. https://doi.org/10.1016/j.wsif.2023.102721

Molodikova, Irina (2020) 'One step forward and two steps back: Migration policy and human trafficking in the Russian Federation since the Palermo Protocol of 2020', *Journal of Human Trafficking*, 6(2): 141–155.

Moore, Barrington (1966) *Social Origins of Dictatorship and Democracy: Lord and Peasant in the Making of the Modern World*. Boston, MA: Beacon Press.

Moser, Caroline O.N. and McIlwaine, Cathy (2014) 'Editorial: New frontiers in twenty-first century urban conflict and violence', *Environment and Urbanization*, 26(2): 331–44.

Mujaj, Endrit and Netscher, Amanda (2015) *Prostitution in Sweden 2014: The Extent and Development of Prostitution in Sweden*. Stockholm: Länsstyrelsen Stockholm. Available at: https://www.lansstyrelsen.se/download/18.35db0 62616a5352a22a1d7a5/1559733783690/Rapport%202015-18%20prost itution%20in%20Sweden%202014.pdf

Nakazora, Moe (2017) 'Infrastructural inversion and reflexivity', in Penny Harvey, Casper Bruun Jensen, and Atsuro Morita (eds), *Infrastructures and Social Complexity*. London: Routledge, pp 309–22.

Neilson, Jeffrey, Pritchard, Bill, and Yeung, Henry Wai-Chung (2014) 'Global value chains and global production networks in the changing international political economy: An introduction', *Review of International Political Economy*, 21(1): 1–8.

Niño-Zarazúa, Miguel (2019) 'Welfare and redistributive effects of social assistance in the Global South', *Population and Development Review*, 4(S1): 3–22.

O'Brien, Erin and Wilson, Michael (2015) 'Clinton, Bush, and Obama: Changing policy and rhetoric in the United States annual trafficking in persons report', in Molly Dragiewicz (ed), *Global Human Trafficking*. London: Routledge, pp 123–37.

O'Brien, Freya, Palmer, Sasha, and Blinkhorn, Victoria (2022) 'Factors that predict the referral of adult Modern Day Slavery cases to the UK's National Referral Mechanism', *International Journal of Police Science & Management*, 24(3), 273–84.

O'Connell Davidson, Julia (1998) *Prostitution, Power and Freedom*. Michigan: University of Michigan Press.

O'Connell Davidson, Julia (2011) 'Moving children? Child trafficking, child migration, and child rights', *Critical Social Policy*, 31(3): 454–77.

O'Connell Davidson, Julia (2015) *Modern Slavery: The Margins of Freedom*. Houndmills: Palgrave Macmillan.

Office for National Statistics (ONS) (2020) *Modern Slavery in the UK: March 2020*. Available at: https://www.ons.gov.uk/peoplepopulationandcommun ity/crimeandjustice/articles/modernslaveryintheuk/march2020

Ollus, Natalia, Jokinen, Anniina, and Joutsen, Matti (2013) *Exploitation of Migrant Workers in Finland, Sweden, Estonia and Lithuania: Uncovering the Links between Recruitment, Irregular Employment Practices and Labour Trafficking.* HEUNI Report. Helsinki: European Institute for Crime Prevention and Control.

Oram, Sian, Ostrovschi, Nicolae V., Gorceag, Viorel I., Hotineanu, Mihai A., Gorceag, Lilia, Trigub, Carolina, et al (2012) 'Physical health symptoms reported by trafficked women receiving post-trafficking support in Moldova: Prevalence, severity and associated actors,' *Biomedcentral Women's Health*, 12(20): 1–9.

Oram, Sian, Abas, Melanie, Bick, Debra, Boyle, Adrian, French, Rebecca, Jakobowitz, Sharon, et al (2016) 'Human trafficking and health: A survey of male and female survivors in England,' *American Journal of Public Health*, 106(6):1073–8.

Organisation for Economic Co-operation and Development (OECD) (1994) *The OECD Jobs Strategy.* Paris: OECD.

Organisation for Economic Co-operation and Development (OECD) (2018) *OECD Due Diligence Guidance for Responsible Business Conduct.* Available at: https://www.oecd.org/investment/due-diligence-guidance-for-responsible-business-conduct.htm

Organization for Security and Cooperation (OSCE) (2004) *National Referral Mechanisms: Joining Efforts to Protect the Rights of Trafficked Persons, A Practical Guide.* Warsaw: OSCE.

Orloff, Ann S. (1996) 'Gender in the welfare state', *The Annual Review of Sociology*, 22: 51–78.

Orloff, Ann S., and Laperrière, Marie (2021) 'Gender', in Daniel Béland, Kimberly J. Morgan, Herbert Obinger, and Christopher Pierson (eds), *The Oxford Handbook of the Welfare State.* Oxford: Oxford University Press, pp 346–64.

Outshoorn, Joyce (2001) 'Regulating prostitution as sex work: The pioneer case of the Netherlands', *Acta Politica*, 36(2): 155–79.

Paasche, Erlend, Skilbrei, May-Len, and Plambech, Sine (2018) 'Vulnerable here or there? Examining the vulnerability of victims of human trafficking before and after return', *Anti-Trafficking Review*, 10: 34–51.

Pajón Laura, and Walsh, Dave (2023) 'The importance of multi-agency collaborations during human trafficking criminal investigations', *Policing and Society*, 33(3): 296–314.

Palmer, Emma (2019) 'Trafficked children and child protection systems in the European Union', *European Journal of Social Work*, 22(4): 551–62.

Panda, Pradeep, and Agarwal, Bina (2005) 'Marital violence, human development and women's property status in India', *World Development*, 33(5): 823–50.

Peksen, Dursun, Blanton, Shannon Lindsey, and Blanto, Robert G. (2017) 'Neoliberal policies and human trafficking for labor: Free markets, unfree workers?', *Political Research Quarterly*, 709(3): 673–86.

Penna, Sue, and Kirby, Stuart (2012) 'Bridge over the river crime: Mobility and the policing of organised crime', *Mobilities*, 8(4): 487–505.

Penna, Sue, and O'Brien, Martin (2018) 'The corruption of politics or the politics of corruption? Reconsidering the role of organised crime in the geo-politics of corruption', in Francesco Chiodelli, Tim Hall, and Ray Hudson (eds), *The Illicit and Illegal in Regional and Urban Governance and Development: Corrupt Places*. London: Routledge, pp 200–20.

Peyroux, Olivier (2015) *Trafficking in Human Beings in Conflict Situations*. Caritas France Progress Report. Available at: https://www.caritas.org/wordpress/wp-content/uploads/2015/06/RESEARCH-ACTION-Trafficking-in-human-beings-and-conflicts-EN-10-juin-2015.pdf

Phillips, Nicola (2015) 'Private governance and the problem of trafficking and slavery in global supply chains', in Louis Waite, Gary Craig, Hannah Lewis, and Karla Skrivankova (eds), *Vulnerability, Exploitation and Migrants: Insecure Work in a Globalized Economy*. Houndmills: Palgrave Macmillan, pp 15–27.

Pinker, Steven (2011) *The Better Angels of Our Nature: The Decline of Violence in History and its Causes*. London: Allen Lane.

Pinker, Steven (2018) *Enlightenment Now: The Case for Reason, Science, Humanism and Progress*. London: Penguin.

Plantin, Jean-Christophe, Lagoze, Carl, Edwards, Paul N., and Sandvig, C. (2018) 'Infrastructure studies meet platform studies in the age of Google and Facebook', *New Media & Society*, 20(1): 293–310.

Poell, Thomas, Nieborg, David, and van Dijck, José (2019) 'Platformisation', *Internet Policy Review*, 8(4): 1–13.

Polanyi, Karl (2001) [1944] *The Great Transformation: The Political and Economic Origins of Our Time* (2nd ed). Boston: Beacon Press.

Polaris (2021) *Polaris Analysis of 2020 Data from the National Human Trafficking Hotline*. Available at: https://polarisproject.org/wp-content/uploads/2022/01/Polaris-Analysis-of-2020-Data-from-the-National-Human-Trafficking-Hotline.pdf

Porter, Theodore M. (1996) *Trust in Numbers*. Princeton, NJ: Princeton University.

Rabe, Heike (2019) *Bekämpfung des Menschenhandels: Empfehlungen an Deutschland von der Expert_innengruppe GRETA*. Deutsches Institut für Menschenrechte Information Nr. 28. Berlin: Deutsches Institut für Menschenrechte.

Raby, Kyla, Chazal, Nerida, Garcia-Daza, Lina, and Mebalds, Ginta (2023) '"No income, temporary visa, and too many triggers": Barriers in accommodating survivors of human trafficking and slavery in Australia', *Anti-Trafficking Review*, (20): 92–110.

Rafferty, Yvonne (2021) 'The identification, recovery, and reintegration of victims of child trafficking within ASEAN: An exploratory study of knowledge gaps and emerging challenges', *Journal of Human Trafficking*, 7(2): 145–67.

Rao, Smriti, and Presenti, Christina (2012) 'Understanding human trafficking origin: A cross-country empirical analysis', *Feminist Economics*, 18(2): 231–63.

Raphael, Jody (2017) 'Returning trafficking prevalence to the public policy debate: Introduction to the special issue', *Journal of Human Trafficking*, 3(1): 1–20.

Reed, Sasha, Roe, Stephen, Grimshaw, James, and Oliver, Rhys (2018) *The Economic and Social Costs of Modern Slavery. Research Report 100.* London: Home Office. Available at: https://assets.publishing.service.gov. uk/government/uploads/system/uploads/attachment_data/file/729836/economic-and-social-costs-of-modern-slavery-horr100.pdf.

Reich, Robert B. (2016) *Saving Capitalism.* London: Icon Books.

Reis, Tara A., Gibbs, Jennifer, C., Howard, Daniel, and Strohacker, Emily R. (2022) 'Prostitute or human trafficking victim? Police discernment of human trafficking', *Policing: An International Journal*, 45(2): 334–45.

Research Network on the Legal Parameters of Slavery (2012) *Bellagio-Harvard Guidelines on the Legal Parameters of Slavery.* Available at: https://www.monash.edu/law/research/centres/castancentre/our-areas-of-work/economic,-social-and-cultural-rights/human-trafficking/bellagio-harvard-guidelines-on-the-legal-parameters-of-slavery

Rijken, Conny (ed) (2011) *Combating Trafficking in Human Beings for Labour Exploitation.* Nijmegen: Wolf Legal Publishers.

Rijken, Conny, and de Lange, Tesseltje (2018) *Towards a Decent Labour Market for Low Waged Migrant Workers.* Amsterdam: Amsterdam University Press.

Rioux, Sébastien, LeBaron, Genevieve, and Verovšek, Peter J. (2020) 'Capitalism and unfree labor: A review of Marxist perspectives on modern slavery', *Review of International Political Economy*, 27(3): 709–31.

Roberts, Kate (2018) 'Life after trafficking: A gap in the UK's modern slavery efforts', *Anti-Trafficking Review*, 10: 164–8.

Robinson, William I. (2004) *A Theory of Global Capitalism: Production, Class, and State in a Transnational World.* Baltimore: Johns Hopkins University Press.

Rodriguez, Robyn Magalit (2010) *Migrants for Export: How the Philippine State Brokers Labor to the World.* Minneapolis: University of Minnesota Press.

Rogerson, Michael, Crane, Andrew, Soundararajan, Vivek, Grosvold, Johanne, and Cho, Charles H. (2020) 'Organisational responses to mandatory modern slavery disclosure legislation: A failure of experimentalist governance?', *Accounting, Auditing, & Accountability Journal*, 33(7): 1505–34.

Romero, Karen, Torres, Tatiana, Jones, Alana, and Dacosta-Reyes, Clara (2023) 'Closing the door on survivors: How anti-trafficking programmes in the US limit access to housing', *Anti-Trafficking Review*, (20): 135–43.

Rose, Nikolas (1999) *Powers of Freedom: Reframing Political Thought*. Cambridge: Cambridge University Press.

Ryan, Louise (2011) 'Migrants' social networks and weak ties: Accessing resources and constructing relationships post-migration', *The Sociological Review*, 59(4): 707–24.

Sanders, Teela (2004) *Sex Work: A Risky Business*. London: Willan.

Sanders, Teela, O'Neil, Maggie, and Pitcher, Jane (2017) *Prostitution: Sex Work, Policy and Politics* (2nd ed). London: Sage'

Satz, Debra (1995) 'Markets in women's sexual labor', *Ethics*, 106(1): 63–85.

Satz, Debra (2008) 'The moral limits of markets: The case of human kidneys', *Proceedings of the Aristotelian Society*, 108: 269–88.

Satz, Debra (2010) *Why Some Things Should Not Be for Sale: The Moral Limits of Markets*. Oxford: Oxford University Press.

Scarpa, Simone, Castles, Stephen, and Schierup, Carl-Ulrik (2021) 'Migration and new ethnic minorities', in Béland, Daniel, Morgan, Kimberly J., Obinger, Herbert, and Pierson, Christopher (eds), *The Oxford Handbook of the Welfare State*. Oxford: Oxford University Press, pp 380–96.

Schäfer, Ortwin (2012) 'Das Dortmunder Modell: Erfahrungen und Vorschläge zur Weiterentwicklung der gewerberechtlichen Einordnung von Prostitution und Prostitutionsstätten', in *Bundesministerium für Familie, Senioren, Frauen und Jugend Regulierung von Prostitution und Prostitutionsstätten*. BMFSJF: Berlin, pp 38–43.

Scoular, Jane, Pitcher, Jane, Sanders, Teela, Campbell, Rosie, and Cunningham, Stewart (2019) 'Beyond the gaze and well beyond Wolfenden: The practices and rationalities of regulating and policing sex work in the digital age', *Journal of Law and Society*, 46(2): 211–39.

Sen, Amartya (1999) *Development as Freedom*. Oxford: Oxford University Press.

Shahadat, Khandkaar, and Uddin, Shahzad (2022) 'Labour controls, unfreedom and perpetuation of slavery on a tea plantation', *Work, Employment and Society*, 36(3): 522–38.

Shaxson, Nicholas (2012) *Treasure Islands: Tax Havens and the Men who Stole the World*. London: Vintage Books.

Shire, Karen A. (2020) 'The social order of transnational migration markets', *Global Networks*, 20(3): 434–53.

Shire, Karen A. (2023) 'Social democratic imaginaries of transformation in conservative gender regimes', *Women's Studies International Forum*, 99. https://doi.org/10.1016/j.wsif.2023.102766

Shire, Karen A., and Nemoto, Kumiko (2020) 'Origins and transformations of conservative gender regimes in Germany and Japan', *Social Politics*, 27(3): 432–48.

Shire, Karen A., and Walby, Sylvia (2020) 'Advances in theorizing varieties of gender regimes', *Social Politics*, 27(3): 409–13.

Sîlkner, Andrea (2008) *Needs Assessment of the National Referral Mechanism for Victims of Trafficking in Human Beings in Ukraine.* Kyiv, OSCE.

Simic, Agnes, and Blitz, Brad K. (2019) 'The modern slavery regime: A critical evaluation', *Journal of the British Academy*, 7(s1): 1–34.

Simon, Jonathan (2007) *Governing Through Crime: How the War on Crime Transformed American Democracy and Created a Culture of Fear.* New York: Oxford University Press.

Skrivankova, Klara (2010) *Between Decent Work and Forced Labour: Examining the Continuum of Exploitation.* Joseph Rowntree Foundation Programme Paper. York: Joseph Rowntree Foundation.

Smith, Adam (1986) [1776] *An Inquiry into the Nature and Causes of the Wealth of Nations.* Harmondsworth: Penguin.

Smith, Charles A. and Miller-de la Cuesta, Brandon (2011) 'Human trafficking in conflict zones: The role of peacekeepers in the formation of networks', *Human Rights Review*, 12(3): 287–99.

Sönmez, Sevil, Apostolopoulos, Yorghos, Tran, Diane, and Rentrope, Shantanya (2011) 'Human rights and health disparities for migrant workers in the UAE', *Health and Human Rights*, 13(2): 17–35.

Sorrentino, Lilianam, and Jokinen, Anniina (2014) *Guidelines to Prevent Abusive Recruitment, Exploitative Employment and Trafficking of Migrant Workers in the Baltic Sea Region.* HEUNI Report No. 78. Helsinki: HEUNI. Available at: http://www.heuni.fi/material/attachments/heuni/reports/Eviel1wVV/Heuni_reports_78_Guidelines.pdf

Sozialwissenschaftliches Frauenforschungsinstitut Freiburg (SoFFi.K) (2005) *Untersuchung zu den Auswirkung des Prostitutionsgesetzes*, BMFSFJ: Berlin.

Spapens, Antonius C.M., Peters, Maaike, and Van Daele, Dirk (eds) (2015) *Administrative Measures to Prevent and Tackle Crime: Legal Possibilities and Practical Application in EU Member States.* The Hague: Eleven International Publishing.

Star, Susan L. (1999) 'The ethnography of infrastructure', *American Behavioral Scientist*, 43(3): 377–91.

Star, Susan L., and Griesemer, James R. (1989) 'Institutional ecology, "translations" and boundary objects', *Social Studies of Science*, 19(3): 387–420.

Statistisches Bundesamt (2020) *Ende 2019 rund 40400 Prostituierte bei Behörden.* Pressemitteilung Nr. 286, 30 July. Available at: www.destatis.de

Statistisches Bundesamt (2021) *Ende 2020 rund 24900 Prostituierte bei Behörden angemeldet.* Pressemitteilung Nr, 314, 1 July. Available at: www.destatis.de

Statistisches Bundesamt (2022) *Ende 2021 rund 23700 Prostituierte bei Behörden angemeldet.* Pressemitteilung Nr 277, 1 July. Available at: www.destatis.de

Strauss, Kendra (2014) 'Unfree labour and the regulation of temporary agency work in the UK', in Judy Fudge and Kendra Strauss (eds), *Temporary Work, Agencies and Unfree Labour: Insecurity in the New World of Work.* London, Routledge: pp 164–83.

Surak, Kristin (2013) 'Guestworkers: A taxonomy', *New Left Review*, (84): 84–102.

Taylor, Chloë (2018) 'Anti-carceral feminism and sexual assault – a defense: A critique of the critique of the critique of carceral feminism', *Social Philosophy Today*, 34: 29–49.

Terwiel, Anna (2020) 'What is carceral feminism?', *Political Theory*, 48(4): 421–42.

Teubner, Gunther (1997) 'Global Bukowina: Legal pluralism in the world society', in Gunther Teubner (ed), *Global Law Without a State*. Brookfield: Dartmouth, pp 3–28.

Theodore, Nik, and Peck, Jamie (2014) 'Selling flexibility: Temporary staffing in a volatile economy', in Judy Fudge and Kendra Strauss (eds), *Temporary Work, Agencies and Unfree Labour: Insecurity in the New World of Work*, Oxon: Routledge, pp 26–47.

Therborn, Göran (1995) *European Modernity*. London: Sage.

Thomas, Chantal (2013) 'Immigration controls and "Modern-Day Slavery"', *Cornell Legal Studies Research Paper*, 13–86. Available at: https://papers.ssrn.com/sol3/papers.cfm?abstract_id=2294656

Toews, Ann (2018) 'Reaching for a new approach: a newcomer NGO builds a network to fight the modern slave trade, 2012–2018', Princeton University, Innovations for Successful Societies.

Tooze, Adam (2007) *The Wages of Destruction: The Making and Breaking of the Nazi Economy*. London: Penguin.

tradebeyond (2023) 'The list of global supply chain due diligence laws keeps growing. Blog updated 6/14/2023'. Available at: https://tradebeyond.com/blog/list-of-global-supply-chain-due-diligence-laws/

Transplantation Society (TTS) and International Society of Nephrology (2008) *The Declaration of Istanbul on Organ Trafficking and Transplant Tourism*. Available at: https://www.declarationofistanbul.org/the-declaration

Transplantation Society (TTS) and International Society of Nephrology (2018) *The Declaration of Istanbul on Organ Trafficking and Transplant Tourism* (2018 ed). Available at: https://www.declarationofistanbul.org/the-declaration

Tünte, Markus, Apitzsch, Birgit, and Shire, Karen, A. (2017) 'Prostitution und Sexarbeit: Alte und neue Kontroversen aus dem Blick der Frauen- und Geschlechterforschung', in Beate Kortendiek, Katja Sabisch, and Birgit Riegraf (eds), *Handbuch Interdisziplinäre Geschlechterforschung*. Wiesbaden: Springer Verlag, pp 845 –53.

Turner, Jackie (2013) 'Violent intersections: Revisiting the traffic in women and girls', in Yasmin Rehman, Liz Kelly, and Hannana Siddiqui (eds), *Moving in the Shadows: Violence in the Lives of Minority Women and Children*. Ashgate: London, pp 59–76.

UK Home Affairs Select Committee (2023) *Human Trafficking*. Human Trafficking - Oral evidence transcripts - Committees - UK Parliament.

UK Gangmasters and Labour Abuse Authority (2023) *What we do*. What we do, Regulation Licensing scheme, GLAA. Available at: https://www.gla.gov.uk/who-we-are/what-we-do/

UK Parliament (1957) *Report of the Committee on Homosexual Offences and Prostitution*. Wolfenden Report, UK Parliament. London: House of Lords.

United Kingdom (UK) HM Government (2021) *2021 UK Annual Report on Modern Slavery*. Available at: https://assets.publishing.service.gov.uk/government/uploads/system/uploads/attachment_data/file/1033986/2021_UK_Annual_Report_on_Modern_Slavery.pdf

United Kingdom (UK) National Crime Agency (2023) *National Strategic Assessment 2023 Modern Slavery and Human Trafficking*. Available at: https://nationalcrimeagency.gov.uk/nsa-modern-slavery-and-human-trafficking

United Nations (UN) (2000c) *Millennium Development Goals*, adopted at the UN Millennium Summit in September 2000. Available at: www.un.org/millenniumgoals/

United Nations (UN) (2015) *Sustainable Development Goals*. Available at: https://www.undp.org/sustainable-development-goals

United Nations (UN) (2021) *UN Global Compact Strategy 2021–2023*. Available at: https://unglobalcompact.org/library/5869

United Nations Conference on Trade and Development (UNCTAD) (2023) *World Investment Report 2023*. Available at: https://unctad.org/publication/world-investment-report-2023

United Nations (UN) General Assembly (2015) *Transforming Our World: The 2030 Agenda for Sustainable Development*. Resolution adopted by the General Assembly, A/RES/70/1. Available at: https://sdgs.un.org/2030agenda

United Nations (UN) General Assembly (2016) *Trafficking in Persons, Especially Women and Children. Note by the Secretary-General*. Available at: https://digitallibrary.un.org/record/16402241

United Nations (UN) General Assembly (2018a) *Intergovernmental Conference to Adopt the Global Compact for Safe, Orderly and Regular Migration*. Available at: https://www.un.org/en/conf/migration/

United Nations (UN) General Assembly (2018b) *Contemporary Forms of Slavery, Including its Causes and Consequences. Note by the Secretary-General*. A/73/139. Available at: https://documents-dds-ny.un.org/doc/UNDOC/GEN/N18/218/69/PDF/N1821869.pdf?OpenElement

United Nations (UN) General Assembly (2018c) *Report of the UN Special Rapporteur on Contemporary Forms of Slavery, Including its Causes and Consequences*. A/HRC/39/52.

United Nations (UN) General Assembly (2019a). *Global Compact for Safe, Orderly and Regular Migration*. Resolution adopted by the General Assembly on 19 December 2018. A/RES/73/195.

United Nations (UN) General Assembly (2019b) *Current and Emerging Forms of Slavery. Report of the UN Special Rapporteur on Contemporary Forms of Slavery, Including its Causes and Consequences.* A/HRC/42/44.

United Nations (UN) General Assembly (2020a) *Resolution on Trafficking in Women and Girls*, 17/158, adopted by the General Assembly on 16 December 2020. Available at: https://www.un.org

United Nations (UN) General Assembly (2020b) *Trafficking in women and girls: Report of the Secretary-General.* A/75/289, 7 August.

United Nations (UN) General Assembly (2020c) *Report of the UN Special Rapporteur on Contemporary Forms of Slavery, Including its Causes and Consequences.* A/75/166, 16 July.

United Nations (UN) General Assembly (2022a) *Contemporary Forms of Slavery: Including its Causes and Consequences.* Note by the Secretary-General. A/77/163. Available at: https://documents-dds-ny.un.org/doc/UNDOC/GEN/N22/425/94/PDF/N2242594.pdf?OpenElement

United Nations (UN) General Assembly (2022b) *Trafficking in Women and Girls: Crises as a Risk Multiplier.* Report of the Secretary-General, 7 August 2022. Available at: https://eca.unwomen.org/en/digital-library/publications/2020/07/a-75-289-sg-report-trafficking-0

United Nations (UN) General Assembly (2022c) *General Assembly Security Council, Peacebuilding and Sustaining Peace.* Report of the Secretary-General. A/76/668.

United Nations (UN) Office of the High Commissioner for Human Rights (OHCHR) (2011) *Recommended Principles and Guidelines on Human Rights and Human Trafficking.* Recommended Principles and Guidelines on Human Rights and Human Trafficking: Commentary, OHCHR.

United Nations (UN) Office of the United Nations High Commissioner for Human Rights (OHCHR) (2014) *Report of the Office of the United Nations High Commissioner for Human Rights on Preventing and Eliminating Child, Early and Forced Marriage.* A/HRC/26/22.

United Nations Office of the High Commissioner for Human Rights (OHCHR) (2023a) *International Standards: Special Rapporteur on Contemporary Forms of Slavery.* United Nations Office of the High Commissioner for Human Rights. Available at: https://www.ohchr.org/en/special-procedures/sr-slavery/international-standards

United Nations (UN) Office of the High Commissioner for Human Rights (OHCHR) (2023b) *Home Page* UN Human Rights Office (ohchr.org).

United Nations Office on Drugs and Crime (UNODC) (2009) *Global Report on Trafficking in Persons 2009.* Vienna: UNODC.

United Nations Office on Drugs and Crime (UNODC) (2011) *The Role of Corruption in Trafficking in Persons.* Vienna: UNODC.

United Nations Office on Drugs and Crime (UNODC) (2012) *Global Report on Trafficking in Persons.* Vienna: UNODC.

United Nations Office on Drugs and Crime (UNODC) (2013) *Abuse of a Position of Vulnerability and Other "Means" within the Definition of Trafficking in Persons.* Vienna: Vienna: UNODC.

United Nations Office on Drugs and Crime (UNODC) (2014a) *Global Report on Trafficking in Persons.* Vienna: UNODC.

United Nations Office on Drugs and Crime (UNODC) (2014b) *The Role of 'Consent' in the Trafficking in Persons Protocol.* Issue Paper. Vienna: UNODC.

United Nations Office on Drugs and Crime (UNODC) (2015) *The Concept of 'Exploitation' in the Trafficking in Persons Protocol.* Vienna: UNODC.

United Nations Office on Drugs and Crime (UNODC) (2016) *Global Report on Trafficking in Persons 2016.* Vienna: UNODC.

United Nations Office on Drugs and Crime (UNODC) (2018a) *Countering Trafficking in Persons in Conflict Situations: Thematic Paper.* Vienna: UNODC.

United Nations Office on Drugs and Crime (UNODC) (2018b) *Trafficking in Persons in the Context of Armed Conflict.* Vienna: UNODC.

United Nations Office on Drugs and Crime (UNODC) (2018c) *Global Report on Trafficking in Persons.* Vienna: UNODC.

United Nations Office on Drugs and Crime (UNODC) (2021) *Global Report on Trafficking in Persons 2020.* Vienna: UNODC.

United Nations Office on Drugs and Crime (UNODC) (2022a) *Global Report on Trafficking in Persons 2022: Collection of Court Case Summaries.* Vienna: UNODC.

United Nations Office on Drugs and Crime (UNODC) (2022b) *Conflict in Ukraine: Key Evidence on Risks of Trafficking in Persons and Smuggling of Migrants.* Vienna: UNODC.

United Nations Office on Drugs and Crime (UNODC) (2023) *Global Report on Trafficking in Persons 2022.* Vienna: UNODC.

United Nations (UN) Secretary-General (2020) *Trafficking in Women and Girls. Report of the Secretary-General.* Available at: https://www.unwomen.org/en/digital-library/publications/2020/07/a-75-289-sg-report-trafficking

United Nations Security Council (UNSC) (2016) *Resolution 2331 Trafficking.* S/RES/2331.

United Nations Security Council (UNSC) (2017) *Resolution 2388* Security Council Reiterates its Condemnation of Trafficking in Persons, Unanimously Adopting Resolution 2388. UN Press. Available at: https://press.un.org/en/2017/sc13081.doc.htm

United Nations Security Council (UNSC) (2022) *Report to the Secretary-General, Peacebuilding and Sustaining Peace,* 28 January, A/76/668-S/2022/66.

United Nations (UN) Special Rapporteur on Contemporary Forms of Slavery (2023) Annual thematic reports. Available at: https://www.ohchr.org/en/special-procedures/sr-slavery/annual-thematic-reports

United Nations (UN) Special Rapporteur on Trafficking in Persons (2023) *Special Rapporteur on Trafficking in Persons, Especially Women and Children.* Available at: https://www.ohchr.org/en/special-procedures/sr-trafficking-in-persons/annual-reports

United Nations (UN) Treaty Collection (2023) *Protocol to Prevent, Suppress and Punish Trafficking in Persons, Especially Women and Children*, supplementing the United Nations Convention against Transnational Organized Crime UNTC.

United Nations (UN) UN Women (2021) *From Evidence to Action: Tackling Gender-Based Violence against Migrant Women and Girls, Policy Brief.* New York: UN Women.

United Nations (UN) UN Women (2022) *Progress on the Sustainable Development Goals: The Gender Snapshot 2022.* Available at: https://bit.ly/gender-snapshot-2022.

United States (US) Department of Labor International Labor Assistance Bureau (2022) *List of Goods Produced by Child Labor or Forced Labor.* Available at: https://www.dol.gov/agencies/ilab/reports/child-labor/list-of-goods

United States (US) Department of State (2017) *Trafficking in Persons Report 2017.* Washington: US Department of State. Available at: https://www.state.gov/reports/2017-trafficking-in-persons-report/

United States (US) Department of State (2022a) *Trafficking in Persons Report 2022.* Washington: US Department of State. Available at: https://www.state.gov/reports/2022-trafficking-in-persons-report/

United States (US) Department of State (2022b) 'Implementation of the Uyghur Forced Labor Prevention Act', Press Statement by Antony J. Blinken, Secretary of State, 21 June. Available at: https://www.state.gov/implementation-of-the-uyghur-forced-labor-prevention-act/#:~:text=We%20have%20taken%20concrete%20measures,help%20U.S.%20companies%20avoid%20commerce

United States (US) Department of State (2023) *Trafficking in Persons Report 2023.* Washington: US Department of State. Available at: https://www.state.gov/reports/2023-trafficking-in-persons-report/

Urry, John (2007) *Mobilities.* Cambridge: Polity Press.

Urry, John (2016) *What is the Future?* Cambridge: Polity Press.

Van Daele, Dirk (2015) 'The administrative approach in Germany', in Antonius C.M. Spapens, Maaike Peters, and Dirk Van Daele (eds), *Administrative Measures to Prevent and Tackle Crime. Legal Possibilities and Practical Application in EU Member States.* The Hague: Eleven International Publishing, pp 191–238.

van der Leun, Joanne (2011) 'EU migration policy and labour exploitation', in Conny Rijken (ed), *Combatting Trafficking in Human Beings for Labour Exploitation.* Nijmegen: Wolf Legal Publishers, pp 425–41.

Varieties of Democracy (V-Dem) (2022) *Democracy Report: Autocratization Changing Nature?* Sweden: V-Dem.

Vaughan-Williams, Nick (2015) *Europe's Border Crisis: Biopolitical Security and Beyond.* Oxford: Oxford University Press.

Verloo, Mieke (ed) (2018) *Varieties of Opposition to Gender Equality in Europe.* New York: Routledge.

Virdee, Satnam (2014) *Racism, Class and the Racialized Outsider.* Basingstoke: Palgrave Macmillan.

Virdee, Satnam (2019) 'Racialized capitalism: An account of its contested origins and consolidation', *The Sociological Review,* 67(1): 3–27.

Vogel, Dita, and Cyrus, Norbert (2017) 'Demand reduction in anti-trafficking debates', *ERA Forum,* 18(3), 381–96.

Vosko, Leah F. (2010) *Managing the Margins: Gender, Citizenship, and the International Regulation of Precarious Employment.* Oxford: Oxford University Press.

Voss, Hinrich, Davis, Matthew, Sumner, Mark, Waite, Louise, Ras, Ilse, Singhal, Divya, et al (2019) 'International supply chains: Compliance and engagement with the Modern Slavery Act', *Journal of the British Academy,* 7(s1): 61–76.

Wacquant, Lois (2009) *Punishing the Poor: The Neoliberal Government of Social Insecurity.* Durham, NC: Duke University Press.

Wagner, Ines, and Shire, Karen (2019) 'Labour subcontracting in cross-border labour markets: A comparison of rule evasion in Germany and Japan', in Nathan Lillie and Jens Arnholz (eds), *Posted Work in the European Union: The Political Economy of Free Movement.* New York: Routledge, pp 185–203.

Waite, Louise, Craig, Gary, Lewis, Hannah, and Skrivankova, Klara (eds) (2015) *Vulnerability, Exploitation and Migrants: Insecure Work in a Globalised Economy.* London: Palgrave MacMillan.

Walby, Sylvia (2005) 'Gender mainstreaming: Productive tensions in theory and practice', *Social Politics,* 12(3): 321–43.

Walby, Sylvia (2007) 'Complexity theory, systems theory and multiple intersecting social inequalities', *Philosophy of the Social Sciences,* 37(4): 449–70.

Walby, Sylvia (2009) *Globalization and Inequalities: Complexity and Contested Modernities.* London: Sage.

Walby, Sylvia (2011) *The Future of Feminism.* Cambridge: Polity Press.

Walby, Sylvia (2013) 'Violence and society: Introduction to an emerging field of sociology', *Current Sociology,* 61(2): 95–111.

Walby, Sylvia (2015) *Crisis.* Cambridge: Polity.

Walby, Sylvia (2020) 'Varieties of gender regimes', *Social Politics,* 27(3): 414–31.

Walby, Sylvia (2021a) 'Developing the concept of society: Institutional domains, regimes of inequalities and complex systems in a global era', *Current Sociology,* 69(3): 315–32.

Walby, Sylvia (2021b) 'The COVID pandemic and social theory: Social democracy and public health in the crisis', *European Journal of Social Theory*, 24(1): 22–43.

Walby, Sylvia (2023a) 'Authoritarianism, violence, and varieties of gender regimes: Violence as an institutional domain', *Women's Studies International Forum*, 98. https://doi.org/10.1016/j.wsif.2023.102677

Walby, Sylvia (2023b) 'What is femicide? The United Nations and the measurement of progress in complex epistemic systems', *Current Sociology*, 71(1): 10–27.

Walby, Sylvia, and Olive, Phillipa (2014) *Estimating the Costs of Gender-Based Violence in the European Union*. European Institute of Gender Equality. Luxembourg: Publication Office of the European Union.

Walby, Sylvia, and Francis, Brian (2023) 'Improving the estimate of trafficking in human beings/modern slavery by integrating data from the ILO/Walk Free/IOM and UNODC'. Unpublished manuscript.

Walby, Sylvia, Armstrong, Jo, and Strid, Sofia (2012) 'Intersectionality: Multiple inequalities in social theory', *Sociology*, 46(2): 224–40.

Walby, Sylvia, Towers, Jude, Francis, Brian, Shire, Karen, Kelly, Liz, Apitzsch, Birgit, Armstrong, Jo, Balderston, Susie, Fish, Adam, Hardaker, Claire, Kirby, Stuart, May-Chahal, Corinne, and Palmer, Emma (2016a) *Comprehensive Policy Review of Anti-Trafficking Projects Funded by the European Commission*. HOME/2014/ISFP/PR/THBX/0052. Final Report. Luxembourg: Publications Office of the European Union. Available at: https://data.europa.eu/doi/10.2837/647655

Walby, Sylvia, Apitzsch, Birgit, Armstrong, Jo, Balderston, Susie, Follis, Karolina, Francis, Brian, Kelly, Liz, May-Chahal, Corinne, Rashid, Awais, Shire, Karen, Towers, Jude, and Tünte, Markus (2016b) *Study on Gender Dimension of Trafficking in Human Beings*. Luxembourg: Publications Office of the European Union. Available at:https://data.europa.eu/doi/10.2837/991766

Walby, Sylvia, Towers, Jude, Balderston, Susie, Corradi, Consuelo, Francis, Brian, Heiskanen, Markku, Helweg-Larsen, Karin, Mergaert, Lut, Olive, Philippa, Palmer, Emma, Stöckl, Heidi, Strid, Sofia (2017) *The Concept and Measurement of Violence against Women and Men*. Bristol: Policy Press.

Walby, Sylvia, Bell, Patricia, Bowstead, Janet, Feder, Gene, Fraser, Abigail, Herbert, Annie, Kirby, Stuart, McManus, Sally, Morris, Stephan, Oram, Sian, Phoenix, Jessica, Pullerits, Merili, and Verrall, Rachel (2020) *Study on the Economic, Social and Human Costs of Trafficking in Human Beings within the EU*. Luxembourg: Publications Office of the European Union. Available at: https://op.europa.eu/en/publication-detail/-/publication/373138c5-0ea4-11eb-bc07-01aa75ed71a1/language-en

Walby, Sylvia, Barbosa, Estela Capelas, and McManus, Sally (2022) 'Costing the long-term health harms of trafficking: Why a gender-neutral approach discounts the future of women', *Frontiers in Sociology*, 7. doi.org/10.3389/fsoc.2022.858337

Walk Free (2018) *Global Slavery Index 2018*. Available at: Global-Slavery-Index-2018.pdf (walkfree.org)

Walklate, Sandra, Fitz-Gibbon, Kate, and McCulloch, Jude (2018) 'Is more law the answer? Seeking justice for victims of intimate partner violence through the reform of legal categories', *Criminology & Criminal Justice*, 18(1), 115–31.

Wallerstein, Immanuel (2011) [1974] *The Modern World-System I: Capitalist Agriculture and the Origins of the European World-Economy in the Sixteenth Century*. Berkeley: University of California Press.

Waring, Marilyn (1988) *If Women Counted: A New Feminist Economics*. San Francisco: Harper & Row.

Weitzer, Ronald (2013) 'Sex trafficking and the sex industry: The need for evidence-based theory and legislation', *Journal of Criminal Law and Criminology*, 101(4): 1337–69.

Weitzer, Ronald (2015) 'Human trafficking and contemporary slavery', *Annual Review of Sociology*, 41: 223–42.

Weldon, S. Laurel, Lusvardi, Amber, Kelly-Thompson, Kaitlin, and Forester, Summer (2023) 'Feminist waves, global activism, and gender violence regimes: Genealogy and impact of a global wave', *Women's Studies International Forum*, 99. https://doi.org/10.1016/j.wsif.2023.102781

Werner, Marion, Bair, Jennifer, and Fernández, Victor Ramiro (2014) 'Linking up to development? Global value chains and the making of a post-Washington consensus', *Development and Change*, 45(6): 1219–47.

Williamson, Sarah Hupp (2017) 'Globalization as a racial project: Implications for human trafficking', *Journal of International Women's Studies*, 18(2): 74–88. Available at: https://vc.bridgew.edu/jiws/vol18/iss2/5

Williamson, Sarah Hupp (2022) *Human Trafficking in the Era of Global Migration: Unravelling the Impact of Neoliberal Economic Policy*. Bristol: Bristol University Press.

Whitehead, John, Jackson, James, Balch, Alex, and Francis, Brian (2021) 'On the unreliability of multiple systems estimation for estimating the number of potential victims of modern slavery in the UK', *Journal of Human Trafficking*, 7(1): 1–13.

Whitehead, John, Jackson, James, Balch, Alex, and Francis, Brian (2022) 'Response to "Misunderstandings of multiple systems estimation"', *Journal of Human Trafficking*, 8(4): 469–73.

Wismer, Sebastian, Bongard, Christian, and Rasek, Arno (2017) 'Multi-sided market economics in competition law enforcement', *Journal of European Competition Law & Practice*, 8(4): 257–62.

Withers, Matt, and Piper, Nicola (2023) 'Decent wages for decent work in Asia: Addressing the temporality-precarity nexus in South-South migration', in Boris, Eileen, Gottfried, Heidi, Greene, Julie, and Tham, Joo-Cheong (eds) *Global Labor Migration: New Directions*. Urbana: University of Illinois Press. pp 297–314.

World Bank Group (2016) *Forward Look: A Vision for the World Bank Group in 2030. DC2016–0008*. Available at: https://thedocs.worldbank.org/en/doc/545241485963738230-0270022017/original/DC20160008.pdf

World Bank Group (2020) *World Development Report 2020: Trading for Development in the Age of Global Value Chains*. Available at: https://www.worldbank.org/en/publication/wdr2020

World Bank Group (2022) *Helping Countries Adapt to a Changing World. Annual Report 2022*. Available at: www.worldbank.org/annualreport

World Bank Group and IOM (2022) *Economic Shocks and Human Trafficking Risks: Evidence from IOM's Victims of Human Trafficking Database*. Washington, DC: World Bank. Available at: https://openknowledge.worldbank.org/server/api/core/bitstreams/6c889575-2e83-51c8-911a-24958d9427c1/content

Xiang, Biao (2012a) 'Labor Transplant: "Point-to-Point" Transnational labor migration in East Asia', *South Atlantic Quarterly*, 111(4): 721–39.

Xiang, Biao (2012b) 'Predatory princes and princely peddlers: The state and international labour migration intermediaries in China', *Pacific Affairs*, 85(1): 47–68.

Xiang, Biao (2017) 'The base: A case of infrastructural governance of labour outmigration in China', *Mobilities*, 12(2): 175–87.

Xiang, Biao, and Lindquist, Johan (2014) 'Migration infrastructure', *International Migration Review*, 48(1): 122–48.

Xiang, Biao, Yeoh, Brenda S.A., and Toyota, Mika (eds) (2013) *Return: Nationalizing Transnational Mobility in Asia*. Durham and London: Duke University Press.

Yea, Sallie (2017) 'Editorial: The politics of evidence, data and research in anti-trafficking work', *Anti-Trafficking Review*, 8: 1–13.

Yeates, Nicola (2009) *Globalising Care Economies and Migrant Workers: Explorations in Global Care Chains*. London: Palgrave Macmillan.

Yen, No (2018) 'Human trafficking: In the shadows of the law', *NTS Insight*, Number IN 18–06, August.

Yohannes, Hyab T. (2023) 'Refugee trafficking in a carceral age: A case study of the Sinai trafficking', *Journal of Human Trafficking*, 9(1): 33–47.

Young, B.R. and Chua, M.M. (2023) 'Can multisector approaches improve victim identification?' in UNODC (2023) *Global Report on Trafficking in Persons*. pp 30–2.

Yttergren, Asa (2012) 'Swedish gender equality for trafficked women? Radical official remedies and ethnic otherness', *feminists@law*, 2(1). https://doi.org/10.22024/UniKent/03/fal.58

Yuval-Davis, Nira, Wemyss, Georgie, and Cassidy, Kathryn (2018) 'Everyday bordering, belonging and the reorientation of British immigration legislation', *Sociology*, 52(2): 228–44.

Zenz, Adrian (2023) 'Coercive labor in the cotton harvest in the Xinjiang Uyghur autonomous region and Uzbekistan: A comparative analysis of state-sponsored forced labor', *Journal of Communist and Post-Communist Studies*, 56(2): 1–32.

Zimmerman, Cathy, Hossain, Mazeda, Yun, Katherine, Gajdadziev, Vasil, Guzun, Natalia, Tchomarova, Maria, et al (2008) 'The health of trafficked women: A survey of women entering posttrafficking services in Europe', *American Journal of Public Health*, 98(1): 55–9.

Index

References to tables appear in **bold** type.